LONGMAN LINGUISTICS LIBRARY

ENGLISH IN AFRICA : AN INTRODUCTION

LONGMAN LINGUISTICS LIBRARY

General editors
R.H. Robins, University of London
Martin Harris, University of Essex

For series list see p. xii

English in Africa: An Introduction

Josef J. Schmied

LONGMAN
LONDON AND NEW YORK

Longman Group UK Limited,
Longman House, Burnt Mill, Harlow,
Essex CM20 2JE, England
and Associated Companies throughout the world.

Published in the United States of America
by Longman Inc., New York

First published 1991

British Library Cataloguing in Publication Data
Schmied, Josef J.
    English in Africa. — (Longman linguistics library).
    1. Africa. English language
    I. Title
    420

    ISBN 0–582–07456–8
    ISBN 0–582–07455–X pbk

Library of Congress Cataloging-in-Publication Data
Schmied, Josef J.
    English in Africa : an introduction / Josef J. Schmied.
        p. cm. — (Longman linguistics library)
    Includes bibliographical references and index.
    ISBN 0–582–07456–8. — ISBN 0–582–07455–X (pbk.)
    1. English language—Africa. 2. English language—Social aspects—
    Africa. 3. English language—Study and teaching—Africa.
    4. African literature (English)—History and criticism. I. Title.
    II. Series.
    PE3401.S34   1991
    306.4′4′09609171241—dc20   90–24693
                                                                        CIP

Set in Linotron 10/11 point Times
by Columns Design & Production Services Ltd, Reading

Produced by Longman Singapore Publishers (Pte) Ltd.
Printed in Singapore

Contents

Figures

Maps

Tables

Foreword

Of all the continents, Africa is the most complex linguistically. Its languages are many and various, numbering between one and two thousand. Upon this ancient and intricate palimpsest European colonial rule inscribed a further pattern of languages: Portuguese, Spanish, French and English, all still used for many purposes, not as mother tongues but as second or auxiliary languages. Among them English appears likely to become, in today's Africa of independent nation states, the most widespread and convenient; not simply because British hegemony was more extensive than that of the other colonial powers, but because English is now the world's most commonly used ecumenical language.

English thus continues to play many roles in Africa, more especially in those states formerly ruled by Britain: in education and administration at different levels, in commerce and journalism, in legislative debate and international assembly, as a medium of literature, as a means of communication between individuals with no other language in common. English has put down roots in Africa and is adapting itself to the various linguistic ecosystems of which it has become part. Living alongside the languages of Africa, it interacts with them; and the study of its implantation, adaptation, growth and development, from region to region and community to community, presents a considerable challenge to the linguistic scholar.

When I first began my own enquiries into English in Africa thirty years ago I was daunted by the scale and complexity of this new field of study. It seemed to me then that the English language specialist would also have to be an Africanist; that descriptive linguistic studies, whether in phonology or grammar

or lexis, would need to be complemented and buttressed by
sociolinguistic observation; and that the traditional methodologies
of historical and dialectal research had little to offer by way of
guidance. I comforted myself with the belief that no single
scholar could in any case adequately cover the whole field, and
that research workers would have to contribute to it piecemeal
over the years, country by country and aspect by aspect. And this
indeed has been the case until today.

Josef Schmied's study is therefore an important milestone. For
here is a scholar able to encompass the whole continent, and
survey and map for us the past and present of English in Africa.
He has all the qualifications for the task: a scholarly background
in English language studies and linguistics, many years of
research experience in Africa, close contacts with African
scholars, familiarity with the now extensive literature on the
subject, and a sympathetic understanding of the different social
and cultural contexts within which English is used in Africa. He
is, I believe, the foremost European spcecialist in this field.

His book marks a significant step in the historical study of
English, for here is a new chapter in the story of the language.
Those who have an interest in the contemporary study of English
and its spread across the world will turn eagerly to it, as indeed
will the linguistic historians of the future.

January 1991   John Spencer

Acknowledgements

A survey of a whole continent is obviously impossible without the help of numerous colleagues and friends who provide not easily available up-to-date information. I am particularly grateful to Alex Johnson (Sierra Leone), Lawrence Boadi (Ghana), Conrad Brann, Augusta Omamor (both Nigeria), Mohammed Abdulaziz, Okoth Okombo, Kembo Sure (all Kenya), Casmir Rubagumya (Tanzania), Teresa Chisanga, James Moody, Youngson Simukoko (all Zambia), Bill Low (Zimbabwe), Manfred Görlach (Germany), Jenny Cheshire, Lorraine Lawrence, Loretto Todd (all UK) and John Holm (United States) for comments and information. Finally I wish to thank my colleagues at Bayreuth, Diana Hudson-Ettle, Franz Rottland, Richard Taylor, and particularly John Spencer for continuous support and encouragement.

Introduction

The aim of this book is to provide an introduction to a relatively new field of linguistic study. The growing interest in non-native varieties of English, often called the 'New Englishes', is documented in the new journals, *English World-Wide* or *World Englishes* (first published in 1979 and 1982 respectively), and in numerous recent book publications (e.g. Bailey/Görlach (eds) 1982; Platt/Weber/Ho 1984; Kachru 1986a; or Cheshire (ed.) 1991). These usually combine theoretical discussion with specific case studies from all parts of the English-speaking world. In contrast, this book attempts to give the reader a more comprehensive picture of the English language on one continent. The choice of Africa for this study is determined by the relative scarcity of published information and the author's own fieldwork experience, as well as by the great variety of functions, forms and problems of English in Africa.

Up to now, no general book on English in Africa has been published. Although some countries (e.g. Nigeria) are covered by several books and numerous articles, others are relatively blank areas on the map of English sociolinguistic research. This does not mean that nobody is thinking about the forms and functions of English in these countries, since many African linguists and English language teachers face related sociolinguistic or grammatical problems in their daily work. Many have even written papers, often mimeographed, on them. Although there is a growing body of literature in the field the scarcity of published information means that there is still insufficient exchange of ideas in written form between researchers inside and outside Africa. 'Insiders' may not be able to obtain access to European publications or to publish their own research material, whereas

'outsiders' may not be able to collect enough research material
themselves.

The problems that arise from this gap are manifold. A minor
problem is, of course, that a 'European' (in the African sense,
which includes American, Australian, etc.) scholar, like the
author of the present volume, finds it impossible to obtain
information regarding many interesting questions and phenomena. Hence some of the generalizations of this book must also be
speculative, in the sense that although the findings reported are
supported by data from one area, they may – hopefully – raise
discussions in others.

The great variety of functions, forms and problems makes this
area of study particularly interesting. It may be difficult to strike
a balance between uniformity and diversity, but by using some
crude labels such as English as a Native/Second/International
Language (ENL, ESL, EIL), or West/East/North/South African
English, I hope to provide a basis for more specific discussion and
research. Although the scope of this book makes it impossible to
provide as much specific information as I would wish, some case
studies and many empirical examples are included to stimulate
comparisons, for it is certainly rewarding to compare such
different 'anglophone' countries as Sierra Leone, Zambia and
Somalia.

When I use terms like West/East/North/South African English,
or generally African English and 'Africanisms' to refer to forms
of English spoken by African speakers, this does not imply that
there is one acknowledged variety or that there are several
distinct varieties of the language, nor that these forms are already
standardized and codified in any way[1]. This is also borne out by
the fact that descriptions of African forms still have to be made
with reference to 'Standard English', which is largely based on
the variety used by educated speakers in Southern England, as it
is codified in the major reference works, such as the descriptions
of grammar by Quirk et al. (e.g. 1985) or that of pronunciation
by Gimson (e.g. 1989). This reference standard is used for
historical reasons and for descriptive and teaching purposes. This
(and related expressions like deviation, change, etc.) may be controversial in some communities, even though no deficit or
inferiority of African forms is implied.

Within the limits of the African continent the book covers all
the major aspects of English in separate chapters, but aims at
demonstrating how closely these aspects are intertwined. Thus
the differences in the historical impact of the English language in
different regions are reflected in present sociolinguistic situations.

The functions of English may even determine which forms are used and accepted within a community. A central factor in the development of forms and functions of English in Africa is education. And a good indicator and propagator of certain forms of English is the development of African literature in English. Additionally, an important, but often forgotten, side-effect of English in Africa is its influence on African languages[2], which in turn influence the forms of English used. It is also worth remembering that a basic question underlying language use in all sectors is the complex phenomenon of language attitudes. Language policies have their impact on many spheres of life and language use and usage; they not only influenced English in Africa in the past but will determine it even more in the future. As a principal aim of this book is to stimulate research in different countries, and on different aspects of English in Africa, it closes with a brief description of research possibilities and problems in the various fields without neglecting the fascinating perspectives for theoretical and applied linguistics that make the linguistic researcher's task so challenging. Finally, as an attempt at covering all aspects comprehensively would be foolhardy, suggestions for further reading and an extensive bibliography provide entry points to more specific questions.

These aspects exemplify the scope of this book and although many more questions will be raised than (even partly) answered, it is a first attempt to penetrate and systematize the network of English in Africa.

This network is related to three other networks of English in the world. When English is used as a mother tongue, as is partly the case in South Africa, it is obviously related to other 'transplanted' varieties of English in North America or Australia, where English-speaking settlers took their language with them and – to a large extent – imparted it to the settlers from other backgrounds. As this aspect of English in Africa is not only limited to one area with its very special linguistic and sociopolitical problems, but also relatively well documented (e.g. Lanham/MacDonald 1979) it is in many ways neglected in this book.

A second network exists between pidgin and creole languages that are mainly related to English lexically. They fall regionally into two parts: the Pacific and the Atlantic varieties. The latter connect West Africa with the Caribbean and even with North America. As they are restricted to one part of the continent they are omitted from the discussion. This network, including its important African wing, is in any case sufficiently covered in recent introductions to pidgin and creole studies. Although this decision is based purely on pragmatic grounds, some linguists (e.g. Elugbe/Omamor, forthcoming) also offer a theoretical justification for separating English in the narrow sense from the new African languages which have often been called English-based, because of the obvious lexical connections. Whether the English continuum from standard to rudimentary broken English is really linked to the pidgin continuum today, or whether they have become completely separate codes, will continue to be debated by specialists in this field, but is beyond the scope of this work. Even if some linguists prefer to assume the latter this does not mean that there is not considerable overlap in everyday or literary usage (cf. chapter 5).

The third network links all varieties of English as a second language throughout the world. English in Africa is thus linked with English in South and South-East Asia, where research on these 'New Englishes' has been most prolific (cf. Kachru 1986a or Platt/Weber 1980). As this network is the most important in Africa and covers also the above-mentioned areas in West and South Africa where the pidginized and the 'transplanted' varieties are used, it is the dominant perspective adopted here. As such it is also a case study of multilingual sociolinguistics in those parts of the world where English is used mainly as an additional language.

This book is an introduction in two senses. First in the sense that it does not presuppose any specialist knowledge on the part of the reader and is written in a simple, largely non-technical style, although it does introduce a number of technical concepts and theories. Secondly, it is introductory in the sense that it offers a synopsis and a broad general framework. This framework, together with some specific examples, should also be seen as an invitation to compare and a challenge to query. As such a wide topic cannot possibly be exhausted, this survey is intended to promote further discussion and research into English in Africa.

Notes

1. It is in fact one of the aims of this study to illustrate the variation in the sociolinguistic processes (e.g. assimilation, norm formation) as well as in the linguistic forms (e.g. pronunciation, vocabulary, grammar). Uniformity of English is a crude theoretical abstraction in countries with an official standard form, as in Europe or America, and the same applies for Africa, where no such norm has been publicly acknowledged. It is, however, a particular challenge to sociolinguistic description to combine hypotheses about general tendencies with concrete examples from specific cases or texts.

2. As far as the spelling of African names and languages is concerned I
have used the internationally familiar terms, which may differ slightly
from the actual names in the respective languages themselves.

This is
the case particularly regarding languages with prefixes, such as
Icibemba, Cinyanja, Silozi, Chitonga and Kikaonde in Zambia, which
all have basically the same Bantu prefix meaning 'language', but are
usually simply called Bemba, Nyanja, Lozi, Tonga and Kaonde by
people not so familiar with the prefixes. Similarly, the ethnic groups
or peoples who speak these languages are usually given the same
name, thus the Tswana are simply called Tswana instead of Batswana
(or singular Motswana), because outside the region or nation these
prefixes may not be used in English contexts. Generally, I chose the
indigenous or more phonetic name (e.g. Igbo for Ibo).

Chapter 1

The Colonial Inheritance

This historical account cannot report all the facts that resulted in the penetration of Africa by English. It can only offer a few key figures and some of the developments which mark the historical process and may explain differences in the penetration in different parts of the continent. It emphasizes the agents involved in this process, trading and mining companies, settlers, soldiers and missionaries, because each of these agents had a different impact on the African people and their learning and use of English. The interplay of European interests and motivations with their associated African reactions led to the present-day sociopolitical and sociolinguistic situations.

1.1 Early trading connections

According to Hakluyt, who in 1598 recorded early British maritime explorations, the English language was probably first heard in Africa in the 1530s when William Hawkins the Elder passed there on his way to Brazil (Spencer 1971a: 8). The English had already prepared to challenge the Portuguese trade monopoly in West Africa in the 1480s (Blake 1977: 60) and British sailors may have been in the service of other nations, but it was not until decades later that British ships and sea captains, like Sir John Hawkins, who sailed along the Guinea coast in 1562 on his ship *Jesus*, came regularly in order to trade in spices, ivory and slaves. After the opening of the London Stock Exchange in 1571 most of these trading enterprises were financed by merchant companies, such as the Company of Merchant Adventurers for Guinea (formed 1561) or the later but more important Royal Adventurers of England Trading into Africa (formed 1660), which soon acquired a monopoly on the slave trade from Cape

Blanco to the Cape of Good Hope. After the defeat of the Spanish Armada (1588), the English, together with the Dutch, French, Swedes, Danes and even the Prussians, sailed on the former Spanish and Portuguese trading routes along the West African coast and across the Atlantic to the Americas. The Guinea coast was one corner of the famous North Atlantic triangle between Africa, America and Europe, with a constant trade flow of slaves, sugar/rum and cloth/industrial products.

The European trading companies built forts on the coast or on islands near the coast, which were abandoned, sold, captured or exchanged frequently (e.g. Gorée Island just off present-day Dakar, originally Portuguese, became Dutch in 1617, French in 1674, British in 1758 and French again in 1783). European presence in the trading posts or castles started as early as the sixteenth century, but was minimal in relation to the overwhelming and almost absorbing African environment, and its influence did not reach far into the hinterland. The Europeans normally did not travel inland (because of disease, especially malaria), but waited for African traders to bring their merchandise to the coast. The most important British forts were situated around the mouth of the Gambia (Fort St James was founded in 1618), in Sierra Leone (Tassa Island in 1663) and along the Gold Coast (Cape Coast Castle 1664, Accra Castle 1672). Outside these areas the British did not have permanent trading places, but many British ships transported goods for other nations. The Spanish, for instance, sold so-called *asientos*, trade monopolies for a certain cargo (e.g. tons of slaves!), and after 1805 almost all goods to and from the Portuguese colonies were transported on British ships. British supremacy in the West African trade built up slowly but gradually until it reached its climax in the early nineteenth century.

Despite the enormous economic influence of the English on the West African coastal trade their linguistic influence is difficult to assess. Historical reports are normally not very explicit and sometimes inconsistent regarding questions of language use. It seems clear, however, that comparatively few English native speakers were involved and many languages were used, mostly quite imperfectly and definitely far from any 'Standard'. According to Dillard (1979: 264), John Barbot reports from a voyage around 1680: 'For many of the coast Blacks speak a little English, or Dutch; and for the most part speak to us in a sort of Lingua Franca, or broken Portuguese and French.' And F. Moore voices a criticism as early as 1738 in his *Travels into the Inland Parts of Africa* (ibid.: 293): 'The English have in the River Gambia much

corrupted the English Language, by words or Literal Translations
from the Portuguese or Mundingoes.' Other documents have
been used (cf. Hancock 1986) to demonstrate the emergence of
English-related pidgin and creole varieties on the African coast
(and not on the ships or in the West Indies).

As the climate along the Guinea coast prevented extensive
European settlement, Africans had to be trained as interpreters.
As early as 1598 Hakluyt's *Travels* reported that Africans were
sent to England to learn English. In 1788 there were about fifty
African mulatto and black children in and around Liverpool who
were being instructed in 'reading, writing and a little arithmetic'
(Crow 1970: 299). Despite the use of English by these Africans,
who were to become the first interpreters in Africa, other
languages, especially a Portuguese creole, seem to have been
more common in the seventeenth and eighteenth centuries along
the coast.

In general, contact between the different trading parties was
restricted and language contact was probably limited to certain
stereotyped situations where only rudimentary knowledge of
languages was necessary to ensure communication. Historical
linguists assume that the developing lingua franca for these
contacts incorporated features of the language used on the early
Portuguese merchant ships, enriched by African and other
European languages. The English variety spoken by the British
sailors (and to some extent by their African crewmen) in those
days, often called maritime or ship English, was characterized by
many non-standard forms, usually from south-western dialects, as
can partly be reconstructed from the logs and documents of the
trading companies. But as the contact of Africans with these
varieties was constantly changing it is difficult to assess their
influence ashore (Hancock 1976 and Bailey/Ross 1988).[1] The
exact reconstruction of how the new pidgin and creole languages
developed and to what extent indigenous and imposed languages
or universal strategies played a role is a matter of debate among
specialists (for an introduction see Todd 1974, for a detailed
discussion Mühlhäusler 1986, Romaine 1988b or Holm 1988).

1.2 The informal empire

Towards the end of the eighteenth century the British lost their
most important colony in the American War of Independence.
After that the government seem to have had no intention of
expanding their territories but rather 'saw their empire as a
collection of parts, islands, and coastal regions, held together by

the navy and dependent on it for prosperity and even survival' (Lloyd 1984: 138). On the other hand, the reasons for this policy were simple: Britain did not acquire more territory because, her French and Dutch competitors having lost ground during Napoleon's time, she could assert herself on a world-wide basis without any need to establish formal territorial 'responsibility' (as it was viewed later). This kept the cost of colonial policy low for a long time. For almost a century British official responsibility in Africa was restricted to two areas, Sierra Leone and the Cape, which in those days represented respectively Britain's humanitarian and political commitments in Africa.

The humanitarian commitment led to the abolition of the slave trade. After Lord Mansfield's judgement (in 1774) that slavery in Britain was not supported by law (which led to the release of slaves in Britain) public opinion in Britain turned more and more against slavery and the slave trade, until it was prohibited in 1807. Although the economic reasons behind the movement should not be neglected, the humanitarian consequence remains. It led to the establishment of the Anti-Slavery Society (1823) and of a 'slave squadron', which patrolled the Atlantic to intercept the trade. Britain's political involvement in Africa was considered necessary only in so far as it contributed towards securing her naval superiority. As the centre of the older, first British Empire (in the seventeenth and eighteenth centuries) lay in the Caribbean (especially Barbados and Jamaica) and that of the developing, second Empire (in the nineteenth and twentieth centuries) was in India, Africa had always been little more than a stepping stone: West Africa was on the way to the West, to the Caribbean, and South Africa to the East, to India. In order to secure such stepping stones the British founded Bathurst (1816) at the mouth of the Gambia, occupied Mombasa (1824–28) and the islands in the Southern Atlantic and Indian oceans (Ascension, St Helena, Tristan da Cunha, Mauritius, and the Seychelles, all 1794–1816), and took over the Dutch possessions in Ceylon and at the Cape (1795/96 by occupation and 1815/16 by legal treaties). Of these acquisitions the Cape was seen to be the most important and became, also because of the climate, the only place in Africa where the British settled in sizeable numbers, particularly later when the Cape Province was combined with Natal, Transvaal and the Orange Free State to form the South African Union.

As a consequence of its humanitarian commitment the British repatriated Blacks to the Freetown area from 1787: the Poor Blacks from England, the Nova Scotians (ex-soldiers of the

British in the American War of Independence), the Maroons
(militant escaped slaves from Jamaica), and liberated Africans
rescued from slave ships on the 'middle passage' to America.
They were settled in Freetown in Sierra Leone and gained
remarkable influence all over West Africa because in the course
of time they became an educated élite in many commercial and
educational centres. In 1827 Fourah Bay College was founded
and soon became a first centre for higher (Western) education.
The linguistic influence of this centre was felt all over West
Africa, and the developing creole language of Freetown, Krio,
left some traces in most West African varieties of English and the
local pidgins.

A somewhat similar resettlement, supported by US American
anti-slavery societies, took place in neighbouring Liberia in the
1820s, and led to the establishment of the first independent Black
African state,[2] which was officially recognized by the USA in
1847. Since then the state and the English language there have
been characterized by considerable American influence and a
wide socio-educational and linguistic gap between the Americo-
Liberians (who came mainly from the United States, but also
from the Caribbean) on the coast and the Afro-Liberians inland.
The impact of Americo-Liberian English on other West African
Englishes, however, seems to have been fairly limited. The
famous Kru-men, whose origins lie within the borders of the
Liberian state but who have always been oriented towards
Britain, and whose language is said to be more similar to Krio,
seem to have been more influential linguistically. For centuries
they worked on British ships and in trading centres from the
Senegal to the Congo, from the time when the *Lion* and *Primrose*
were the first English ships to come to the Liberian coast in 1553
(Singler 1981).

During the period of Lord Palmerston's Foreign Secretaryship
(1847–65) the Empire was in a kind of equilibrium. While the
British dominated the oceans their involvement on land was
minimal, although the state had taken over all British trading
settlements by an Act of 1821. A government report in 1865 even
recommended handing over all trading posts and colonies in
(West) Africa, except Sierra Leone, to African rulers. The
British reluctance to annex territories can be seen in the
following letter written by Cameroon chiefs to Queen Victoria in
1879, which is also an interesting linguistic document:

Dearest Madam,
We your servants have join together and thoughts it better to write
you a nice loving letter which will tell you about all our wishes. WE
wish to have your laws in our towns. We want to have every fashion

altered, also we will do according to your Consuls word. Plenty wars
here in our country. Plenty murder and plenty idol worshippers.
Perhaps these lines of our writing will look to you as an idle tale. We
have spoken to the English Consul plenty times about having an
English Government here. We never have answer from you, so we
wish to write ourselves. When we heard about Calabar River, how
they have all English laws in their towns, and how they have put away
all their superstitions, oh we shall be very glad to be like Calabar
now.

(Quoted in Mbassi-Manga 1973: 19)

The imperial equilibrium was the basis for two non-govern-
mental forces in Africa: the traders and the missions. For the
only cause of British involvement on land, besides trade, during
most of the nineteenth century, was the missionary interest. This
is why Sierra Leone, a centre of the Church Missionary Society
(CMS), always remained a key possession, although its revenue
did not cover the cost of government. It was the missionary effort
that brought systematic education (including the teaching of
Standard English) to West Africa, from the CMS centre in
Freetown to the Baptist Missionary Society in Fernando Poo and
Victoria in Cameroon (Spencer 1971a: 17). Whereas in West
Africa the Cross followed trade, in Central and Eastern Africa
the missionary came first. And the missionary was David
Livingstone. In general, the impact of the British inland was
minimal before the introduction of breech-loading rifles and
quinine (for the treatment of malaria), which allowed the
Victorian missionary and late-nineteenth century imperialist zeal
to change matters in Africa drastically.

Linguistically, the most important legacy of this era was the
transplantation of English mother-tongue speakers to West and
South Africa (those who came to East and Central Africa later
were much less important). Both the missionaries in the West
and the settlers in the South still looked upon England as their
model in matters pertaining to the language standard (although
most of them did not speak Standard English themselves). It was,
however, only in their immediate environment that English was
now used as a second language, i.e. in administration and above
all in (Christian) education. The early, and possibly undue,
importance attached to English in preaching in the early days can
be inferred from the following comment by an American
missionary in 1857:

Most of the missionaries in Africa preach in English. In Sierra Leone,
Liberia, and at some other places, the native must understand English

or live and die without hearing the gospel, though it is administered
regularly in the town. Very few of those who pretend to understand
English, can comprehend what is said in the fine classical style by the
missionary. Sometimes the preacher is a German, whose accent
would puzzle an Englishman, much more an African.

(Quoted in Spencer 1971a: 18)

In the rest of Africa English was not yet used in second
language functions, but only as the most important contact
language in trade. Although its function was still rather limited it
is interesting to note that English had wider regional currency
during the period of the informal empire than after the
establishment of formal imperial rule. An interesting example is
Katanga (Zaïre), which became part of the Belgian Congo in
1908, after having been a Free State (as regards trade) before:

> The first newspaper to appear in Elizabethville (weekly) was the
> *Etoile du Congo* (first issue on May 26, 1911) and it was trilingual:
> English, Flemish, and French. It was soon followed by the weekly
> *Journal du Katanga* (first issue on August 5, 1911), which had an
> 'English page' and published government notices in the three
> languages. But two years later English had virtually disappeared from
> its pages, a sign that measures against that language were taken quite
> early.
>
> (Fabian 1986: 176)

Similarly, when the Germans moved into East Africa and the
Cameroons (later to become basically Tanzania and Cameroon)
in the 1880s, the Africans were surprised that these Europeans
did not speak English; and whereas the Germans supported the
use of Swahili in East Africa, they reluctantly had to use Pidgin
English in Cameroon, as they wished to oppose any form of
British Standard English, which was so persistent in 'their
territory that it had to be banned from official use by special
order in 1913 (Mbassi-Manga 1973: 42).

1.3 The heyday of imperial rule

Towards the end of the nineteenth century British supremacy in
the world in general and in Africa in particular was challenged.
France and Germany began to create formal empires where state
administration and military protection secured the activities of
traders and settlers. For a long time Britain had refrained from
wasting money on expanding or formalizing the Empire: as late
as 1868 the Abyssinian expedition under General Napier con-
quered Ethiopia in order to release imprisoned Europeans – and

left the country soon afterwards. The acquisition of Suez canal shares by Disraeli (1875) is in line with the basic principle of securing the British naval routes to India – a strategy still in force when Egypt (1882) and British Somaliland (1884) were occupied. At this point the British government felt forced to follow their expansion-minded citizens by imitating Belgian, French and German examples in neighbouring territories. Cecil Rhodes, who expanded British rule (or rather that of his British South Africa Company) from the Cape to Rhodesia (1888–91), is the most famous example. This was not only felt to be necessary in order to keep territory out of the hands of countries that might set up tariffs against British goods; but other motives, too, contributed to this drastic change of attitude: the endeavour to secure raw material for British industry (e.g. from what became the Zambian Copper Belt), strategic considerations (e.g. to prevent Boer or German penetration of Bechuanaland, later Botswana, in 1885) and a general colonizing spirit, most characteristically expressed in Kipling's phrase about 'the white man's burden'. This led to an expansion of the West African coastal trading posts in Ghana and Nigeria into the hinterland until the British encountered their French opponents doing the same from their coastal stations.

The British imperial dream of a land connection from Cairo to the Cape became clearer with the establishment of the colony in Uganda (1895) and of the Anglo-Egyptian condominium of the Sudan (1899). The Boer War (1899–1902) filled the first gap in the connection between the two cornerstones of British interests in Africa, the League of Nations' mandate over Tanganyika (in 1919) the second.

As the British Treasury's philosophy was still based on the assumption that territories should only be taken over when it was economically viable to do so, they either left the administration in the hands of chartered companies (the Royal Niger Company, the Imperial British East Africa Company or the British South African Company) or they tried to attract settlers who would pay for their own local administration from the revenue of their plantations (particularly in Northern and Southern Rhodesia and Kenya). Although initial grants-in-aid were given to the young colonial administrations, they were kept small (Johnston was sent to Nyasaland with £10,000 and could thus only afford seventy-five Indian soldiers and one British officer, for instance) and were virtually extinguished by 1914. An important consequence of this philosophy was that education was largely left to the missions, who had not only to train their own preachers but also to educate

a small native administrative élite. The latter was necessary
because after it had been developed successfully in Northern
Nigeria the British tried to establish their principle of 'indirect
rule' wherever possible. This reliance on indigenous hierarchical
structures was accompanied by a *divide-and-rule* policy, i.e.
small-scale native structures were preferred because they were
considered less dangerous and more manageable for the colonial
superstructure. This superstructure varied according to local
requirements: in Egypt, which became officially independent as
early as 1922, and the (Northern) Sudan the British impact was
much less felt than in the settler colonies, for instance. On the
whole, the British were far less keen than other colonial powers
to assimilate their African subjects to a European or British way
of life, and protected them even to some extent from the
demands of the settler 'aristocracies'. Although the principles
varied in place and time, they constitute a fairly stable basis for
sociolinguistic development during this period.

When the British were finally drawn into the 'scramble for
Africa', which took place in the early 1880s and ended with the
partition of Africa among the European imperial powers at the
Berlin conference in 1884, formal imperial rule was established in
all territories. This meant, of course, that an English-speaking
superstructure was imposed with appropriate administrative,
legal and educational substructures.

The administrative, legal and educational language in the
British African colonies, protectorates and dependencies was
English; but to a certain extent African languages were also used
officially, and at times even encouraged, at the lower levels. The
relationship between English language expansion and British
imperialism was not, however, a straightforward one. On the one
hand British colonial officers had to learn African languages
before they went to Africa, and their subsequent promotion
depended to some degree on passing African language tests (cf.
Abdulaziz 1991). On the other hand even non-British missions
often started English classes either because they wanted to obtain
special government grants that were only available for English-
medium education or because they wanted to cater for Africans
who wanted to 'complete' their education.

From an African perspective English had some advantages.
People soon realized the usefulness of English for economic
advancement, and saw English as being synonymous with
education in general. This position, that Africans willingly took to
English, is not undisputed however. There is a school of thought
that argues that English was imposed on Africans, for example

through a system of 'certification'. English, according to Omolewa
(1975), was not really made compulsory, but to obtain government employment Africans had to have a certificate – and in
order to obtain a certificate a candidate was expected to be
reasonably proficient in English.

The colonial perspective is reflected in the report of a
commission sponsored by the Phelps–Stokes Fund, based on a
visit by the commission to West Africa in 1921 and to Central and
East Africa in 1924/25. The report neatly summarizes the aspects
to be considered in deciding the issue of languages in education
(Jones n.d.: 25f):

> The elements to be considered in determining the languages of
> instruction are
> (1) that every people have an inherent right to their Native tongue;
> (2) that the multiplicity of tongues shall not be such as to develop
> misunderstandings and distrust among people who should be friendly
> and cooperative;
> (3) that every group shall be able to communicate directly with those
> to whom the government is entrusted; and
> (4) that an increasing number of Native people shall know at least
> one of the languages of the civilized nations.
> In determining the weight of each of these elements it is of course
> necessary to ascertain the local conditions. It is clear that there is
> comparatively little, if any advantage, in the continuation of a crude
> dialect with practically no powers of expression. It is also evident that
> the need for a common language is not essential to a large group of
> people speaking the same language and living under conditions that
> do not require much intercommunication. It may even be true that
> some one of the Native languages may be so highly developed as to
> make possible the translation of the great works of civilization into
> that language. With due consideration for all of these elements and
> the modifying circumstances, the following recommendations are
> offered as suggestions to guide governments and educators in
> determining the usual procedure in most African colonies:
> 1. The tribal language should be used in the lower elementary
> standards or grades.
> 2. A lingua franca of African origin should be introduced in the
> middle classes of the school if the area is occupied by large Native
> groups speaking diverse languages.
> 3. The language of the European nation in control should be taught
> in the upper standards.

These principles remained more or less the same in most parts of
British Africa during the whole of imperial rule, but the weight
given to them changed, causing modifications from more
paternalistic to more assimilationist approaches in different

territories and by different colonial governments. The better
integration of the African perspective, or what the colonizers saw
as that, is reflected in general development theory as well as in
language policy (cf. 8.1). After the First World War, Lord
Lugard, Britain's most influential African administrator, developed his Dual Mandate, which implied that the colonial
powers had an obligation, not merely to govern justly, but also to
promote the colonial peoples economically and politically. The
combination of African languages for the lower ranks and
English for the higher ones also reflects the Dual Mandate. On
the whole the British were by no means completely pro-English
in their language policies, which were admittedly rather *ad hoc*
and sometimes inconsistent.

For a long time British administrations in Africa did not want
to invest much money in the education of Africans. It was thus
left to 'voluntary agents', and therefore the influence of the
missions on language in education was very significant. In
consequence missionary language policies, which were often
more consistent than those of the colonial administrations, came
into being. Generally speaking, Protestants tended, in accordance with their tradition since the Reformation, to favour African
mother tongues in church and school, while Catholics favoured
the European language, if there was no major African language,
or lingua franca available (cf. Spencer 1971b). The complexity of
the subject and the arguments associated with it can be inferred
from the following letter by the local Baptists of Duala to the
Basel Mission in Switzerland:

> We your humble petitioners be respectfully to forward to you our
> complaint the sort of teaching given our children in the Duala
> language. It is quite against the reason that our children should be
> educated in a barbarous tongue instead of a civilized one either
> German or English. We have reason for protesting against this and
> two of our principal reasons are that the children could never obtain
> employment under the German Government or under any civilized
> person, or persons whatever when they are grown up, because they
> could never understand what to do. Also the Duala language is not
> our tongue. We have spoken to the mission out here about this
> matter but excuse has been made that it should not be altered without
> your committee's sanction.
>
> (Quoted by Mbassi-Manga 1973: 39)

In territories under British rule the Anglican Church Missionary Society usually played an important role in studying, using
and expanding African languages. Although they showed much

concern about 'the people's tongue' in evangelization and work among the people, it was natural for them to use English for the higher levels of church organization and education.

It is very interesting to note that the contrast between the colonial administration and the missions led to some regional differences in (Nigerian) English, which can still be seen today. For it was in those early days that the seed of the often-mentioned dialect differences between Southern and Northern speech was sown, i.e. the fact that graduates from the élite schools in the North have a pronunciation system that is closer to RP than those from the mission schools in the South:

> . . . in the North, the colonial administration maintained schools mainly for the children of the powerful Hausa/Fulani oligarchy or feudal class. For example, Nasarawa School was founded in 1909 and Barewa College years after. Barewa College had as its first principal an Etonian and most of the other members of staff were said . . . to belong to the cream of English aristocracy, i.e. mostly products of English public schools and graduates of Oxford or Cambridge, and so they taught an accent that was distinctly R.P.; a situation which contrasts with the South where most of the teachers were mostly missionaries who saw as their primary assignment the spread of the gospel and teaching of English only as secondary.
>
> (Awonusi 1985: 43)

1.4 Towards independence and after

After the Second World War, which had shown the logistic value and economic possibilities of African colonies, and after the independence of India (in 1947), it became clear to the British that self-government (within the framework of the Common-wealth) would one day also come to Africa. And although they thought, despite growing African resistance, that it might still take half a century, they started putting their African colonies on the path towards modernization. Although this strategy was obviously aimed at securing British political and economic influence, it gave African countries a boost towards development. Besides extensive agricultural and industrial schemes an expansion of educational systems began. Whereas before the war generally apathetic colonial governments managed to provide two to four years of schooling for perhaps a quarter of their young citizens (Oliver/Fage 1975: 215), now secondary schools were expanded and a few universities founded: University College of the Gold Goast for what became Ghana, Ibadan for Nigeria and Makerere in Uganda for East Africa. The English language was considered a key factor in this strategy, as can be seen from the following document:

116. English is important to Africans for three main reasons; as a lingua franca; as a road to the technical knowledge of modern inventions; and a means of contact with world thought.
117. The movement of population and rapid improvement of communications is bringing together people from scattered regions of Africa, so that Swahili [or another major African language, for that matter] no longer has a wide enough spread to be a useful lingua franca, even in East Africa. As the territories develop closer associations the need for English will steadily increase.
118. Africans are avid to secure the technical knowledge and skill which will, they hope, raise them out of poverty and the ever-present fear of drought and famine, and they know that this knowledge in any amount is only available to the man who can read English. Every week new links are forged through trade with the outside world and so the utilitarian reasons for learning English grow stronger.
119. The knowledge of English introduces the reader to the vast storehouse of English literature and indeed of world literature, for more foreign books have been translated into English than any other language. Now broadcasting and films penetrate into the remotest parts and can only be fully enjoyed by those who understand English.

(Great Britain 1953: 82)

The British post-war policy of modernization was more than ever before conceived and implemented through the medium of English. Since English was straightforwardly equated with modernization it gained enormous prestige. More and more Africans themselves demanded as much English as possible, or petitioned for 'English as early as possible' in schools. Now the same disputes between 'orientalists' and 'modernizers' or 'anglicists' in educational administration took place as in India (where they had been fought for almost a century since Macaulay's famous minute; cf. Kachru 1986a: 35). When African politicians (who had already started to form political organizations like the African National Congress in South Africa in 1912 and the West African National Congress in 1918) joined in this demand for English, as part of their campaign for equal education for Africans, and the abolition of separate education for Europeans, Indians and Africans, they had a second motive, too: for them English was also the language of emancipation and liberation.

The great African leaders like Nkrumah, Nyerere and Kaunda found support for their liberationist ideas from European socialists and philosophers, and began to use the colonizers' legacy against the colonizers themselves. They adopted the English language because they also needed it to criticize and

attack their rulers in international contexts. It is interesting to see
the parallel with South Africa today: there many Blacks bitterly
resent the denial of access to education through English, since
this isolates them from the outside world and deprives them of
their common weapon in the fight for liberation. This became
evident in the 1976 Soweto unrest, which was caused by the
government's attempt to place Afrikaans on an equal footing
with English as a medium of instruction in Black secondary
schools.

It is not surprising therefore that the newly independent
African governments continued on their modernizing English-
dominated path at least for the first few years after their
independence in the early 1960s.[3] Under these conditions it may
be less surprising that some commissions even considered
whether 'literacy in English should be the immediate goal, rather
than a subsequent goal after literacy has been achieved in a
vernacular' (UNESCO 1964: 84). Although African politicians
owed part of their success to the African languages which had
been used in 'grass-root politics' to mobilize the masses, they did
not replace the colonial language at the same time as the colonial
system. In fact, the English language proved far more durable
than other parts of the inheritance (e.g. the Westminster model
of government was soon given up in favour of a one-party system
or even military rule in most African Commonwealth states).

Since the time most African colonies gained independence the
status of the English language has not drastically changed (as will
be seen in chapter 2). Despite the withdrawal of the British
colonial administration the English language was retained as a
kind of oil which kept the administrative, military, political, legal
and educational systems running smoothly when the switch-
boards of power were handed over. It goes without saying that
this state of affairs caused controversy in some of the new
nations. Sometimes conscious and determined language policies
have been used to weaken or strengthen the position of English
(see chapter 8) and such attempts are likely to continue. A few
general reasons why this part of the colonial inheritance has been
so largely retained must suffice here.

For purely pragmatic reasons it was much easier for the
government machinery to maintain the linguistic status quo and
concentrate on more immediate and acute issues. Whereas after
independence many African nations embarked on ambitious
modernization programmes, today they are so absorbed in day-
to-day problems that they have neither the energy nor the means
to attempt fundamental changes in the sociolinguistic situation.

For pure reasons of national cohesion many governments have
so far not chosen to use indigenous languages with sub-national
ethnic affiliations in a national context, in case this endangers the
ethnic equilibrium within the nation. Whereas this is a question
of political feasibility in multiethnic nations (e.g. Nigeria or even
Gambia), it is one of economic feasibility in smaller nations with
their international dependency (e.g. Malawi or Lesotho). Few
countries, apart from Tanzania, where Swahili is seen as a supra-
ethnic lingua franca, or Somalia, which is exceptional in being a
state with only a single ethnic and linguistic group, with strong
national feelings, were in a position to use an African language as
a national means of communication; most preferred to rely on
other symbols to demonstrate their Africanness and intensify
national unity.

For international purposes English has become more, not less,
important since colonial times, and this is not only because the
influence of the British as the leading world power has in many
ways been replaced by that of the Americans. Although for many
Africans the feelings about English may subjectively be very
mixed, it is an objective necessity for discussing national
problems and expressing national points of view in pan-African
and international forums (such as OAU or UNO) and for
claiming a fair share of international communication processes,
be it in the political, economic, or technological fields.

Finally, in order to summarize the colonial linguistic inheritance, a map of Africa (Map 1) shows the main areas and
duration of British influence. It is worth noting that even nations
that had never been colonized by the British still need English
today because of its world-wide importance in international
communication.

Notes

1. I tend to play down the influence of these early trading contacts on
   the development of African English in contrast to English-related
   creoles, because I emphasize the role of language learning in the
   formal educational system, which was not introduced systematically
   until 1882, when the first colonial educational ordinance was passed
   to regulate educational practices in the Gold Coast and Lagos areas
   (Adesina 1977). For the actual implementation and expansion of
   English it was important that it provided voluntary agency schools
   with special grants when English was used as a medium of instruction.
   If British dialectal influence plays a role it is more important to
   analyse the later missionary English or settler English than the early
   white and creole settler English. The continuity and influence of these
   early varieties on the standard varieties of the language beyond
   pidgins and creoles is very difficult to determine.

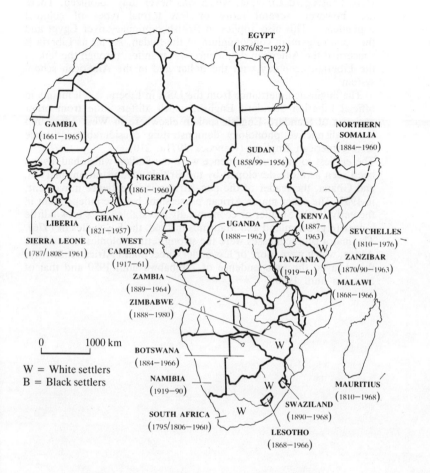

EGYPT
(1876/82–1922)

GAMBIA
(1661–1965)

NORTHERN
SOMALIA
(1884–1960)

SUDAN
(1858/99–1956)

NIGERIA
(1861–1960)

LIBERIA

GHANA
(1821–1957)

UGANDA
(1888–1962)

KENYA
(1887–1963)

SEYCHELLES
(1810–1976)

SIERRA LEONE
(1787/1808–1961)

WEST
CAMEROON
(1917–61)

W

ZANZIBAR
(1870/90–1963)

TANZANIA
(1919–61)

ZAMBIA
(1889–1964)

MALAWI
(1868–1966)

ZIMBABWE
(1888–1980)

0   1000 km

W = White settlers
B = Black settlers

W

BOTSWANA
(1884–1966)

NAMIBIA
(1919–90)

W

MAURITIUS
(1810–1968)

SOUTH AFRICA
(1795/1806–1960)

W

SWAZILAND
(1890–1968)

LESOTHO
(1868–1966)

MAP 1   The colonial inheritance

The years after the country name give the beginning and end of formal British colonial rule, with the exception of Namibia, which was South African, and Liberia, which had never been a formal colony of the United States; several figures indicate different stages in colonization. International borders and the names of African states represent the present-day standard; dotted lines within states separate former British provinces from others.

2. Here I disregard Ethiopia, which was never fully colonized. There are, however, several more or less formal types of colonial dependency. This also applies to British supremacy over Egypt and the Anglo-Egyptian condominium of the Sudan. As far as Liberia is concerned the American dominance was manifest through the link of the Liberian economy with the dollar and in the American school system.

The linguistic inheritance from the USA in Liberia is felt mainly in official Liberian Standard English, which 'differs little from other varieties of Standard English spoken elsewhere in West Africa but has a distinctive phonology demonstrating considerable influence from American English' (Hancock 1971a: 210).

3. The earliest to gain independence were the Sudan, which had always been seen as more developed by the British administration, in 1956, and Ghana, the leader of the pan-African independence movement, in 1957. The other major African possessions became independent in the early 1960s. Smaller or economically less stable states took a little longer (e.g. Swaziland and Mauritius in 1968, the Seychelles in 1976). The major problem cases were the strong settler colonies in Southern Africa, which were more or less under direct South African influence; this delayed the independence of Zimbabwe until 1980 and that of Namibia until 1990.

Chapter 2

The Sociolinguistic Situation

The position of English as a language in a country is determined by its official status, as laid down in the constitution or in other regulations. This affects the knowledge and use of it within the state. This chapter will give various examples illustrating the sociolinguistic position of English in African states and use a broad classification of English as a native, a second and an international language, to compare and categorize African states according to the macrosociolinguistic status of English.

2.1 Official status

One crucial factor determining the position of English in a nation-state is of course the government's language policy. Many language functions, such as the use of languages in administration, parliament, jurisdiction and education, are allocated officially by laws, government circulars and syllabuses. As official language attitudes can be either more or less explicit, in some countries English is proclaimed the 'official' language, whereas in others the term is avoided and it can only be deduced from actual practice that English has some semi-official status.[1] Many small regulations add to the official status of a language. In Zimbabwe, for instance, fluent English is required and tested for acceptance into the police force, and army recruits have to undertake English lessons on joining their unit. In Lesotho and Zambia every student entering the university must have a pass in the Cambridge Overseas School Certificate in English, in Botswana even a credit. In Malawi English is compulsory in Parliament and all MPs are required to pass a stringent test. In Gambia, where the government is the only sizeable employer outside farming, the local languages have no standardized orthography and all employees have to use English in administration. Official and semi-official English requirements have already been firmly entrenched in the minds of the people: 'No constituency in Ghana would elect someone, no matter how good he is, to represent them in parliament if he could neither read nor write English because it is the language of all official occasions' (Saah 1986: 373).

The relationship between the terms official and national language is not very clear,[2] except if both terms are used within the same national 'judicial-status continuum' (cf. Eastman 1983: 37); European languages would normally be called 'official', African languages 'national'. But the question whether there is a certain difference of status and symbolic value involved can often only be answered indirectly from the way the two adjectives 'official' and 'national' are used, and this usage often tells us a lot about associated attitudes (cf. chapter 7). All depends on the sociolinguistic and sociopolitical context of the respective country. If national is associated with nationalistic it is because of the nation's language policy (cf. chapter 8). If national means nation-wide, which would be sociopolitically desirable, few languages would qualify, but if it means associated with ethnic nationalities, which is sociopolitically less desirable, most would. Some Africans may say that English is *only* the official language, whereas an African language is the national language, and in their intonation one can hear their pride in this symbol of African independence and identity. Others may admit that an African 'vernacular' is one of the national languages, but emphasize that English is still *the* official language, and in their intonation you can hear their pride in being able to speak this official language. Because of this vagueness in expression and terminology the categorization in Map 2 must be tentative in some cases, especially since there may be regional differences within a nation (e.g. between the Arabic Northern Sudan and Black Southern Sudan) or there may be differences in the institutions (e.g. in parts of tertiary education). It is also noteworthy that in many African nations there is a huge discrepancy between official declaration and actual practice in language policy. Many governments pay lip service to African languages by giving them the status of national languages, but they do not necessarily promote their active development or use. On the other hand

English, too, has its problems. Efficient communication is
hindered when English is imposed in situations where the
parameters of language use, e.g. topic, place and interlocutors,
do not match. The following critical interpretation of the
problems involved is reported from Botswana (Coangae/Let-
sididi/ Nyati 1987: 92–3, 94):

> In Parliament the official means of communication for conducting the
> official business and debates is English. The practice is a strain on the
> verbal competence of most members of parliament, who have not had
> a high standard of education. To some the use of English is a real
> impediment to meaningful communication and hinders their
> contribution to parliamentary debates. The result is that most
> parliamentarians make up for their lack of proficiency by supporting
> the evening parliamentary review programme, entitled 'Dikgang tsa
> Palamente', which is conducted in Setswana. In this programme
> parliamentarians fight to be allotted time to say to the nation what
> was communicated inadequately in English during the debates.

In such cases the official language, English, seems difficult to
maintain. In the traditional system in customary courts, however,
everything works in Setswana:

> [an accused is] charged of an offence against a western-type law
> through the medium of English. To ensure the rights of the illiterate
> and uneducated Motswana part of the way, interpretation is provided
> by the police officer who has arrested the culprit. The charge sheet is
> written in English for the convenience of a Western type trained
> magistrate, prosecutor, judge and defence lawyer. . . . All court
> proceedings are in English. Such a situation is convenient for the
> public servants, though not necessarily for the interpreter, whose
> proficiency in English may be low and may succeed in promoting
> inadvertent miscarriage of justice.

In many cases a flexible situation, where a lot of code-switching
takes place (cf. 7.5), is the result. Although indigenous African
languages have taken over certain functions from English in some
countries (e.g. Somali in Somalia), English is spreading, partly at
the expense of African languages, in others, especially in
urbanized areas (e.g. in Zambia), if not in relative numbers of
speakers at least in absolute ones.

When speaking of language functions one must bear in mind
that straightforward opposition between a European and an
African language can only be found in special cases of very crude
slogans and campaigns for a particular language policy. This
relationship has been described as diglossic[3] with English as the

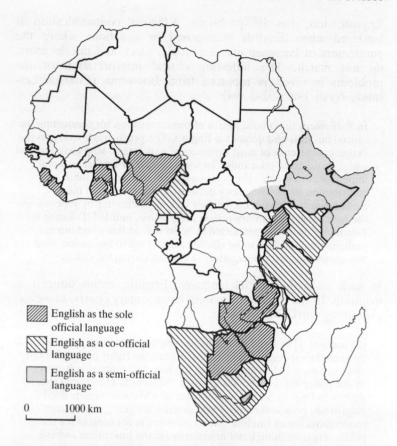

MAP 2   The official status of English in African nation-states

H(igh) and an African language as the L(ow) variety (cf.
Ferguson 1959 and Fishman 1965). Usually the term polyglossia
is more correct, as the multilingual situation is normally much
more complex, involving at least three types of language: a
European lingua franca, an African lingua franca, and African
ethnically related, or local, languages. This situation has been
called trifocal (e.g. by Whiteley) with the hierarchy partly
determined by geographical range: indigenous languages of
ethnic affiliation used in local (often rural) communication, the
African lingua franca in regional communication (even across
national frontiers) and the European lingua franca (in this case
English) in national or international communication. Among the
most important African lingue franche are Hausa, Yoruba and

Igbo in Nigeria, Akan/Twi in Ghana, Swahili in Tanzania, Kenya and Uganda, Bemba and Nyanja in Zambia, Tswana in Botswana and Shona in Zimbabwe. All of them are national or quasi-national languages in coexistence with English. It should be noted that it is an advantage for the spread of lingue franche and their acceptance as national languages if they are ethnically more or less neutral, i.e. if they have few native speakers and are used mostly as second languages. Ethnic languages are normally not accepted as national languages wherever other ethnic groups fear 'tribal dominance' and prefer English, which is 'tribally neutral'. Only tribally neutral lingue franche have any chance of taking over certain functions from English as national languages (as Swahili may eventually in Kenya); otherwise English (in whatever form) may retain these functions and establish itself as the national lingua franca, often called, perhaps euphemistically, a link language (e.g. in Nigeria), because it links those parts of the country that are separated by different ethnic languages or lingue franche. On the whole, however, the delicate bi- or trifocal sociolinguistic pattern has remained remarkably stable in many African countries over the last few decades.

2.2 Knowledge and use

Calling African nations anglophone is obviously a gross exaggeration, because all of them – including the nations with a sizeable number of English mother-tongue speakers – are primarily 'afrophone'. When the term anglophone is used, it should only be applied with caution and a due understanding of its special and restricted meaning in the African context. In this sense, it can refer to the whole range of sociolinguistic situations (as described more systematically below), and means that English is the country's official or at least its first foreign language. Anglophone is thus used in contrast with francophone or lusophone (French- or Portuguese-speaking) African states, for which the same reservations hold. Even then it must be borne in mind that the English-speaking and English-using section of African nations is only an educated minority (with the notable exception of the Republic of South Africa).

It is always difficult to answer the question concerning the number of Africans who actually know English.[4] As the only exact way of finding out would be to ask all Africans which languages they speak, linguists have either to rely on data already available or calculate the numbers indirectly, if they cannot interview a 'representative' sample in an extensive field-study. There is, however, a general scarcity of empirical data about Africa. The existing national censuses, normally the only nation-wide data sources, are unreliable and, what is more, their questionnaires hardly ever include more than one linguistic question, that of the informant's mother tongue. A further possibility would be to ask sample groups a series of linguistic questions and draw conclusions from their answers. This is done in large-scale sociolinguistic surveys. One of the most extensive and well-known was the Survey of Language Use and Language Teaching in Eastern Africa (SLULTEA), sponsored by the Ford Foundation and carried out between 1968 and 1972 in Ethiopia, Kenya, Uganda, Tanzania and Zambia. The publications resulting from this survey now provide a basis for further sociolinguistic research.

In the case of Zambia, for instance, the 1969 census just tells us that 41,434 informants (1 per cent of the total population) claimed to speak English as a mother tongue. One of the SLULTEA surveys gives more detailed information about the knowledge of languages: it reports that 26.1 per cent of the informants in a sample survey named English (as opposed to 56.2 per cent Bemba or 5.3 per cent Lunda, the largest and the smallest of Zambia's seven national languages). It also shows that this number of speakers of English is rather unevenly distributed, since only 19.0 per cent of those in rural but 45.3 per cent in urban areas claim to speak it, with differences between the Copperbelt, Kabwe, Livingstone and Lusaka. Furthermore, as English is usually an additional language used by polyglots and acquired through formal teaching in schools, it tends to be the language of males (more than females) and the language of Zambians with at least upper primary education (all data from Kashoki 1978).

Even sociolinguistic surveys have their weaknesses, since it is often impossible to gain data that conform to the strict rules of empirical social science research, in terms of representativeness and generalizability. They tend to be biased in favour of the urban, developed and accessible areas. Yet, this is where national decision-making takes place, which might finally affect all inhabitants. It must also be recognized that the majority of the population is not used to standardized questionnaires or inter-view techniques, and that their answers will be heavily deter-mined by their personal attitude towards the interviewer and less by so-called objective factual accuracy. Research and survey techniques more adapted and appropriate to African situations are still being developed. Some problems associated with the informants' responses are even more fundamental than these methodological inadequacies. It is, for instance, by no means clear what people mean when they say that someone knows or speaks a language. Many children in African villages will greet white visitors by shouting 'How are you?' or a stereotyped 'Good morning, teacher', which shows that they know certain fixed expressions from English, but it is not difficult to discover that there is little variation or depth in their knowledge of English. As far as passive competence[5] is concerned, it is obvious that most Africans in anglophone states can read simple signs or instructions like to POST OFFICE or TOWN HALL, if they live in areas where these exist. Listening to petty traders in African markets, for instance, shows that there is a threshold level above: 'Buy this, friend, only ten shillings, good price' or even 'Dis one only one tousan'. When one counts only those who can also react correctly to simple questions in normal, i.e. not pidginized English, just a minority can talk about simple everyday facts and events in a reasonably intelligible way – and even then it may take a foreigner some time to get used to their pronunciation and usage, whereas other Africans are said to be able to understand more easily, because intelligibility is a subjective skill dependent on experience.

Informants' self-evaluations about the languages they 'know' are often unreliable; first, because they may really not be able to tell objectively, since they cannot know what degree of proficiency is considered a minimum requirement by the interviewer, and secondly because their answer may be biased by the fact that knowledge of languages in general and of English in particular is normally seen as a status symbol, a sign of importance, influence or education. It is always advisable either to ask more specifically, whether the informants understand greetings, speeches, jokes, whether they can write a letter or read a newspaper, or briefly to test the informants' knowledge of English. Another possibility is to compare their answers to other questions, e.g. on education. In most anglophone African countries there is a clear correlation between English competence and length of schooling, becoming particularly conspicuous in countries where less English is used within the nation (see 2.3). Where English is a foreign language formal education is the only means of language acquisition, whereas if it is a second language it may be possible to pick up a certain amount of English in town streets, work places, etc., although this may never go much beyond very rudimentary English, which English films, radio and television programmes may improve where they can be received. At a higher level, the comparison of educational figures can give a fairly adequate estimate of the English speakers in a country (see chapter 4).

Such methodological and conceptual problems make it difficult to give more than a broad picture of the knowledge and use of English in Africa. As has been seen in the case of Zambia above, the most important determinant in a country is education, including literacy: the higher the percentage of English speakers, and the longer a person stays in the educational system, the higher his or her standard of English will be. Closely connected to education are the other determinants of age, sex and religion. Most educational systems in Africa have expanded enormously since independence, hence there are more speakers of English among young adults than among older ones. The schools' intake is often unbalanced between the sexes, since parents sometimes still think that schooling is more important for boys than for girls, and in consequence in many African states about twice as many males speak English as females, if we can go by the rough semi-official estimates by ministries of education or other specialized institutions or the few case studies available (e.g. Heine/Köhler 1981). Similarly, the religious factor plays a decisive role: in predominantly Islamic areas education, especially girls' education, is regarded as less important than in Christian areas; but even among Christian denominations differences in the knowledge of English are noticeable because of the different language policies in different missions (as has been stated in chapter 1, protestant missionaries always made a greater attempt to teach Africans in their mother tongue than Catholics normally did). Another factor is associated with 'regional development', which subsumes the well-known urban–rural, coastal–hinterland and central–peripheral contrasts. In the central areas the proportion of multilingual and English-speaking people is higher, because of relatively broader and higher education, more interaction with other ethnic groups, development experts or tourists, and the selective nature of the migration process (usually the more educated, innovative and active people leave the village, the others stay behind).

It is nevertheless true that such broad parameters can indicate only vaguely the number and nature of English speakers in any given African country or region. The number must primarily depend on the sociolinguistic position of English in the nation or state, and especially in its educational system. This accounts for the variation between over 30 per cent claimed for Ghana to about 5 per cent of the total population estimated by specialists in and for Tanzania. In most countries where English is a second language the percentage should be between 10 and 20. Again Liberia, with its unique settlement history and relation to English, is the exception with 40 per cent (Bokamba 1991). A second question about language use is concerned with language choice. Even when an African can include English in his language repertoire (and it is obviously this minority only to whom the following statements apply) English is normally only his second or third language, if not in importance, then at least in order of language acquisition. Apart from a very small élite in the few urban centres, for the majority English is always an additional (second, third, fourth, etc.) language. Which language a speaker chooses to use in a particular communicative situation depends on a number of variables: the addressee(s), the place, the topic and the (formality of the) situation. All this is implied in Fishman's (1965) famous definition of sociolinguistics as being about: 'Who speaks what language to whom and when?' This again raises difficulties in research and the question has been tackled in various ways. Some researchers asked their informants to keep a diary for several weeks, others participated and themselves observed what happened, others used standardized questionnaires. The quantitative analysis of such data has proved particularly difficult. One must, for instance, distinguish between continuous use of a language in one conversation, code (language or variety) switching within one and the same conversation, and code mixing within the same syntactic unit or sentence.

In oral communication the role of English is sometimes very limited. In the family, for instance, English is rarely used by non-native speakers, except perhaps when educated, urban parents want to help their children to acquire English at home or when ethnically-mixed couples have no African lingua franca as a common ground. Otherwise, family life, which in Africa often still means the extended family, is the domain of the mother tongue (except in very 'modern' families). The reasons for this are manifold, not only because language choice in the family is usually most persistent (older members being used to the language choices of their youth) but also because it is difficult to express the traditional African deferential relationship towards the older members in English. English emphasizes status in a modern sense based on education and material success and not the traditional one based on age and social rank, thus it would be inappropriate in many family situations (cf. Siachitema 1991).

Outside the home, African lingue franche (including pidgins) become more important, but administrative and business offices are English-dominated. Nevertheless, language choice varies according to whether a friend, a colleague or a formal visitor is addressed. In schools (see chapter 4) and hospitals English is usually heard because a technical vocabulary is needed, which may not be available in African languages, or because all the records are kept in English. Generally speaking, it is often used as the language of specialized information. Whereas news and politics are the domain of African languages, economics, natural sciences and often even literature are discussed at least partly in English. Another sociolinguistically interesting factor is ethnicity (tribal background). In ethnically homogeneous groups the mother tongue is used, whereas in mixed African groups African lingue franche (among the less educated) or English will be chosen. With Europeans most Africans will show that they know English, if they do, either to demonstrate their education or simply to make communication easier for the foreigner. Immigrants from India and the Middle East, who formerly acted as middle-men between black and white in trade, often still occupy a linguistic middle position, i.e. they talk to Africans in African languages and to Europeans in English.

In written communication the role of English is normally much more prominent, partly because writing is more élitist and selective anyway. Writing letters requires literacy in English or an African language and some familiarity with the formal system of mailing, and as a result English is – in absolute terms, in contrast to African languages – chosen in writing much more often than in speaking even when the same people are involved in the communication. Besides writing, choice in reading is also important, but here language choice is determined by the availability of reading materials, be it from bookshops or libraries. In many countries it is much easier to obtain books, periodicals and even newspapers in English than in African languages. And again, there is an increase in the percentage of English from literary, social science, economic to natural science books, and of course, from popular to scientific literature. However, in questions of language choice the prestige factor should not be underestimated: in many anglophone African societies it is fashionable to read the English edition of a newspaper if available rather than the African one, although they may be very similar in content and even style.

Finally, it must be pointed out that the use of English not only depends on the knowledge of the language, the communicative situation and the speakers' attitudes towards it but also on the development of the African languages available.

2.3 Describing the position of English within African nation-states

The position of the English language in the different African nation-states is complex and varies considerably. In order to describe and understand this diversity several categories have been used. It is thus customary (cf. Moag 1982, Platt/Weber/Ho 1984) to apply the following broad terms to countries as well as to individual speakers:

ENL English as a native language (or English as a mother tongue or first language);[6]
ESL English as a second language;[7]
EFL English as a foreign language.

In recent years another category has been added, subdividing EFL into EFL proper and

EIL English as an international language.[8]

This means that English is referred to as EIL when used among non-native speakers and EFL when used by non-native speakers talking to native-speakers. As English is used by many Africans to communicate with Europeans, irrespective of whether they are English native speakers or not, and even by members of francophone African states (with French as a second language) to communicate with their anglophone neighbours, the term EIL seems to be more appropriate as often only non-native speakers are involved.

Although the labels EIL, ESL and ENL, in this order, generally imply an increase in the functions the language fulfils, they are obviously very broad abstractions when applied to whole nation-states. It must be emphasized that the theoretical framework of features (as summarized in Table 2.1) is still rather tentative, but it can serve as a basis for the following more detailed discussion. One also has to bear in mind that the categorization is not always clear-cut (because there are also intermediate cases), that the classification of countries is often determined by an educated, politically dominant minority, and that the typological categories themselves are rather complex and

TABLE 2.1 Sociolinguistic and linguistic features of English as a native (ENL), second (ESL) and international language (EIL) in idealized oppositions

Features	ENL	ESL	EIL
official status	uniquely recognized	explicitly supported	
communicative range	intranational	intra-international	international
multi-lingualism		societal	individual
acquisition from	parents	environment formal education	formal education
motivation for language acquisition	expressive	integrative	instrumental
prestige	(taken for granted)	very high	high
adapted to speaker identity	(taken for granted)	partly accepted	not accepted
target norm	indigenous national	indigenous national	utilitarian international
variation	social and regional	ethnic and educational	educational
interference		strong	strong
generalization		very strong	strong
fluency	very important	important	restricted
stylistic range (registers)	very broad	broad	restricted

do not have only one defining feature. In fact, the categorization in ENL, ESL and EIL nations is based on differences in many sociolinguistic and linguistic features.

In theory, whereas ENL and ESL countries use English for intranational (as well as international) communication, EIL countries use it only for international communication, albeit as their most important medium. English certainly functions as an international language, when it is used in communication with international development agencies, even by Africans in their own country. In practice, however, it is sometimes not easy to decide whether English really has an intranational function, for instance, just because it is used as the language of instruction in an African university, because most of the books are in English and possibly produced in Europe or America and because many lecturers come from abroad. Also, in theory, in ENL and ESL nation-states English should have an official status, laid down in the country's constitution or legislation. In practice, we notice that some African governments hesitate to grant this official status to a former colonial language. We often find various, partly contradictory, official statements and it is not clear whether earlier ones have been superseded or are still valid; later, previous statements may be re-emphasized and others 'neglected'. Furthermore, due to its intranational functions multilingualism in ESL countries comprises large sections of society, whereas in EIL countries it is basically only individuals who are polyglots as a result of their special training or individual experience. But where is the absolute or relative borderline?

Similarly, other sociolinguistic features are a matter of degree. It is certainly true to say that mother tongues are usually learnt from parents (hence the name) and international languages in formal education; second languages can be acquired in social contacts, especially among peer groups, but also in the home or in early formal education. The prime motivation for learning the mother tongue (if we can call it 'motivation' as first language learning is obviously less conscious than additional language learning) is the need to express all personal wishes, thoughts or aims; for learning EIL it is to use the language for restricted communicative purposes in one's occupation or holidays; ESL is learnt, it is said, because a learner wants to integrate into the ESL speech community which normally enjoys high prestige, English being often used as an indicator of class. But can these motivations really be separated from one another? The prestige of English certainly appears to be highest in an ESL community, because it is associated with a successful élite and with the degree of formal education (though this may not apply to other second languages), but how can this be measured objectively? The speaker's identity, culture and authenticity are normally symbolized by and in the mother tongue, but latest developments (e.g. in Nigeria) show that certain modern aspects of identity (cf. 7.5) can also or even only be expressed in a European second language, if there is no accepted supra-ethnic lingua franca.

This is clearly reflected in literary production. Uganda, for instance, had a very active tradition of writing in English, partly under the influence of the university at Makerere. Unfortunately this has suffered as much as that in the Southern Sudan, where English is much more important than in the North of the country; the importance of English for the Southern identity is attested by the fact that most English contributions in the monthly *Sudanow*, for instance, were written by Southerners.

As sociolinguistic phenomena usually have linguistic correlates, it is interesting, though not easy, to investigate the formal linguistic features of English as used in ENL, ESL and EIL countries. A very important linguistic question is which target norm, model or standard of English, is accepted in the speech community. This norm may be used in language teaching, propagated in books or in broadcasting, and codified in books on usage and grammar and in dictionaries. Growing linguistic awareness in independent nation-states goes hand in hand with growing political awareness, because both are aspects of a developing national identity. Thus, the political independence of ENL nations from Britain was often followed by a desire for linguistic independence. This happened in the United States, in Australia and in the Republic of South Africa, especially as far as pronunciation and ranges of vocabulary are concerned (cf. chapter 3). Interestingly enough, a similar development seems to be taking place in some ESL nations, for example in post-independent India or Nigeria, both being countries which have found it difficult to express national identity in *one* unifying indigenous language. It is, however, not certain whether this process will in fact touch all ESL nation-states. For EIL nations it is usually not possible to accept their own national standard because their international partners may find communication difficult when a distinct national variety is used. Thus a more neutral 'working English' is considered to be preferable; such an international target variety has been called *Utilitarian English* (Wong 1982). This concept was suggested as an alternative for the new nations of the Third World to Quirk's *Nuclear English* 'that would contain a subset of the features of natural English; . . . [it] would be intelligible to speakers of any major variety and could be expanded for specific purposes' (Quirk et al. 1985: 9). Whereas Quirk wants to introduce planned simplification to make the variety easier for the learner, Wong (1982: 270) claims that *Utilitarian English* 'is already spoken in many parts of the Third World, in regions where English has merely an auxiliary and instrumental role to play in the non-native speaker contexts'. For many parts of Africa these could be viable pragmatic, not necessarily prestigious, solutions for the future; today however both concepts are still largely theoretical and detailed descriptions for pedagogic use are not available.

Even if a certain norm is generally accepted in a country, be it in the codified form of an institutionalized norm or only as a performance norm, there will still inevitably be a degree of variation. In ENL situations this variation is usually along social and/or regional dimensions. In ESL situations it tends to correlate with ethnic background and educational achievement, which is often closely linked with socio-economic status. In EIL situations it will vary primarily with educational background, that is the amount of schooling and amount of English language teaching available.

One linguistic reason for deviations from the native speaker norm in ESL and in EIL nations is the interference from other languages spoken, especially the mother tongue. Then the pronunciation of English, for instance, is closer to some common African sounds which are similar, but not identical to those of international English, because the African speaker tries to make use of his native African sound system as far as possible. Or (Standard) English structures are not 'properly' used, underused or not used at all, because they do not occur in the mother tongue. Other linguistic reasons, besides these interlanguage influences, can be found within English itself. For instance, when common target language structures are (over-)generalized, a generally correct English rule is extended to words, structures, etc. to which normally more specific rules apply (e.g. *Today meat is costing a lot* expands a construction used with dynamic verbs in Standard English to include stative ones). Such intralinguistically determined deviations in frequency and acceptability may occur more often in ESL than EIL nations because of the pressure to use English more spontaneously in certain situations, even when only few English structures are known to the speaker.

It is a commonplace that ENL speakers can talk more fluently than ESL and of course EIL speakers. Similarly, native-speaker English is more elaborate and has more registers at its speakers' disposal, whereas ESL speakers are more restricted, and EIL speakers normally have only a small range of expression in formal style.

When the broad categories of ENL, ESL and EIL are applied to specific African nation-states, the problems raised by abstract categories become evident. There is no African state which could be called an ENL nation in the same sense as the United Kingdom or even Eire, Canada or Jamaica, where an absolute majority speaks English as a mother tongue. In Africa today, only Liberia[9] and the Republic of South Africa have a sizeable proportion of ENL speakers, even though in both cases they constitute only a small minority. They are both settler colonies, albeit of a very different nature (see p. 10).

The British settlers were latecomers to the Cape, the Dutch having arrived more than 150 years before, in 1652. There were several distinct waves of British settlement, starting with the working-class Cape settlers in the 1820s and the more aristocratic Natal settlers in the 1850s (cf. Lanham/MacDonald 1979). Today there is a wide spectrum of mother-tongue Englishes, not only among White South Africans but also among Indians, Coloureds and some Black Africans. Nevertheless, Afrikaans is equal to English, not only in terms of numbers of mother-tongue speakers (the offical ratio is even about 60 per cent to 40 per cent in favour of Afrikaans) but also in official status.

The Republic of South Africa can be characterized as an ENL country, for a substantial amount of the population uses English as its first language, between 6 per cent (monolingual) and 11 per cent (bilingual with Afrikaans). But the Republic of South Africa is an ESL country for the majority of the population who speak Bantu, Khoi-San, Afrikaans, Indian and other immigrant languages as mother tongues. This example shows that speech-communities are not homogeneous, certainly not on the national level.

The descendants of the settlers in Liberia form the dominant political and economic group in the country, at least they did until the 1980 revolution. As a reflection of the continued strong political and economic influence of the United States, Liberian English has always had an Afro-American stamp. Whereas the descendants of the former settlers, the Americo-Liberians, who spoke different forms of English creoles and Black American English as their mother tongue, are concentrated in urbanized areas, the majority of Afro-Liberians live in the peripheral hinterland and are mainly still illiterate. Among them only an educated elite uses English as a second language. Even after the 1980 revolution English has proved extremely persistent. Thus the distinction between English-speakers and non-English-speakers, which used to be along ethnic lines, establishes itself more and more along socio-educational lines, although the two overlap, as those who were born into high social positions are also those whose parents have the economic means to finance a good English-medium education.

A similar sociolinguistic case seems to be Sierra Leone, where the same marked political and linguistic dichotomy exists between the Freetown area, with the descendants of the repatriated English-speaking American Blacks, called Krios, and the hinterland Africans, mostly Temne- and Mende-speaking. But the Americo-Africans' mother tongue Krio, although historically an English-derived creole, should be seen as a language in its own right. English (in the sense of Standard English) is thus a second language, which is acquired by Sierra Leoneans who have the opportunity of receiving some formal education. This is particularly so in view of the fact that the internal balance of power shifts from the coastal Krios to the inland groupings.

When calling Liberia and the Republic of South Africa intermediate ENL-ESL cases today, it may be interesting to note that historically Kenya, Zimbabwe (as Rhodesia) and Namibia (as South-West Africa) were similarly ENL-dominated. Whereas in Kenya many British settlers left during the Mau-Mau period or subsequently, in the 1950s and early 1960s, a similar retreat occurred from Zimbabwe 20 years later, although the ENL speakers there are still much more prominent in terms of number and influence. In Namibia this dominance is still partly upheld by the South African presence. On the whole and in view of future developments, it seems safe to categorize Kenya, Zimbabwe and Namibia as ESL (or even intermediate ESL-EIL) countries.

The most typical ESL nations are those which cannot agree on the choice of one unifying indigenous lingua franca, and rely therefore on English for nation-building purposes. They use English as a medium of instruction, even in primary schools; some from Standard 1, most of them only from Standard 4 or 5 onwards (see ch. 4). There may also be regional differences in this respect, with English medium classes starting earlier in ethnically-mixed or urban schools than in ethnically-homo-geneous or rural schools. Another almost certain indicator of an ESL country is the fact that English is used in the national parliament, because this is inevitably a politically sensitive domain. Almost the same applies to local administration and courts, although in Africa these domains often show a discrepancy between official regulations and actual language use, since problems of practical communication make it impossible to follow the theoretical regulations given by administrations from above. Typical former British colonies in Africa that have developed into and will certainly remain ESL nations are Nigeria, Zambia and Ghana.

Although there has been a debate about adopting a Ghanaian

language (usually Akan) as a national language, English is the language used in government and administration. It is the language of instruction in all government schools from primary four onward (the few 'international schools' using it from the beginning) and the language of the second national radio programme and the television station. All daily newspapers are in English. Ghanaian creative writing is in English (except for a few religious works, oral literature and some drama) and its authors publish in local popular magazines of the entertaining and moralizing type as well as in the major international series. Through the general decline of the economy and education the once famous national standard of English has also suffered, and the influence of the mother tongues and even Nigerian English is clearly felt, mainly from Ghanaians working in the rich neighbouring country in the 1970s.

A particularly interesting case is Cameroon, since it is officially an ESL and an FSL (French as a second language) nation at the same time, although in practice French predominates quite clearly. Two colonial inheritances, British in the small Western part and French in the Eastern part, are partly responsible for this unique experiment in official bilingualism[10].

It is also interesting to note that some nations, such as Malawi, Lesotho, Zimbabwe and Kenya maintain an ESL status, although they have an indigenous majority language or lingua franca (Chewa, Sotho, Shona and Swahili, respectively) which could take over some functions from English.

Some African nations use African (either first or national) languages in primary and partly in secondary schools but still maintain English as a medium in higher levels of education, with many other aspects of public life dominated by one or another African language. These nations must therefore be seen as belonging to an intermediate ESL–EIL category. The difference between ESL and ESL–EIL countries can be illustrated by comparing the domains of English in East African states (cf. Table 2.2, adapted from Hancock/Angogo 1982: 311, who seem to be overemphasizing English in some countries). Again it must be stressed that strict labelling is practically impossible because some public aspects of language use can easily be recorded by participant observation, whereas others are a matter of degree and can only be stated tentatively, even after specific enquiries and discussions (e.g. private correspondence).

In contrast to ENL–ESL countries, ESL–EIL territories were only partly penetrated historically by the British. For instance, Tanzania became British only after the First World War (named

TABLE 2.2 The domains of English in East African states

	Zambia	Zimbabwe	Malawi	Uganda	Kenya	Seychelles	Somalia	Tanzania	Ethiopia
High court	+	+	+	+	+	+	−	+	−
Local court	*	*	*	*	*	*	−	−	−
Parliament	+	+	+	+	+	+	−	−	−
Civil service	+	+	+	+	+	+	+	−	−
Primary school	+	+	+	+	+	*	−	−	−
Secondary school	+	+	+	+	+	+	+	+	+
Radio	+	+	+	+	+	+	+	+	+
Newspaper	+	+	+	+	+	+	+	+	+
Local novels	+	+	+	+	+	*	*	+	+
Local records	+	+	+	+	+	−	−	−	−
Local plays	+	+	+	+	+	*	*	−	−
Films (not dubbed)	+	+	+	+	+	+	+	+	−
Traffic and vehicle signs	+	+	+	+	+	+	+	−	−
Advertising	+	+	+	+	+	+	+	*	−
Business correspondence	+	+	+	+	+	+	+	+	+
Private correspondence	+	+	+	+	+	+	*	−	*

Key
+ = English used
* = English only sometimes used
− = English not used

Tanganyika instead of German East Africa), Somalia only in the northern part (then called British Somaliland) and Ethiopia remained formally independent and was occupied by British forces only partly and very briefly after they had helped to drive out the Italians (1941–54). Although this may be the most important reason for the weaker position of English in these countries, there is also another one: the respective governments promote their own national languages in order to unite the different groups in their territories. This is relatively easy in Somalia, where practically everybody speaks a variety of Somali as a first language, and also in Tanzania, where Swahili is the generally accepted and widely known national language. In Botswana the situation is historically different, because British penetration started earlier and the South African influence (in English) is still dominant, but it is similar with respect to the nation-wide lingua franca, because Tswana is spoken by more than 80 per cent of the population as a mother tongue and understood to some extent by most others. From an internal sociolinguistic perspective English could easily be 'reduced' to the status of an international language, if the country were not so small and heavily dependent on its international relations and their internal repercussions.

The transition from ESL–EIL to EIL nations is marked by the Sudan, since although once under British rule, it has Arabic as its dominant language, especially in the North, whereas English still holds some second language functions in the South. Arabic is, in fact, the national and international language for the whole of Northern Africa, so that there remains little room for other international languages, but American English is gaining ground even at the expense of the traditional international language, French.

Again, there is variation in degree between EIL countries, such as between countries where English is the first European language learnt in school and others like Mozambique, which inherited Portuguese as a second language but teaches English as it is completely surrounded by ESL countries, and Togo, which is economically, culturally and linguistically embedded in the West and Central African francophone community, but still needs English to communicate with its big ESL neighbours, Ghana and Nigeria. In Senegal, where French is also the second language and English very little used, courses of English for Special Purposes (ESP) are taught in the five technical *lycées* of the country; in the other *lycées* English is taught not only as an international language to 95 per cent of the students (5 per cent take German) but also to strengthen the envisaged confederation with Gambia. There is also an English for Academic Purposes (EAP) course for students in most university degree courses.

In this categorization only those countries are called EIL that do not have another European language with more official functions because of their specific problems (e.g. in teaching English at university level). Other countries, such as Algeria, seem to use English to reduce unilateral dependencies: although Algeria's relationship with France is particularly long and complex the government follows a policy of Arabization, with the long-term perspective of using English and French as international languages of equal status, which is far from the sociolinguistic reality nowadays. Maintaining two international languages may be particularly difficult (cf. however Cameroon p. 40). In order not to exaggerate unduly it may therefore be wise to restrict the term EIL nation to those that use it as the first non-national international language, although there may be many 'exceptions' on the personal level of individuals who use English in a state with, for instance, French as an international language. A good example of an EIL country is Egypt. English is the medium of instruction (except in civics, religion and Arabic) in only a small number of fee-paying primary and secondary schools in Cairo and Alexandria, but there are also French-medium schools. When it comes to higher education the medium is (officially) English in many institutions, particularly in the Higher Nursing Institutes or the university departments of medicine, pharmacy, dentistry, science, veterinary service, engineering and architecture. The other university departments, which teach in Arabic, use English as a library language and postgraduate theses include at least a summary in English. Among the general public English is *not* widely used, except with tourists and foreign experts. But there is a national daily newspaper in English and English language films are very popular. Creative writers, however, publish in Arabic.

A final overview is provided by Map 3. Despite the weaknesses of such categorizations explained above it offers a useful comparison of the position of English in all African states.

Notes

1. Apart from the political sector, the semi-official status of English is also visible in the (more or less independent) mass media. In Nigeria, for instance, most of the broadcasts of the federal broadcasting corporation are in English, and there are more than a dozen daily newspapers in English, each with a circulation of between half a million and a million copies: *The Times, Punch, New Nigerian Concord, Sketch, Tribune, Herald, Star, Observer, Chronicle, Echo*, etc. In contrast, of the more than four hundred indigenous languages, there are only two weekly newspapers, one in Hausa and one in Yoruba, both with a circulation of less than fifty thousand.

2. These terms have been discussed and interpreted in various ways. Brann (1985a: 1) sees the reason for the ambiguity of 'national' in 'diachronic overloading'; that is why Fishman distinguished between nationist (referring to the nation-state) and nationalist (referring to strong ethnic nationality; for a summary see Fasold 1984: 72–9).

3. There are other definitions of diglossia today which would emphasize the difference between educated and broken varieties of English, which is presented as a continuum in 3.1.

4. The figures of English speakers in Africa in Crystal (1985) are misleading as he lists the total population of some African countries as speaking English as a second language (e.g. Ethiopia 32.2

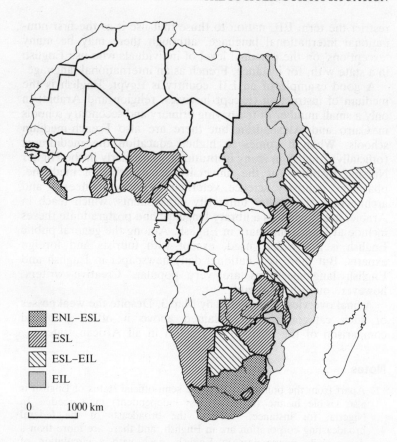

MAP 3 The position of English in African nation-states

ENL–ESL

ESL

ESL–EIL

EIL

0   1000 km

million). Such figures do not refer to actual, but rather to potential
English speakers.

5. The notion of competence has led to much confusion in theoretical
linguistics and applied/sociolinguistics, because Chomsky's grammatical concept, even when he talks of pragmatic competence, is
much narrower than Dell Hymes' sociolinguistic one (Taylor 1988).
A further complication arose when the concept of communicative
competence became fashionable, usually in reference to language
learning and teaching. In relation to African multilingualism the
sociolinguistic concept (emphasizing the communicative value) and
the proficiency concept (emphasizing the fluency and acceptability)
must be kept apart.

6. All these terms have been criticized, because 'first' in the sense of a
first-learnt language may be forgotten later through disuse, while

"native" has pejorative overtones for some Africans and Indians. "Mother tongue" may mean the language spoken from birth, the language of the mother or even father, the language used in the home, the language one thinks in, etc. Thus "primary" language has been suggested as an alternative, emphasizing the dominant use. On account of such criticism, a "native" speaker has been redefined as someone who learns the language from childhood *and* continues to use it *and* has reached a certain level of fluency in terms of grammatical well-formedness, speech act rules, functional and variational diversification. This allows us to separate the concept of native speaker from that of native competence and to see very highly educated Africans as having native competence in several languages, including English.

7. With reference to language speakers and learners the term ESL is used in two completely different sociolinguistic situations: first in an immersion situation when immigrants or migrants come to a basically monolingual ENL country, where the dominant culture is clearly English, second in a multilingual society when English is an additional language and expresses only part of the national culture. This also explains the fate of the mother tongue: in a dominantly monolingual ESL situation, as in the USA, it tends to be given up more easily than in a multilingual ESL situation, as in anglophone Africa. For the African situation an attempt of "the conceptualization of ESL" was made by Afolayan/Awolowo (1987).

8. Lubega (1987) isolates four senses of the term international language: as a contact language for specific international contacts in education, business, diplomacy and travel; as a language of handling international affairs, as a language that provides links between individual countries and as a language that facilitates social interaction between persons of different nationalities within the same country. For the formal side of these functions he suggests that "instead of creating a pan-cultural [artificial] language to function as EIL in order to guarantee mutual intelligibility among all users of English, we should regard the educated versions of the various varieties of English as the desired forms to function jointly as EIL" (ibid. 63).

9. Because English in Liberia is unique in Africa – when I consider Krio as a language separate from English – I will not go into the discussion as to whether or not is should be called English as a second dialect (ESD), with a low variety as a mother tongue and a high variety as an American-related Standard, which is the reflection of the economic, cultural and educational ties with the USA.

10. Actually the term bilingualism is misleading, because this official bilingualism must include at least the mother tongue and both official languages, and must thus be at least trilingual (cf. Tadadjeu 1975).

Chapter 3
Language Forms

The variation in the forms of English in Africa is as wide as the variation in the sociolinguistic environment in which it is learnt and used. Referring to these forms in the past simply as 'English' was certainly a gross, and dubious, overgeneralization. But, although English in Africa naturally often differs in some respects from the British varieties of Standard English (including its variant pronunciations), its 'Africanness' is very elusive and any supposed homogeneity far from the reality of the African situation. This does not mean that such features cannot be found in other non-standard native-speaker varieties or in American English for instance, and even British authors may exhibit similar features in some styles. 'Africanisms' form a glide from clear cases, where Africans are almost surprised that other English speakers do not use these forms, to others, which seem only slightly more frequently used and are thus hardly consciously recognized. Nevertheless, there are several ways of classifying the forms of English spoken in Africa and there are several reasons for the origin and persistence of its distinctive character. This can be shown at all levels of linguistic description, e.g. pronunciation, grammar, vocabulary, meaning and discourse.

3.1 The range of variation in English in Africa and its categorization

One of the broadest categorizations of the English used in Africa is suggested by Angogo/Hancock (1980: 71), who distinguish the following types according to speakers:

(a) native English of African-born whites and expatriates;

(b) native English of locally-born Africans;
(c) non-native English spoken fluently as a second language;
(d) non-native English spoken imperfectly as a foreign language.

The first category, White African English, is relatively insignificant today – with the notable exception of South Africa – although its influence on language development may have been considerable. The other three categories of (Black) African English constitute a continuum of English forms parallel to our sociolinguistic categorization (in chapter 2), which ranges from ENL to ESL and EIL varieties. It is worth noting, however, that these categories were used to illustrate differences between entire nations, especially in the process of developing (hypothetical) national varieties of English; when it comes to analysing language forms which are actually used in Africa, intranational and intrapersonal variation, the individual speaker's sociolinguistic background and the actual speech-act situation must be taken into consideration. At the individual level, the type of English spoken by Africans depends largely (i.e. if we ignore personal differences in use with special interlocutors and degree of exposure to English on the radio, television, etc.) on two factors: (a) their education, i.e. the length and degree of formal education in English, and b) their occupation, i.e. the necessity for and amount of English used in everyday life.

The two factors may correlate in countries with strict governmental man-power management planning or they may be completely unrelated in countries with free movement of labour. It is clear that the two parameters themselves depend on other variables, such as family background and regional origin (with more prosperous and influential family background and more central, developed regional origin likely to produce a 'higher' education, occupation and variety of English). If we also take the national sociolinguistic background into consideration we can construct a rough and ready theoretical continuum of English varieties (see Table 3.1) or 'cline of bilingualism' (Sey 1973: 18), which may not be valid for all individuals but indicate general societal guidelines. As labels for the linguistic levels the categories of acrolect, mesolect and basilect (with increasing deviation from the target language) are used, which are applied in research on pidgin and creole languages as well as in that on 'New Englishes' (cf. Kachru 1986a or Platt/Weber/Ho 1984). These names were transferred from pidgin and creole research, because both types of language show a similar cline in the

TABLE 3.1   Continuum of English varieties in the African sociolinguistic environment

Cline of English varieties	Cumulative length of English education	Degree of formal education		Characteristic jobs and occupations	
		ESL	EIL	ESL	EIL
acrolect	14 years	university in home country	university in English-speaking nation	newspaper editors, lawyers, senior officers in civil service and business firms	university lecturers, medical doctors, business managers
mesolect	8–14 years	secondary school	university in home country	junior civil servants, senior nurses, secretaries, typists	senior civil servants, newspaper editors, lawyers
basilect	7–10 years	primary school	secondary school	shop assistants, taxi drivers, clerks, nurses	medical assistants, junior civil servants, typists, secretaries

development of reduced forms of the target language, especially when second-language learners regard themselves as socially separate from the language's native speakers and when they use the target language only for a limited range of functions.[1] To what extent the different varieties are spoken in any given African country will obviously depend on the sociolinguistic background as well as educational and occupational possibilities in the national context.

The linguistic characteristics of the varieties defined hypothetically above are very difficult to categorize, but the following model may give a tentative approximation (Table 3.2 developed from Criper 1971: 9), although it neglects paralinguistic features, timbre and pitch, for instance. It is interesting to note that the acknowledged reference model is still largely (British) Standard English (StE). It must however be emphasized that Standard

TABLE 3.2 Model of linguistic differences in African varieties of English

	Phonetics	Phonology	Grammar	Lexis	Semantics	Discourse	Content
(StE)							
acrolect	−	~	~	~	−	−	−
mesolect	−	−	−	~	−	−	~
basilect	~	~	−	~	−	−	~
(pidgin?)							

Key
~ = similar to category above
− = different from category above

English itself is not homogeneous and, when spoken, does not necessarily involve Received Pronunciation. Although even the most elevated level of English, the acrolect, differs from Standard English in phonetics, semantics, discourse and content, it is fairly similar in phonology, grammar and lexis. This means that the phonological system, the structures used and the overwhelming majority of the words are still the same, but the actual phonetic form of words varies slightly, their meaning may be a little different, the subtle differences of formality may be disregarded, and the subject matter discussed is often related to the African environment (e.g. festivities or plants). From the mesolect downwards, mergers of vowels change the whole phonological system and grammatical structures often become more and more 'distorted', if judged from a prescriptive Standard English perspective; and thus a basically new system evolves. At the lower end of the continuum, the basilect, which is still English although often Africanized to unintelligibility for those who are not used to it, is difficult to identify, especially in areas where it coexists with an English-related pidgin (as along the Guinea Gulf coast). Whether the forms of pidgin can be added at the bottom end of this scale or whether they are completely separate is a matter of debate.

Although education and occupation may be the major parameters in internal language variation in Africa, the other 'big three' are sex, age and ethnicity/first language. The few studies that exist (e.g. Awonusi 1985 or Jibril 1982a) suggest that – as in most sociolinguistic studies around the world (cf. several studies in Cheshire (ed.) 1991) – female Africans are closer to the standard variety than male ones (because they tend to avoid stigmatized features) – if they have the same level of education, which is still unlikely in some areas. The age parameter is usually judged impressionistically, as most studies only use professionals or students as informants. Although the general claim in Africa is that 'in the old days' the standard of English was much higher, the quantitative aspect must not be overlooked. In late colonial days the few élite schools, such as Katsina College in Northern Nigeria and Alliance High School in Kenya, educated what is now politically, economically and intellectually the leading class, whereas today more young Africans than ever before learn English in many more, mostly less well-equipped schools. Ethnicity, which is often defined in terms of first language, cultural practices and traditions, is still an important factor in many African nation-states and in many ways the most important emotional determinant of social and even sociopolitical behaviour. It is therefore of significance whether intranational differences are more salient than international ones, or whether the ethnic differences are being levelled out, as Jibril (1986: 59) hypothesizes. Up to the present time ethnic differences are still very much perceived and stereotyped in most African societies. The well-known pronunciation 'problems' of neighbouring groups are certainly perceived and sometimes even ridiculed by people in Kenya (Schmied 1991a) and Nigeria (Jibril 1986), particularly when they occur not only more or less frequently but almost consistently. Africa (1983: 16) also claims that 'many Zambians are able to say whether a fellow Zambian speaking English has Tonga, Lozi, Bemba or Nyanja as his/her first language and this information is derived mainly from phonological indices'. Such differences may, however, be used for political argumentation and played up, as by Southern Sudanese in contrast to the North, or down, as by most politicians emphasizing nation-building. This can also be seen in its extreme form (of variational complexity), in South Africa, where ethnic heterogeneity is reflected within the various varieties of English (cf. Mesthrie 1988).

Whereas variation has so far been described as variation according to language user, it is essential to consider also the one according to language use: i.e. according to the situational setting (home–public), the topic (personal–technical), the medium (spoken–written), the purpose, etc. The choice of style is, like the choice of language, not controlled by objective features but by the participants' perception and interpretation. Such stylistic variation is often called stylistic switching in Africa to form a parallel to code switching between languages. Other terms for a similar phenomenon are code-sliding and style-shifting, which emphasizes that features and styles of several varieties may form an overlapping continuum. Scotton (1972: 53) observes that in Africa interlanguage switching can serve the same function as intralanguage switching (cf. 7.5). Intralanguage variation also depends on the extension of language use across several domains. As English tends to be used more in formal and African languages in informal domains, interesting questions concerning the formality of African forms of English arise. African English is often generally said to be formal, possibly because features associated with formality usually signal politeness, and are therefore valued highly in traditional African societies (see 3.7). This leaves little room for informal registers of English. So far only few ESL communities in Africa seem to have developed informal styles (cf. Moody 1982). But on some occasions formal style may even be impolite since it can also be used for interpersonal distancing. This may lead to communicative misunderstandings (particularly between ENL and ESL cultures) and shows that it is not only the forms but also the related attitudes that are important. As it is the culture of a society that determines its language patterns, style becomes a relative concept. Style associations may be conventionalized differently in a speech community.

A particular problem of style in a second-language community is for the investigator to discover to what extent a speaker's stylistic repertoires overlap with varying degrees of competence. Thus whether or not a particular item should be considered as marked becomes problematical. Speakers may want to impress their listeners with their formal command of English, but with no intention of striking a more formal tone in the relationship. Zuengler (1982: 117) mentions the use of English forms that would be considered as strangely archaic or overtly formal in first-language English, but are used in situations not perceived as such by Kenyan speakers and Gregory/Carroll (1978: 92f.) observe: 'Some quite proficient Nigerian speakers of English have difficulty hitting the right tone in informal tenors; perhaps because they tend to use their native language in more familiar or intimate situations. Their informal English tenors often sound out-of-date, as though they have been learnt from the novel literature of a few decades ago.' This observation has raised the concern that whereas monolingual speakers exhibit fluent style variability in a single language, their mother tongue, multilingual speakers may sacrifice this ability to the less optimal command of several languages (which is sometimes called subtractive bilingualism). But a limited range of speech forms in one language does not necessarily mean a limited communicative potential. When the overall communicative system consists of more than one language multilingual speakers obviously still maintain high competence in conversational interaction when they are free to choose their language according to the context. This also explains why the ability of speakers to vary English styles is a function of nativization on the EIL–ESL–ENL continuum: when English is used for more functions variability increases to a parallel degree.

3.2 Reasons for African forms of English

The reasons for the occurrence of African forms different from Standard English ones are manifold and can basically be attributed to at least four factors as far as their origin is concerned.

R1: General language-learning strategies

The influence of general psycholinguistic processes that take place when languages are learnt is very difficult to assess because they take place in the human brain, which is a black box in the sense that it is not possible to see what is going on within; it is only possible to compare input and output and guess that certain processes must have taken place. There is some evidence that language learners in general use simplification strategies at an early stage and try to reproduce memorized phrases from the target language later, irrespective of the linguistic and pragmatic context. From a certain stage onwards learners enjoy complicating their language and even tend to exaggerate typically English features (which is called overgeneralization or, when the higher social prestige associated with a feature is aimed at, hypercorrection). When the learning process does not progress normally, certain developmental errors, which occur regularly in first and second language acquisition, become fossilized, i.e. they become permanent features. Often explanations of these strategies are combined with theories of markedness, which assume that unmarked features or structures are easiest to acquire for the second-language learner. All these creative strategies of language learners must have played a certain role in the development of African varieties of English.

R2: Influence of the learners' mother tongue and other African languages

The mother-tongue hypothesis rests on the assumption that features and strategies previously known to the learner are likely to be transferred to the target language system. It has long been seen as the basic cause for African variation in English, because it obviously influences the pronunciation, often distinctly:

In every major linguistic area in the world where English is learnt as a second or foreign language, there is a characteristic set of deviations from authentic [?] English, each of which is a point of easy transfer from the mother tongue into English. With the passage of time these deviations become institutionalized and give a specific stamp to Indian English, African English in its various forms, Spanish English, and so on. In an area where one generation supplies the English teachers to the next, mother-tongue interference can be cumulative so that, with time, English in that area can deviate more and more from accepted norms.

(Lanham 1965: 198)

This view of 'deviations from authentic English' reflects an early view and uses the term African English very loosely and generally. From today's perspective mother-tongue influence seems to have been overestimated in this case, as in second language acquisition in general. The use of plosives [t,d] instead of fricatives [θ,ð] has often been attributed to African substratum influence, but it also occurs in Irish and Brooklynese, for instance (Wells 1987: 63). Furthermore, because English is for many Africans only one possible choice in their verbal repertoire, which will include more than one African language, it may be safer to assume the influence of a common substratum of the African languages known by the English user. Interestingly enough, some speakers of African English exhibit 'interference features' although they do not derive from their mother tongues but from other languages used in the area.

Today, when the vast majority of English teachers in Africa are – apart from a sizeable number of Indians – Africans who speak African English themselves, it is not surprising that this African dialectal influence is much more dominant than a theoretical British norm, which is still upheld in books but rarely experienced in use in present-day Africa.

R3: Exposure to the written language
The fact that in many societies, including African ones, the written word has an authority exceeding that of the spoken form has far-reaching consequences for English language learners, particularly in a situation where native speakers of English are becoming relatively rare, even in language teaching. Thus African speakers of English tend to reproduce characteristics of written English even in the spoken form. Grammatical constructions and lexical items from relatively formal registers or spelling pronunciations will often be used. This explains the articulations of /h/ in *heir* or of /b/ in *debt* and generally the tendency of the

central vowel /ə/ to assume the sound value 'suggested' by the
orthographic symbol that represents it (e.g. agem [again]). As
Shakespeare and the Bible have until recently – when they were
supplemented or replaced by modern African writers' texts –
been most commonly used for teaching the target language,
African varieties have also tended to have an archaic flavour.
This feature often overlaps with the problem of register
mentioned above. For a long time the 'four dangers connected
with colloquial and literary English' have been noted:

(a) The danger of using colloquial English in writing.
(b) The danger of using literary English in speech.
(c) The danger of using too much colloquial English in speech.
(d) The danger of using too much literary and old-fashioned English
    in writing.

Of those four faults, the last is the commonest.

(Tregidgo 1959: xv)

R4: Influence of various English native speakers as models
As not only African English but also native-speaker English
exists in considerable variety, it should not be assumed that
African learners have been exposed to a uniform native speaker
target language. Even when colonial administration and education were still largely in the hands of English native speakers, the
administrators, missionaries and settlers working and living in
Africa very often spoke different kinds of English and passed
features of these on to their African pupils. Thus, Wells (1982:
634) attributes certain features of English in Malawi to the
dominance of Scottish missionary activities there – but the
characteristic /r/, for instance, may also be explained through
first-language interference. Awonusi (1985: 46) explains some
peculiarities of Igbo English (e.g. the tendency of central vowels
towards ð in Igbo English compared with that towards [a]
in Yoruba English) as 'Scottish', as the result of the influx of Irish
and Scottish teachers from the Roman Catholic Mission in
Igboland.

Whereas ENL missionaries could be found in all anglophone
African countries, ENL settlers were only common in the East,
Central and South African highlands. In South Africa, for
instance, different groups of settlers brought different dialects
with them; the original linguistic differences between the 1820
working-class settlers on the Cape and the 1850 'higher-class'
settlers in Natal (cf. p. 38) have repercussions on the extreme and
respectable varieties of South African English even today (cf.

Lanham/MacDonald 1979). Here historical British forms have to
be compared with South African usage, otherwise Afrikaans
influence may be exaggerated (cf. Lass/Wright 1986).
    Similarly, Hancock/Angogo (1982: 312) write: 'All East
African varieties have a more or less discernible substratum of
South African English phonology.' This suggests considerable
linguistic influence from (white) South African settlers, who did
indeed move northwards as far as Zambia and even Kenya –
albeit in such small numbers that this connection is much less
likely than another one also put forward by Hancock/Angogo: 'In
fact, the phonological similarities to South African English may
be better attributed to the influence of a common Bantu
[Black] substratum than to direct influence from [White] South
African English' (ibid.). The Central African region is much
more likely to provide formal evidence of an overlap between
British and South African forms, such as the famous examples of
tsotsi (thug) and *robot*, which is used officially instead of the
equally current *traffic lights* there.
    Another strong influence exerted by non-standard English
speakers derives from Americo-Africans and Krio speakers in
West Africa, particularly where they worked as teachers (cf.
chapter 1). Whereas this influence may have been significant in
the past, today the growing importance of American English
should not be underestimated, not only through their economic
dominance, but also through educational and technical development aid. It is particularly noticeable in Northern and parts of
West Africa. Cameroon is a particularly interesting example (cf.
Mbangwana 1989), because in this officially bilingual state
English is overshadowed by French, and in this situation
American English expressions are sometimes supported by
French parallels, as in the case of *tribunal* for 'court', *apartment*
for 'flat', *profundity* for 'depth', *reservation* for 'booking', each of
which may be pronounced with a French rather than an
American accent. These differences are, however, not categori-
cal, but rather a matter of frequency. They are also examples of
how various influences can complement or support each other.
    For in general, the deviations that cause the distinct 'African-
ness' of African varieties of English may be accounted for by a
combination of all these characteristic elements in the language
acquisition process in Africa (Figure 3.1). It is therefore possible
that several factors combine to generate the distinctive 'Africanness'. The pluralization of non-count nouns (*furnitures*) may, for
instance, be attributed to ignorance of target-language subrules,
i.e. semantic restrictions to pluralization rules, or to interference

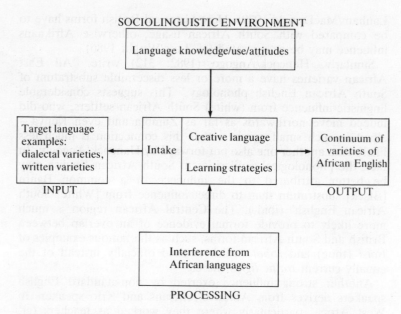

SOCIOLINGUISTIC ENVIRONMENT

Language knowledge/use/attitudes

Target language examples: dialectal varieties, written varieties

Intake

Creative language

Learning strategies

Continuum of varieties of African English

INPUT

OUTPUT

Interference from African languages

PROCESSING

FIGURE 3.1   Elements in the acquisition process of African English

from African languages. And if there is a choice between two formal alternatives forms with more factors supporting them may gain higher frequency. As in creole studies the 'universalist' and 'substrativist' positions can be combined (cf. Mufwene 1986).

As in most parts of Africa nowadays language learning (in classrooms through the conscious study of grammar, etc.) is more important than language acquisition it is worth bearing in mind that learning advances only through comprehensive input. Input does not equal intake because (in Krashen's (1981) monitor model, for instance) input may be disrupted by the activity of the socioaffective filter, where sociopsychological concerns – whether the learners can identify with attributes ascribed to a language, its speakers and its roles in and outside their speech community – play a decisive role.

Besides the factors which contribute to the origin of African forms, those contributing to their maintenance and persistence are worth consideration, both unconscious and conscious ones. Here again language attitudes play a central role. The question is whether describing African English is still the surest way to kill it as maintained by Sey (1973: 10). If however self-assurance in language is based on a positive self-evaluation of African identity, including its formerly foreign language elements (cf. 7.5), then maintenance and even cultivation of African forms seem certain.

The factors that play a part in the acquisition of English in Africa act very differently on the individual in different countries, regions and towns; that is why linguists or linguistically conscious listeners who are used to these forms from their own experience can indicate a speaker's home area or tribe from the way he speaks English. Whereas Nigerians recognize Yoruba speakers because they tend to replace the English dental fricatives [θ,ð] with alveolar plosives [t,d] and Hausa speakers with alveolar fricatives [s,z], Kenyans recognize Luos from their lack of [ʃ] (*sure* pronounced as [suɛ]) and Kikuyus from intrusive nasals before plosives (as in [saland]) or their [l] (as an [r]), and so on. These and many more are stereotypes. It would be otiose to list all the pecularities already recorded in the relevant literature, and would not afford in any case a systematic view. The alternative is to construct generalizations of varieties of African English, even though the description of actual linguistic data, including their variation, is still insufficient. As it is obviously very difficult to offer generalizations for the entire continent or in some cases even for large countries, the following tentative examples of tendencies, constructions or feature catalogues may be seen as a stimulus and challenge to further research, which can show how widespread they are socially and geographically. It is interesting to note that the deviations occur at all levels of linguistic description, albeit with different strength and salience.

3.3 Pronunciation

The pronunciation of English in Africa is of particular importance because (non-standard) pronunciation features seem to be the most persistent in African varieties, i.e. they are retained even in the speech of the most educated speakers. This may be because in many languages pronunciation seems to be the most flexible element, which can be used (subconsciously) to express subtle sociolinguistic messages of speaker identity and of distance from or solidarity with the listener (cf. 7.5). English appears to be particularly fluid at this level, because even the supposed norms in Britain have moved so far away from the institutionalized written form that the graphemic system cannot symbolize the diverging phonemic systems any more (although mistakes in the form of phonetic spellings allow conclusions on the pronunciation even from written texts). The features characterizing African pronunciations of English can be found at subphonemic, phonemic and supraphonemic levels.[2]

Differences at the phonemic level are important because here differences of lexical meaning are maintained. This can be illustrated in minimal pairs, i.e. words where only one different phoneme in Standard English signals a completely different meaning, e.g. *ram* and *lamb*, *beat* and *bit*, or *show* and *so*. Many Africans would not distinguish clearly in pronunciation between the elements of such pairs tending towards the same pronunciation (homophony). Differences in sound interpretations can also be seen in the change of place names, thus independent Zimbabwe changed Umtali to Mutare and Gwelo to Gweru. Among the consonants, /r/ and /l/ are a particularly infamous pair for many Bantu speakers, both rendered as one and the same, often intermediate sound between /loli/ and /rori/ instead of /lori/, for instance. Occasionally the sets voiced and voiceless fricatives around the alveolar ridge /tʃ/, /ʃ/ and /s/, and /dʒ/, /ʒ/ and /z/ are not distinguished clearly either. Other problematic consonants are /ð/ and /θ/, which often deviate in the direction of /d/ and /t/ or, sometimes, /z/ and /s/ or even /v/ and /f/. These examples show the general tendency:

P1: Fricatives tend to be avoided or merged

Most of these deviations, however, are not very salient or pronounced. They may be registered as peculiarities, but they do not endanger the consonant system as a whole, which would be the case if there were too few minimal pairs retained to ensure differentiation and thus intelligibility.

At the subphonemic level, which is not important for differences in meaning, but gives the English spoken a particular colouring, an interesting consonant in many varieties of English is /r/. As in most English varieties including RP (Wells 1982: 218–22), it is usually only articulated in pre-vocalic positions, which means African accents of English are non-rhotic; and its pronunciation varies considerably (whether it is rolled or flapped). Interestingly, the ever increasing influence of American English seems to have had little effect so far (except in some areas such as Liberia). Other subphonemic 'problem areas' are, for instance, (dark/velar) /ł/ generally, and word-initial plosives, which tend not to be as aspirated as in RP, or are realized as implosives, so that the aspiration is not audible. In general it is important that when sounds are not pronounced in isolation they tend to influence one another, and this assimilation in African English is often different from (European?) Standard English.

A comparison of the English phoneme system with that of most African languages would show that whereas there are at least as many consonants in African languages as in English (but in fewer consonant combinations), there are fewer vowel contrasts compared to those in the extensive English vowel system. The consequences of this contrast are: consonants may deviate at the subphonemic level, but the major distinctions at the phonemic level can usually be kept; vowels deviate at the phonemic level, they merge, because the extreme range of the English vowel continuum is not covered by the underlying African systems of, for instance, the Kwa languages in West Africa and the Bantu languages in East Africa (see Figure 3.2 below). On the whole three basic generalizations may be made for English vowels:

P2: Length differences in vowels are levelled down and not used phonemically, i.e. to differentiate meanings systematically

Usually short vowels are longer and more peripheral than in RP, especially closed /ɪ/ and /ʊ/ or /ʌ/.

P3: The central vowels /ʌ/, /əː/ and /ə/, as in *but*, *bird* **and** *a*, **are avoided and tend towards half-open or open positions [ɔ,ə,a]**
This conforms to the tendency towards more extreme articulatory positions of the tongue in general (as in P2). It leads to the phenomenon that whereas vowels in full syllables tend to be underdifferentiated, those in unstressed ones may be overdifferentiated; thus the difference between *policeman* and *policemen* or between the suffixes *-ance* and *-ence* may be clearer than in Standard English.

P4: Diphthongs tend to have only marginal status and to be monophthongized
This is certainly true for the closing diphthongs /eɪ/ and /əʊ/, where the second element is hardly heard in many African varieties, thus almost coinciding with the /eˑ/ and /oˑ/ phonemes. Diphthongs with a longer glide are preserved, but they are not really pronounced as falling diphthongs, i.e. with less emphasis on the second element than on the first, but rather as double monophthongs (e.g. /ɔɪ/, /au/). All the centering diphthongs (/ɪə, eə, uə/) tend to be pronounced as opening diphthongs or double monophthongs (/ɪa, ea, ua/; cf. tendency P3).

These general observations on vowel pronunciation seem to hold for so many African varieties that this cannot be interpreted merely as a product of mother-tongue interference – although some groups are said to speak better than others (again Hausa speakers in contrast to Yoruba speakers in Nigeria, as mentioned above) because their mother tongues have a more differentiated vowel system. Some of these features of 'Africanization' have already been predicted by Gimson (1989: 318f) in very general terms (without any reference to Africa) because of the particularly complex structure of the English vowel system:

> . . . the full systems (20 V and 24 C) must be regarded as complex compared with the systems of many other languages. In particular, the opposition of the close vowels /i:/-/i/, /u:/-/u/, the existence of a central long vowel /ə:/ and the delicately differentiated front vowel set of /i:/-/i/-/e/-/æ/ + /ʌ/, together with the significant or conditioned variations of vowel length, will pose problems to many foreign learners.

Finally, it is worth considering vowel systems as a whole in African varieties of English. It seems possible to categorize these systems on a broadly regional basis. Whereas West African varieties tend to have a basic seven- (to nine-) vowel system, East African varieties tend towards a basic five-vowel system at the basilectal end of the spectrum. This distinction becomes clear in Figure 3.2. Black South African varieties largely correspond to East African ones, forming a general Bantu English. The White South African system is included in the chart, because on the one hand it may play a role in shaping a common South African English and on the other this juxtaposition points out the difference between the white varieties, South African English and RP, and the black varieties, West African English and East African English (cf. Hancock/Angogo 1982: 314, Trudgill/Hannah 1982: 25). An interesting single parameter in this respect is the deviation of the RP long central vowel /ə:/: it tends toward a back vowel /ɔ/ in West African varieties, towards a front vowel /a/ in Eastern and towards /e/ Southern African varieties, but these tendencies are not uniform in a region, neither across all ethnic groups (Igbo speakers tend towards /e/ and Yoruba speakers towards /a/), nor across the lexicon (*girl* tends towards front and *turn* towards back pronunciation).

Other important features of African English are supra-phonemic, that is they relate to the pronunciation of larger sound units, to word stress, to intonation and to general rhythmic patterns. Many of these phenomena are very difficult to describe, but some examples from two aspects, consonant clusters and word stress, may suffice.

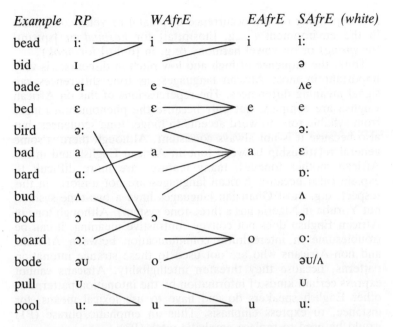

FIGURE 3.2 Vowel systems of English in Africa compared

Consonant clusters are a major phonotactic problem, as many African languages have a relatively strict consonant–vowel syllable structure (often CV–CV–CV, for instance). This explains African English tendencies with regard to consonant clusters and final consonants.

P5: Consonant clusters tend to be dissolved, either by dropping one/some of the consonants involved or by splitting them through the insertion of vowels

Final consonants are dropped when there are two or more in a sequence, e.g. in [ncks] for *next* and [hæn/hen/han] for *hand*. But this tendency also occurs in native-speaker English (especially in rapid speech in American English) and its frequency seems to vary in different parts of the continent. The general rule appears to be that if plosives are preceded by fricatives, they are dropped in word-final position; if they are preceded by other plosives or occur in non-final position they are split by vowels inserted between the consonants. A similar phenomenon occurs when final vowels are added to closed syllables, i.e. syllables ending in consonants. The vowels inserted or added are normally [ɪ] or [ʊ], depending on the occurrence of palatal or velar consonants in the environment (e.g. [hosɪpɪtal] for *hospital* or [spɪrɪŋɪ] for *spring*) or on vowel harmony (e.g. in [bʊkʊ] for *book*).

Tone, the sequence of high and low pitch in discourse, is very important in most African languages, as tone differences can signal meaning differences. The repercussions of this on African English are complex, not only because the phenomenon ranges from syllable tone to word accents to longer tone sequences, but also because it is not always consistent. Although there is some general relationship between tone in African English and in the African mother tongues, many features are more difficult to explain (also because African languages are not uniform in this respect, e.g. most Ghanaian languages have a two-tone system, but Yoruba in Nigeria has a three-tone system). Although tone in African English does not convey contrastive meaning, it can be troublesome in intercultural communication between Africans and non-Africans who are not used to these strange intonation patterns, because they threaten intelligibility. Africans cannot express certain kinds of information by the intonation patterns as other English speakers do and have to use lexical means, for instance, to express emphasis. Thus an emphatic phrase (P1) would be used to replace emphatic pitch (P2):

(P1) Aṡ fòr Kòfí hè iṡ thè cúlprit.
(P2) 'Kofi is the 'culprit.

Word stress is a particularly complex phenomenon in English due to the mixed nature of its vocabulary. Words from the Germanic stock and old integrated loanwords tend to have the stress on the stem syllable and to retain it, regardless of affixes; the great number of words and their derivations that came later into the language have movable stress, often but not always on the penultimate syllable. This creates considerable uncertainty on the part of second-language speakers, especially with words that are infrequent or relatively long. It is difficult to express these changes in general rules, because many factors play a role. The number of syllables is important as it leads to secondary stress in American English and secondary stress appears to support the African tendency towards more regular stress rhythms. The recognition of prefixes and suffixes leads to regular pronunciation; -'ize and particularly -'ate endings tend to receive final stress, for instance. The frequency and familiarity of words normally supports the 'correct' British English pronunciation. In many cases better known, etymologically related or similar words

TABLE 3.3 Differences in word stress between Nigerian and British Standard English (' indicates principle stress)

British English		Nigerian English	Possible influence
(a)	initial >	stem	
	'admirable	ad'mirable	ad'mire
	'affluence	af'fluence	
	'protestant	pro'testant	pro'test (v)
	'supervisor	super'visor	
(b)	initial >	penultimate	
	'democrat	de'mocrat	de'mocracy
	'arbitrator	arbi'trator	nar'rator
	'epilepsy	epi'lepsy	
	'escalator	esca'lator	
(c)	initial >	final	
	'alternate	alter'nate (v)	alter'nation
	'attribute (n)	attri'bute	
	'comment	com'ment	
	'dominate	domin'ate	
(d)	stem >	penultimate	
	ad'ministrative	adminis'trative	
	ad'vertisement	adver'tisement	NigE/AmE adver'tise
	af'firmative	affir'mative	
	pre'paratory	prepa'ratory	
(e)	stem >	final	
	ac'climatize	acclima'tize	
	dis'organized	disorga'nized	
	dis'sociate	dissoci'ate	
	ex'terminate	extermi'nate	

Note Although the examples are all taken from Nigeria (Kujore 1985), similar tendencies and examples have been observed in Kenya and Zambia.

may serve as models. As there are no comprehensive quantitative analyses available, the above lists (Table 3.3) provide some examples of the most common tendencies. In many cases stress on the stem is considered appropriate when the initial syllable is stressed in British English (a). Penultimate stress is customary, even for some frequent words with initial stress in British English (b); but in this uncertain situation other stress shifts are also possible (c–e).

Some English words even have different word stress depending on their word class, whether they are nouns, adjectives or verbs. This is often regularized in African varieties in the sense that the same pronunciation applies, and even where the word forms are not identical there is a tendency to maintain the same stress for the derivationally related noun, adjective or verb forms (*am'biguity* from the adjective *am'biguous*, *pro'testant* from the verb *pro'test*). The direction of these regularizations is usually towards the more familiar and frequent word. There are also other forces at play, such as the need to maintain essential contrasts of meaning (*can'not* for *'cannot* or *can't* where the first vowel of the positive form *can* is not different from the negative one in African English).

In general African English is more marked in sentence stress patterns than in the pronunciation of individual words. There is a general tendency towards a syllable-timed, rather than a stress-timed rhythm, which means that all syllables are more or less equal in duration.[3] This also accounts for the tendency to give too much weight to the unstressed syllables and weak forms of English, and combines with the tendency to insert vowels to avoid consonant clusters (as is also manifested in loanwords from English into African languages, see chapter 6).

Even more general are suprasegmental features such as speed and length of pausing. Some Africans are said to speak more slowly on average (although this conceals vast differences according to urban/rural and educational background, even if general proficiency and fluency are identical), if white and black South Africans are compared, for instance (Chick 1985: 309). This can have far-reaching effects: when black communication partners fail to take the opportunity to speak because they do not perceive the pause inviting them 'to take their turn', or when they experience white English speakers interrupting their normal flow of speech; or equally, when white listeners to black speech get the impression that black thoughts are not presented coherently or they feel uncomfortable because of pauses of 'undue length'. All this can lead to negative stereotypes, which can not only make intercultural communication difficult, but even living in the same community.

3.4 Grammar

An outline of the grammar in African English varieties is even more difficult than that of their pronunciation: first, because there is no easily available and generally acknowledged descriptive system of grammar (or of language-learning strategies if the acquisitional aspect is stressed); second, because it is never quite clear whether grammatical alternatives really express the same meaning (or even style); and third, because deviations in grammar occur in much lower frequencies than those in pronunciation, not only because there are many more categories, but also because grammatical deviations are more stigmatized. In this section the grammatical description of African English will therefore be presented in broad categories of word class type, independent of any specific syntax or (interpretation according to) language-learning theories.[4] Although this leads to overlaps of explanations with underlying semantic structures, such as the count–non-count distinction, which has repercussions on plural formation as well as determination (cf. N2 and N3 below), although with different frequencies (the pluralization *advices*, for instance, seems to be less frequent than *an advice*). The features will also be found at the upper end of the cline of African varieties, such as can even be found in African newspapers (cf. Tingley 1981 from Ghana) or in educated speech of university students (cf. Yankson 1989a from Ghana and Nigeria). They do not occur consistently each time a construction is used and are very often related to subrules of more general rules, which are not affected. It is therefore safe to say that the basic grammatical system of Standard English is retained but certain additions, omissions or modifications are made, often in a very logical and sometimes even less irregular way than in Standard English. It is not quite clear whether the following so-called African tendencies really occur in the whole of Africa. But they have been found used by speakers with different first languages and in such diverse contexts that they are at least the most likely cases. On the other hand this does not mean that these tendencies do not occur in other second-language varieties too, or even in some first-language varieties in Britain, America or Australia. Partly at least English varieties all seem to develop in similar directions, as for instance in terms of simplification and regularization. Frequency, consistency, systematicity and the developmental, regional and social distribution over various spoken and written text types are a matter for further research as well as the discovery of implicational hierarchies in frequency and acceptability.[5]

As far as verbs are concerned, the following tendencies have been noted:

V1: Inflectional endings are not always added to the verb, but the general, regular and unmarked forms are used instead
This applies to the regular endings of the third person singular present tense (V1a) and of the past tense (V1b) as well as to irregular verb forms (V1c). It may be related to the fact that

auxiliaries are not inflected in Standard English. In (V1d), for instance, *seem* is semantically close to a modal auxiliary (*may be*), but formally different:

(V1a) If she real<u>ize</u> that you are not following in English she switches to Swahili (Platt/Weber/Ho 1984: 67).
(V1b) Ocol protes<u>t</u> his wife and insul<u>t</u> her.
(V1c) Tundi's father wanted to punish him, but Tundi <u>run</u> away.
(V1d) It seem_ that he has returned.

Example (V1a) shows how inconsistent the marking can be, *-s* is omitted after the first verb (*realize*) but not after the second (*switch*). Occasionally the reverse (hypercorrect) type of deviation, i.e. *-s* after infinitives or other unmarked categories, can also be found. The omission in (V1b) is supported by the pronunciation of the verb stem ending in a *t*-sound anyway, and when a similar sound is to be added to express the past, it seems to be more easily omitted than when the final sounds are different. Pronunciation may also play a role in (V1c) because *ran* and *run* tend to have the same pronunciation in Africa. Possibly the omission also depends on semantic features: Platt/Weber/Ho (1984: 76) suggest that it occurs more often with non-punctually used verbs, such as *live*, than with others. In general, the tense marking is redundant when adverbials or adverbs clarify the time context.

V2: Complex tenses tend to be avoided
This tendency occurs particularly with the past perfect (V2a) and conditionals (V2b) and is also common in less formal native-speaker usage today. It affects mainly the sequence of tenses, which is taught in school grammars, particularly in the case of subordinate clauses in past contexts (V2c) and when modality (*irrealis*) is expressed (V2d).

(V2a) It would have been much better if this delicate, technical and complicated matter <u>was</u> dealt with by competent men like legislators and lawyers.
(V2b) The proposal that the President <u>will</u> have a final say on ministerial appointments is not good.
(V2c) They could have lived a happy life if they <u>were</u> not [had not been] told . . .
(V2d) She behaves as if she <u>has</u> seen me before.

Very often past tense forms are not used to express modality as in Standard English (as in *I had better* or *If I went* . . .), *will* constructions are used instead.

V3: The use of *be* VERB *-ing* constructions is extended to all verbs

This affects the distinction between the non-stative and the stative use of verbs and applies particularly to some verbs that are used with *-ing* forms only in marked, specific meanings.

(V3a) I <u>am having</u> your book (Odumuh 1987: 63).
(V3b) I <u>was</u> not <u>liking</u> the food in the hotel.
(V3c) This hat <u>was</u> not <u>belonging</u> to you.
(V3d) Madame commandant who <u>was loving</u> with the engineer was known as a very shy woman.

Sentence (V3d) also suggests that it may be difficult to decide whether the writer means to use a continuous form to express an action going on at the moment of speech or whether no such meaning is intended. With sentence (V3a) the decision is relatively easy, but with other constructions it may be more difficult. Deviations are often due to the attempt to mark the habitual aspect in customary actions or states in a different way than in Standard English, where the continuous form would never be used in (V3b and 3c). And where the latter is applied to mark an (unfinished) action in progress it can only be with verbs in non-stative use (this is why Sey 1973 calls this the perfective use of imperfective verbs). Apart from the formal problem there are semantic ones accompanying the use of the continuous form. This becomes obvious to the uninitiated when they are told by Africans 'I am coming', when the speaker is however not moving closer, but turns round and goes away, so that 'I am coming' actually means 'I will come back in the near future.'

V4: Phrasal/prepositional verbs are used differently

Prepositions are an important word class in English, because they occur in adverbial phrases, in idioms and in combinations with verbs, where they are used in word-formation parallel to prefixes. The use of fixed prepositions with many verbs is more expansive in English than in African languages, and the idiomatic preposition may follow semantic, morphological or even traditional Latin rules, which are often difficult for learners.

(V4a) I will pick you _ at eight tonight.

(V4b) They protested _ the price increase.
(V4c) A cheque is attached <u>with</u> this letter.
(V4d) He did not like to participate <u>with</u> the discussion.
(V4e) They are advocating <u>for</u> free primary education.

Platt/Weber/Ho (1984) establish the following grid (not only for African English!) using the formal descriptive categories of omission, substitution and addition customary in error analysis:

particle compared to StE	phrasal verb	prepositional verb
omission	crop [up], pick [up]	apply [to], provide [with]
substitution	throw out (arms), put off (fire)	deprive from, congratulate for
addition	lock up, voice out	discuss about, stress on

Some of these constructions are influenced by parallels in Standard English that are similar in form or meaning (*pick* with the meaning of *pick up*; *wait for* instead of *wait on*; *participate with* instead of *in* because of *co-operate with*; *attached with* instead of *attached to* because of *enclosed with*). They do not result from confusion only, however, but can be very logical (e.g. *to discuss about*); they can also be found in native varieties (such as V4b above in American English). Prepositions are very often omitted when they are 'obvious' anyway (e.g. *put* [*in*], *protest* [*against*]), as the verbs normally do not occur without them, at least not in Standard British English. The substituted particles are often consistent with the meaning of the verb or the prefix morpheme (e.g. *deprive from* instead of *deprive of*). The additional particles would often be logically possible, but are considered redundant according to Standard English norms (e.g. *join with*, *comprise of*, *mention about*, *attend to*, which may be seen parallel to *put together with*, *consist of*, *talk about*, *go* to, or others).

Besides analogy with other English verbs (cf. Sey 1973: 48f.) interference from African languages is indirectly important because the English prepositional system is unusually complex. A polysemy of various local meanings exists, for instance, in Swahili, where *mwituni* can be translated as *at*, *to*, *in/inside*, *by/near/next to* and *from the forest*. Similarly, the few prepositions in Hausa have to be rendered by various English ones (Jibril 1991):

Yaa zoo <u>da</u> saafe.   He came <u>in</u> the morning.
Yaa tafi <u>da</u> akuyaa.   He went <u>with</u> the goat.

Musa da Audu sun zauna.	Musa and Audu sat down.
Na ganshi a gida.	I saw him at home.
Na ganshi a mota.	I saw him in (a) car.
Na ganshi a babur.	I saw him on (a) motorcycle.

It is also interesting to note that prepositions supported by inter- and intralinguistic tendencies, are more likely to develop into stable Africanisms, such as *congratulations for your promotion* (ibid.).

V5: Verb complementation (infinitives, gerunds, etc.) varies freely
As verb complementation is usually a matter of individual lexemes rather than rules this feature would have to be listed or taught with the individual verb lexemes. This also determines how stigmatized the expression is (V5a is for instance much more stigmatized than V5c). Often Africans try to solve the apparent irregularity by applying semantic criteria. Then *let* and *allow* (V5a) and *force* and *make* (V5b) should follow equivalent structures, but they don't according to British norms. Sometimes two similar constructions are confused (as *decide to* +INFINITIVE and *decide on* +-ing in V5d). The subtle distinction between infinitive and gerund constructions tends to be neglected and the choice is apparently random.

(V5a) Allow him _ go.
(V5b) They made him to clean the whole yard.
(V5c) It will be necessary here highlighting the difference between
the two types.
(V5d) He decided buying a new car.

As far as noun phrases are concerned the following features of African English have been found:

N1: Noun phrases are not always marked for number and case (by inflectional endings)
This applies to certain plural endings (N1a), especially when they seem redundant, since the plural is indicated by numerals (N1b) or indefinite pronouns (determiners) anyway.[6] It also applies to genitives (N1c) and relative pronouns (the inflected forms *whom* and *whose* are avoided in favour of invariable *which* constructions as in N1d).[7] Whereas the pluralization of uncountable nouns (cf. N2) is very often seen and heard (e.g. *informations*), the singularization of mass nouns is typical for learners and

stigmatized (e.g. *a cattle, an advice*). In some cases the genitive noun is simply put in front of the modified noun without any formal marker, as if they were compounds (N1c). In others the *of* genitive is used even with human determinants where Standard English would use the *-s* genitive. Or, to put it differently, the overlap when there is a choice between the two constructions is much greater.

(N1a) Many varieties of fish with different colour_ will need different aquarium.

(N1b) On the market we found only three farmer_ selling vegetables.

(N1c) Ocol_ conflict was that he was too much used to the European culture.

(N1d) Adult education <u>which</u> its main purpose is to help adults to learn how to read and write faces many problems.

N2: The use of *-s* plural markers is overgeneralized

This tendency is quite common and in most cases semantically correct, i.e. although they can be seen as collective units, several individual pieces can be distinguished, e.g. with *luggages*, *furnitures*, *firewoods* or *grasses*. But it ignores the grammatical distinction of count vs. non-count nouns, which does not always correspond to the semantic one. Sometimes this tendency conflates more or less subtle semantic differentiations in Standard English, such as between *hair–hairs, food–foods, work–works, people–peoples*, sometimes it merely regularizes (historical) morphological Standard English irregularities, such as *childrens, fishes* or (*three*) *dozens*. In Standard English plural *-s* is not added to nouns that are considered collective or mass and thus non-count (N2a–c) nor to some historical irregular forms (N2d), whereas in African English this occurs frequently. Some of the non-countables may occur in the plural in special meanings (e.g. *works*) or contexts even in Standard English (e.g. *experiences*), and then differences are often a question of interpretation and frequency. A related tendency is to individualize mass nouns simply by using the singular article in front, instead of *a piece/ bottle/pair of*, etc. (N2e). English *pluralia tantum*, which have a plural ending because they consist of two symmetrical parts (e.g. *trousers, scissors*), can also be found in the singular and when they are used in the plural form often more than one pair is meant.

(N2a) He had too many <u>luggages.</u>

(N2b) The situation of two governments has caused some <u>discontents.</u>

(N2c) I would listen to what my parents gave me, i.e. good <u>advices.</u>
(N2d) There were many <u>fishes</u> in the pond.
[(N2e) Kola went to the market to buy a new <u>trouser.</u>]

N3: Articles and other determiners tend to be omitted in front of nouns

This tendency may partly be an overgeneralization of British usage (*I am going to church/school*, etc. for N3a). Often, subrules of Standard English grammar are neglected, e.g. the rule that a definite article is used when nouns are postmodified by *of*–genitives or relative clauses (N3b). In (N3c) the basic function of the definite article, to refer back to something mentioned earlier in the discourse, is not fulfilled ('others' refers to specific persons, family members, not generally 'other people'). In contrast to the system in Standard English some linguists (e.g. Platt/Weber/Ho 1984: 52–9) even see a completely different system of articles in 'New Englishes': whereas Standard English uses the definite/indefinite system (known/not known) as the basic distinction, the 'New Englishes' prefer to use the specific/ non-specific (particular/not particular) system, as in the Standard English determiner pair *a certain – any*. In this system[8] non-specific reference is expressed by no article (as in N3d and N3e) and specific by *the* (N3f), *one* or even *this/these* and *that/those* (the relationship of articles to demonstrative pronouns is generally very close in many languages, as it is, historically, also in English). The tendency of omitting determiners also expands to indefinite, possessive and demonstrative pronouns.

(N3a) I am going to __ post office.
(N3b) It is unfortunate that the factory has to start with fuel oil when
     possibilities for __ use of coal are there.
(N3c) She accepted to remain at home, while __ others went on the
     tour.
(N3d) Give me __ meat.[9]
(N3e) They all have [an] African background.
(N3f) And thus he became the educated boy.

N4: Pronouns are not always distinguished by gender

The three possibilities of third person singular pronouns, *he, she, it* in subject roles (N4a and N4b) and *his, her, its* in possessive roles (N4c) are often used indiscriminately, especially when their pronunciation is only distinguished by one consonant, as in the case of *he* and *she*. This can be accounted for as simplification, or else as interference from mother tongues that do not have sex distinctions in pronouns (e.g. languages that have only one class for animate or human beings in general). Pronunciation may also overlap in the case of *her* and *a* (N4d).

> (N4a) Lawino said that she didn't like the behaviour of Tina, because
>   <u>he</u> got abortion.
> (N4b) Did you see my sister? <u>He</u> went out just now.
> (N4c) The poor girl had lost <u>his</u> exercise-book.
> (N4d) The man holds a girl who is not <u>her</u> wife.

N5: Adjective forms tend to be used as adverbs
The unmarked adverbial form is correct in very few cases in Standard English (*hard*, *first*, *high* in certain contexts or sayings like *take it easy*, etc.; N5a), but it occurs not only in African, but also in some American and British English varieties (N5b). Since it is often associated with non-standard usage, some African rule-conscious speakers may use semantically or formally hypercorrect forms (such as N5c and N5d). The tendency N5 may also be supported by the fact that some Africans elide final syllables in English generally, which is itself related to penultimate syllable lengthening in (some) African languages.

> (N5a) I can obtain the food <u>easy</u>.
> (N5b) Do it <u>proper</u>.
> [(N5c) I jumped <u>highly</u> (Sey 1973: 38).
> (N5d)   She ran <u>fastly</u> because the train was coming.]

As far as the larger syntactic structures are concerned, the following deviations have been noted:
S1: Pronouns tend to be copied as so-called resumptive pronouns[10]

This implies the use of anaphoric personal pronouns to take up the subject of the sentence, especially after long and complex subjects (complex through partitive constructions as in S1a, inserted examples, infinitives or relative clauses), the use of anaphoric personal pronouns to take up the head of a relative construction (i.e. the syntactic position of the relative pronoun is filled twice in the relative clause; as in S1b) or the use of redundant possessive pronouns to premodify the head of a relative construction (i.e. the possessive pronoun and the relative clause subject refer to the same person, in the case of the first person pronouns in S1c the speaker). Some of these constructions could also be explained as a transfer of spoken English grammar, including its hesitation phenomena and truncated or incomplete sentences, to written language. Redundant pronouns occur most often in front of the verb (as an equivalent of African verb prefixes), but not exclusively (as in S1d). They are seen as learners' features in Africa (although they also occur in native varieties in Northern England and Scotland) and are thus stigmatized. The example also shows pronoun omission in the answer (which also occurs with the particle *so* in reference to complete sentences).

(S1a) Many of the fish they have different colours.
(S1b) I choose fish which they can live together.
(S1c) I tell you about my journey that I had from home to school.
(S1d) 'Have you brought it the food?' – 'I have brought __.'

S2: Negative yes/no questions are confirmed by responding to the form of the question and not to the absolute 'inner logic'

Those used to the Standard English system may receive what they see as 'confusing forms of response' (Sey 1973: 41) after direct questions (S2a) as well as after tag questions (S2b) and after questions with interrogative intonation and declarative word order (S2c). This can be particularly confusing, when the tags are omitted and only the particles *no* or *yes* are used. This derives from a different frame of reference: The African sees that the negatively stated question queries the accuracy of the statement and thus asserts (*Yes, what you say is true.*) or denies the basic statement *He is good* (*No, what you say is wrong.*).

(S2a) He isn't good? – Yes [, he isn't]. Or: – No [, he is].
(S2b) You don't know this, do you? – Yes, I don't.
(S2c) So you did not get what you wanted to buy? – Yes.

This can be explained by the tendency in Standard English to choose the particle in accordance with the answer (*Yes*, i.e. as in the negated base form, *he is not good*) and in African English in accordance with the question (*No*, i.e. contrary to the negated hypothesis, *he is good*, or *It is [not] as you say*).

S3: Question tags tend to occur in invariant form

As tag questions are unusually complex in Standard English because their form depends on the main clause verb, the gender of the subject and its affirmative or negative character, they tend to be generalized (in African varieties as in others, e.g. Welsh

ones). This means that the tag is neither adapted to the verb form
nor to the subject of the main clause and *is* and *it* occur with all
verbs and subjects. This can be explained as reference to the
complete main clause. Often the tag is used indiscriminately in
the negative form, after affirmative (S3a) as well as after negative
clauses (S3b). Thus subtle Standard English distinctions in
speaker assumption between positive and negated tags disappear.
Occasionally non-verbal particles with the same functions are
added; *not so* (S3c) has an equivalent in many African languages,
e.g. *sivyo* in Swahili, but there is also the common init in non-
standard urban ENL speech.

> (S3a) He came here, <u>isn't it</u>?
> (S3b) That doesn't matter, <u>isn't it</u>?
> (S3c) You wanted to leave for Nairobi, <u>not so</u>?

S4: The basic interrogative word order is maintained in indirect speech and questions

Indirect speech which used the word order of direct speech could
be interpreted as correct in spoken English where one cannot
distinguish between the direct and indirect versions – if it is
marked by a different intonation and a break marking a question
mark (after *know* in S4a) or a colon (after *guess* in S4b, for
instance). That may be the reason why this feature occurs also in
non-standard native-speaker English. Sometimes usage cannot be
explained in this way (S4c), sometimes it seems rather erratic
(S4d). A related problem may be the omission of the Standard
English subrule that inversion (plus a pro-verb) occurs also after
clause initial negative sentence adverbs (S4e).

> (S4a) Do you know what <u>will be the price</u>?
> (S4b) Try to guess whose house <u>is this</u>.
> (S4c) I cannot tell you what <u>is the matter</u>.
> (S4d) Have you checked her background well, or <u>you are</u> simply
>   infatuated by her long hair and white skin?
> (S4e) Only when it was too late, <u>he discovered</u> that she was very
>   determined.

Maintaining the question word–verb–subject word order seems to
contradict another tendency, i.e. to retain the most normal
subject–verb–object order wherever possible, but it must be
interpreted as a simplification or regularization of the formation
rules for all types of questions, direct and indirect.

S5: The strict English word order rules are weakened, especially for adverbs
Whereas some adverbs tend to come as an appendix but often without a break at the end of the clause or sentence (e.g. *already* or *often* in S5a or comment adverbs like *unfortunately* in S5b), others can be found at the very beginning (S5c). Such positions do not seem to emphasize the adverb as is possible in Standard English (S5d). 'Inappropriate' emphasis also occurs frequently with emphatic pronouns (as in S5e).

(S5a) She went <u>often</u> to see them.
(S5b) He did not arrive in time <u>unfortunately</u>.
(S5c) <u>Always</u> the tank must be clean.
(S5d) <u>In my family</u> we are many.
(S5e) <u>Myself</u>, I am leaving now.

In general, word order is much more flexible and can be used to express emphasis and focus more readily than in Standard English (in this respect it can be seen as being closer to colloquial spoken English). The following examples of topicalization, i.e. putting the topic in initial clause position, are all from Dominic Mulaisho, *The Tongue of the Dumb* (London: Heinemann 1971), although literary language does not, of course, always reflect actual language use (cf. 5.4):

This new teacher from the mission, he and his wife don't get on well together? (p. 5, l. 25)
These young women you bring in the village, these women have two ears and ten eyes. (p. 17, l. 28)
This beer, who brewed it? (p. 17, l. 28)
This teacher at your village. You think he is an honest man? (p. 62, l. 33)
The red maize which Simbeya planted that year, where did it come from? (p. 74, l. 26)
That woman, do you believe that she did not help the teacher? (p. 83, l. 32)

It goes without saying that the fifteen tendencies listed above can only serve as a few basic examples of grammatical features of English in Africa, but they are perhaps the most widespread in terms of geographical range and frequency of occurrence. Other possible cases of grammatical 'Africanisms' might be:

(1) a tendency to overlap *to*-infinitive and gerund constructions after verbs (Sey 1973: 36);

(2) a tendency to use exceptional forms of negations,
   such as 'He is not almost happy' (Sey 1973: 36);
(3) a tendency to use unusual premodifications,
   such as '. . . to solve this our common problem' (Platt/
   Weber/Ho 1984: 64);
(4) a tendency to use conjuncts (adverbs) such as *also* or *so* as
   conjunctions to begin a clause;
(5) a tendency to use negations after semantically negated
   verbs,
   e.g. 'His father refused that Obi can't marry Clara';
(6) a tendency to 'simplify' comparative constructions, either
   by omitting the comparative particle *than* or, more often,
   the inflection *-er/-est*,
   e.g. 'African people get *low* wages than European'.

Other tendencies, which are well-known as interlanguage features, are heavily stigmatized,[11] such as the tendency to omit
certain verbs altogether, especially *be* in certain uses, e.g.
existential *be* before adjectives as in

   In the aquarium not good to keep salt-water fish.

3.5 Vocabulary

The following excerpts from a Kenyan and a Ugandan newspaper
illustrate the use of 'unusual' vocabulary in African English,
which derives from lexical borrowing from African languages:

   The government in conjunction with the Chamber of Commerce and
   Industry is committed to providing technical skills to the business
   community in Kenya to improve the economic status of the wananchi.

   A manamba whose matatu was travelling from Likoni to Mwembe
   Tayari was yesterday set upon by two Karate-chopping women who
   tore his shirt and knocked him down before he ran for cover.

   Chiefs and their assistants in Kitui district should join forces with
   agricultural officers in persuading wananchi to plant and eat a wide
   variety of foodstuffs.
   (*Sunday Times*, 23 March 1986, 3; all based on Kenya News Agency)

   Government should implement taxing of landlords, ligalise [sic]
   Kibanda and tax it.

A total of the official rate is 25,000 shs while on the parallel market (*Kibanda*) it is over shs 70,000.

The workshop is also engaged in the production of a very durable economical *jiko* (stove). Explaining the advantages of the particular stove over the ordinary ones used in many homes, Mr Kamlega said that in an average family which would require four sacks of charcoal in a month, the *jiko* stove uses only one sack for the same period.

The company had become a household name in Kenya's motor industry where it is credited with building some of the most outstanding and modern luxurious coaches, buses, lorries and the 'luxury' matatu which won a Special Design Award.

(*New Vision*, 12/8/89: 7; all by *Vision* reporters)
[small capitals JS, italics original]

Although it is usually possible for readers used to the context to guess from the general sense what these Africanisms mean, they may constitute a serious problem for those unfamiliar with them. Many lexemes are assumed to be known by the readership, only few are explained by a Standard English equivalent in brackets or as a compound head (*jiko* stove), and some are not even marked in italics as belonging to another language system but treated as completely integrated (*matatu*). And since lexical Africanisms are taken over from the first languages and/or depend on the national context, even speakers from neighbouring African countries may find them difficult to understand (the Swahili word *matatu* from Kenya in the Ugandan newspaper above is an obvious exception). For them dictionaries of regional English are compiled.

The oldest such lexicon of book length in Africa, leaving aside some short word lists, is Charles Pettman's *Africanderisms. A Glossary of South African Colloquial Words and Phrases and of Place and Other Names* (1913). He wrote down all the words that sounded unusual to his British ear, mainly those of his Dutch fellow-settlers, who in speaking English borrowed many words from Afrikaans, their local African variety of Dutch. This early tradition was followed up by Jean Branford's *A Dictionary of South African English* (*Third Edition*) (1987),[12] which is much wider in scope and, if we do not count Fyle/Jones' *Krio-English Dictionary* (1980), because Krio is best regarded as an independent language today, the only regional dictionary of African English. Regional dictionaries are more important than regional grammars, because the words peculiar to African English are often borrowed from regional source languages and cannot be interpreted by those unfamiliar with regional usage, whereas grammatical deviations usually can. Thus basically the same stringed musical instrument is called *zanza* in West Africa, *mbira* in East Africa and *kalimba* in Southern Africa.

For the whole of Africa, there is Dalgish's *Dictionary of Africanisms* (1982), which is only a beginning, however, because it lists 'unknown' words of African origin in newspaper texts about Africa rather than from Africa and neglects a few vital problems. It is, of course, difficult to decide whether a word is an individual *ad hoc* or nonce borrowing or formation, whether it is jargon with a limited range,[13] or whether it is already firmly integrated into general usage. Another vital distinction to be made is between proper names, fixed terminology, etc., e.g. *shilling* (currency unit), *moran* (Maasai warrior/youth) and more general Africanisms. A further categorization could be according to the users: is the expression used by all educated Africans or only by special groups, or is it used by white experts and tourists? Much more research on the basis of large representative text collections will be necessary before a comprehensive dictionary of Africanisms with appropriate usage labels can become available.

In this short section, it will suffice to cover three specific and interesting aspects: the range of the Africanisms, the areas of life in which Africanisms occur and the origin of Africanisms, from external sources, i.e. from other African languages, or from internal material, i.e. through word formation.

The first issue deals with the question of how far Africanisms are used and understood in the English-speaking world. Very old borrowings, such as *askari*, *baobab*, *bwana*, *fetish*, *palaver* or *safari*, have already been incorporated into general English and are thus codified in general large dictionaries of World English, the *Oxford English Dictionary* with its supplements, for instance, because they entered World English relatively late. Their range transcends African English by far, and some have even been borrowed into other European languages. They are, however, restricted to African contexts and thus have a more specific meaning in general English than in the particular regional English. A well-known example is the Swahili word *safari*. In East Africa it means any journey (*journey* is seldom used, possibly because of pronunciation difficulties), but for European tourists it always refers to a small expedition to see and shoot game (with gun or camera), normally in National Parks. Interestingly enough, *safari* in Standard English also refers to the group of people setting out on such a *safari*, a semantic expansion which is not possible in Swahili. Another example that has entered Standard English is *Kwashiorkor*; its West African origin is forgotten and it is used world-wide as the name of a severe protein deficiency disease, unfortunately only too often still to be found in Africa. Very few Africanisms have such a secure existence in general English, most of them being marginal and only used to render meanings in an African context (see chapter 5). This becomes understandable when one examines the areas of life or domains in which most Africanisms occur. The following list (Table 3.4) shows a few examples from East Africa, mainly from Swahili, grouped in the major domains of Africanisms. As can be expected, the African environment is inadequately reflected in the Standard English lexicon and is supplemented by African names for characteristic landscapes, plants or animals. African loans cluster around 'African' domains just as English loans cluster around 'European' domains. Even persons often have 'English names' and 'African names', 'home names' or even 'day names', as they are called in Nigeria and Ghana. It is interesting to see that the semantic expansion of Standard English lexemes may create problems of distinction as in the case of *potatoes*, where Africans often have to specify *European potatoes* or *sweet potatoes*. In general, the preferred staple food dish is hardly ever translated: Tanzania's *ugali* is Uganda's posho or Zimbabwe's *sadza* (maize dish; polenta). Why should a Nigerian translate *akara* as 'bean cake' instead of calling it by its usual African name? The field of food is probably culture-specific everywhere, but in many African countries there is a marked contrast between European and African food (and eating habits) because Europeans in Africa have tended not to adopt African food, in contrast to the British in India (cf. Spencer 1991). Interestingly, many African words for kin relations in the intimate family and beyond are retained, especially when used as a form of address. Where African clothing is still worn it is, of course, referred to with African names. Other African customs, which have to be rendered in African words, are concerned with traditional customs or pastimes, e.g. *lobola* ('bride-price') from Bantu and *dagga* ('cannabis') from Khoi languages in South Africa, or with rules of politeness. An important domain of Africanisms today is politics. As African languages have often played a major role in mobilizing the masses, even before *uhuru* (independence in East Africa) was reached and before *amandla* (power in South Africa) is in black hands, many politicians wish to demonstrate their local roots by including African vocabulary in their speeches even when they are talking in English. In order to avoid European stereotypes, a comrade is a *ndugu* in Tanzania and a *mukoma* in Zimbabwe (both literally 'brother'), but the concept as such is marked and is more or less fashionable in different ideological climates. This also shows that some words can only work in a specific national context (as also indicated in Table 3.4).

TABLE 3.4 The domains of lexical Africanisms in East African English

Environment	baobab*	(tree)	panga#	machete
	dudu(s)	insects	pori	bush, rural areas
	jembe	hoe	shamba#	field
	miombo#	(type of woodland)	simba?	lion
Food	bajia	(roasted potatoes)		
	chai#	tea	supu	(bone in 'soup')
	githeri	beans/ vegetable dish	ugali	(staple maize dish)
	dagaa?	small fish	uji	porridge
	maandazi	(wheat cakes)	vitumbua	(rice cakes)
	piripiri/ pilipili#	(red pepper)	soda	soft drink
People	askari*	watchman, policeman	fundi	craftsman
	baba	man	mama	woman
	babu	grandfather, old man	manamba	labourer
			mzee	(old man's title)
			mzungu	white man
	bwana*	Mister, master, Lord	(plural wazungu)	
			ndugu#	comrade, brother
	bibi#	grandmother, Lady	watoto?	children
	daktari?, mganga#	medical doctor		
Clothing	buibui	Islamic veil	khansu/ khanzu	men's cloth
	Kaunda suit	African suit	kitenge#,	women's
	khanga/	women's cloth	lesso	cloth
	kanga#			
Customs	bao	(board game)	ngoma#	dance, drum

TABLE 3.4 *cont.*

	habari(s)	(greetings, news)	pole	expression of sympathy
	jambo	hallo		
	marimba#	xylophone	pombe#	traditional beer
Politics	boma#	(administrative headquarters)	magendo nyayo K	black market national philosophy
	bunge	parliament	Uhuru	independence
	chama?	party; the Party	ugamaa T harambee K	'African socialism'
	kujitegemea T	self-reliance		
	Mwalimu	President Nyerere	wananchi	fellow countrymen
Others	dawa	medicine, cure	matatu#	collective taxi
	debe#	container (for about 4 gallons)	daladala T	priviate bus service
			pikipiki	motorbike
	duka#	shop	pole pole	slowly
	kiondo/ Kikapu	basket	safari*	journey
	mabati	corrogated iron (sheets)	sufuria	cooking pan

Key
* = Contained in *Concise Oxford English Dictionary*
# = Contained in *Oxford English Dictionary* (especially Supplements)
K = Nation-specific use in Kenya
T = Nation-specific use in Tanzania
? = Rarely used.

The parallel list of Nigerianisms is categorized according to the same domains in Table 3.5, but it contains the additional category of titles, which seem to be more important in West than in East Africa. Although this list was gathered from newspapers and other documents in Nigeria, most of them appear to be in use in Ghana (cf. Sey 1973) and Sierra Leone (cf. Pemagbi 1989) as well. Whereas most of the borrowings in East Africa come from Swahili those in Nigeria originate in several languages, particularly the major three, Hausa, Yoruba and Igbo; this reflects differences in the sociolinguistic setting. Origin, however, also raises usage questions, not only related to user but also to sociocultural reference: Is *juju* (charm, diviner) only used by the Hausa or also by the Yoruba and Igbo? If so, does it refer only to Hausa *juju* or to *juju* generally, even Yoruba and Igbo *juju*? These steps show different stages in the process of taking over words from an ethnically related language and culture into the national variety of a language. These processes also apply in East Africa, but as Swahili is considered a generally accepted second language there, the ethnic relation may be felt less strongly.

TABLE 3.5 The domains of lexical Africanisms in Nigerian English

Environment	harmattan	North wind	obeche	(tree/timber)
	iroko Y	hardwood tree		
Food	akara Y	beancake	iyan Y	Yam dish
	amala Y	yam flour	jolof rice	rice with gravy
	arrozo	special rice		ceremonial dish)
	dodo Y	fried plantain	ngwongwo I	goat dish
	eba Y	cooked gari	nono/nunu H	milk sauce/ drink
	edikanifong	vegetable sauce	Ofe I	sauce/soup (in
	egusi Y	melon-seed soup		compounds)
	fufu (foofoo) Y	yam porridge	ogbono I/ akpon	soup with balls
	gari Y	cassawa meal/ drink	okasi I	(soup)
	isiewu I	goat head pepper soup	suya/soya H	to roast/fry
			tuwo H	(cereal staple food)
People	alawada Y?	jester, joker	Osun/Oshun	river godess
	babalawo Y	diviner	oyibo Y/ oyinbo	white man
	dandoko H	carrier, porter	Shango Y	god of thunder
	dogo H	tall person	talakawas	the masses/ poor
	Ogboni Y	secret society		
Titles	Are Y	chief	Oga Y	headman
	Oba Y	king		
Clothing	adire Y	women's cloth	buba	male shirt

TABLE 3.5 *cont.*

		male gown	lappa	women's cloth
	agbada Y	male gown	lappa	women's cloth
	ankra	wax print	sokoto Y	male trousers
	babaringa H	male tunic		
Customs	calabash	container (from fruit skin)	juju H	charm diviner
			.	
			kwaghir?	puppet-show
	gangan Y	traditional drum	miliki	frivolous fun
	Iwarefa Y	cult	Odun Y	(festival)
Others	agbo Y	medicine	nna a-kedu I	greeting exclamation
	haba Y	(exclamation)	ogbeni Y	greeting exclamation
	kalabule	black market	rankadede	greeting
	molue	minibus	ogogoro	top
	sharia H	Islamic law	yeye Y	useless

Key
H = from or related to Hausa
I = from or related to Igbo
Y = from or related to Yoruba
? = rarely used.

The word-list in Table 3.6 adds examples of how language-internal material is used to create new words, i.e. it distinguishes loanwords taken from other African languages from English word material derived through word-formation processes which are possible though not utilized in Standard English. Affixation, composition and specification or expansion of meaning (cf. 3.6) can be used to express African nuances, which may be deduced easily by Europeans familiar with the African scene. Thus a *co-wife* (or even a *second*) and a *sugar-daddy* (which is associated with American English), *womanizer* (casanova), and, of course, *rainy* and *dry seasons* are known almost everywhere in Africa.

Some words from West Africa entered Standard English via the 'middle passage'; that is, they were used in the Caribbean and by Black Americans first, included in American and British usage later and are now listed in the Webster and Oxford dictionaries. Some of these words even lost their African connection *en route* and are not lexical 'Africanisms' in Africa today but (Black) Americanisms (e.g. *jazz, banjo, guy, bogus*).

Another developmental aspect of African words concerns not only their origin and their integration into English, but also their disappearance. Although most of the words in Table 3.6 are used in connection with the new modern African life-style, some such as *smallboy* have a colonial connotation or a generally unpleasant ring, so that they appear only in certain contexts. Similarly *chop box*, *chop money* and *catering/bush resthouses* belong more or less to (mainly white) colonial African English and have almost disappeared. Some words and word meanings may have gone out of use in England today (e.g. *to pass* in the sense of 'proffer' food or drinks) but are still used in Africa. 'Film African English', as the well-known *daktari*, is not really used by Black Africans, they use other expressions instead, such as *mganga* in East Africa, but not in Southern Africa, where *sangema* is still restricted to an African witch-doctor. There may, however, also be a connotational difference as far as the expected form of treatment is concerned. The entrance routes of African words into World English have changed, too: first they came via the slave trade and America, later via the settlers and colonial administrators, and finally, today, via tourists and African news agencies.

TABLE 3.6   The origin of some Africanisms in West African English

alkali	Arabic	magistrate, judge
alligator pepper	folk etymology	Malagrotta pepper
Asantihene	Akan	(Ashanti ruler)
been-to	composition	(someone who has been to Europe, usually for education)
booker	suffixation	(someone who collects passengers at lorry stations, etc.)
bush*	expansion	rural area (also in meat game)
camwood*	Temne folk etymology?	hard red wood (from *Baphia nitita*)
chew(ing)-stick	composition	(stick for cleaning teeth)
chiefly	suffixation	(adjective of chief)
chop	Pidgin	food; to eat (box, money; World English chopsticks)
cloth	specification	traditional garment for women
coaster	suffixation	European resident (in Africa)
cocoyam	composition	food plants (*colocasia esculenta xanthosoma sagittifolia*)
couscous*	Arabic	(dish: wheat vegetables/meat)
dash	Fanti?	tip, bribe, commission
fetish*	Portuguese	amulet, enchantment object
groundnut stew	expansion	(dish: meat groundnut (oil))
head-load	composition	(carry) goods on head

TABLE 3.6 *cont.*

head-tie	composition	woman's
high-life	specification	music style combining Jazz + West African elements
iroko*	Yoruba	mulberry tree + fruits
juju*	French	amulet, fetish
kente#	Akan	Ghanaian cloth
kola*	Temne	nut, tree (also in Coca Cola)
kwashiorkor#	Akan	(protein deficiency disease)
lappa#	specification	traditional women's garment (< Standard English: wrapper)
linguist	specification	spokesman (of a chief)
lorry/car station, motor park	composition	'bus station'
market-mammy#	Creole + compos.	woman trader, marketwoman
oba#	Yoruba	Yoruba chief/king
on seat	specification	present in office/at desk
palaver*	Portuguese/Pidgin	dispute, quarrel
pass	old usage	serve, proffer (food/drinks)
pickin	Portuguese	small child
smallboy	composition	servant (colonial)
stool	expansion	chief's throne in Ghana (also: to enstool, destool)
tapster	derivation	man who taps palm trees to collect/sell palm wine
watchnight	composition	night-watchman

Key
* = Contained in *Concise Oxford English Dictionary*
\# = Contained in *Oxford English Dictionary* (especially Supplements).

The taking-over of some English words into African usage can also give rise to connotational problems. Forms like *blackmail* or *black market* are stigmatized because the word *black* is used to characterize activities beyond what is permitted by law. It is therefore not surprising that many language-conscious Africans object to these terms and replace them. This is why Africanisms for *black market* occur almost as frequently all over Africa as the phenomenon itself, e.g. *magendo* in Tanzania, *kibanda* in Uganda and *kalabule* in Nigeria and Ghana. Such darker sides of the economy tend to change expressions rapidly, however, and once *kola* in Nigeria and *chai* in Kenya are known to the general public as expressions for a bribe, they are replaced already in the inner circle of users. The connotation 'African style' occurs in many areas of the informal sector or petty trade, from the infamous *parking boys*, who force car owners to pay them for 'looking after their cars' in Nigeria, to the *mishanga* boys (petit traders in Zambia), the *tsotsis* (thugs in Southern Africa) and the *jua kali* artisans, who follow their craft in the 'hot sun' and not in a shop or garage in Kenya. These examples illustrate that it is necessary to pay attention not only to denotative but also to connotative meanings and associations.

3.6 Meaning

Even if the words used in African English are unchanged traditional English words, their meanings may be quite different. Although word usage may depend on the specific linguistic and extralinguistic context and although individual words may show many different deviations, some tendencies may occur more generally. One possible categorization[14] starts from the assumption that words always combine a certain meaning with a particular form in a particular environment or context. This correspondence may be changed in many ways, as for instance when a particular meaning is expressed more than once in the same context (M1: redundancy); when the fixed correspondence between form and meaning is changed in form (M2: idiomaticity); when words extend (shift or occasionally restrict) their meanings in some contexts (M3: reference expansion); or when a certain, particularly close combination of words is altered by lexical replacements (M4: collocation). The examples quoted here are mainly from Kujore (1985 s.v.) for Nigeria, but they also occur in Kenya and Zambia at least. Such African 'particularities' are of course very common and there are numerous lists (e.g. Odumuh 1987 for Nigeria and Sey 1973 for Ghana).

M1: The level of semantic redundancy tends to be higher
Examples of redundancy can be found on many levels. The repetition of semantic elements may occur in connection with word formation (e.g. the suffix *-able* expresses the same as the modal auxiliary in M1a) or with modifying elements. This occurs when the meanings of the modifying words, adjectives, adverbs or prepositions, are already included in the meaning structure of the modified words, nouns (e.g. one defining element of a *ballot* (in M1b) in Standard English is that it is held secretly) or verbs (e.g. the element *together* is already contained in *pool* in M1c, the element *perhaps* in the modal *may* in M1d). Sometimes a (Latin) prefix correponds to a Germanic particle (as re- and *back* in M1e), when both are used this is considered tautological in Standard English. Other meaning elements may be reinforced

because they seem to have lost part of their meaning, as the feature 'duration' immanent in *during* (less so in *in*), which is emphasized a second time by *the course of* (in M1f), or the element absence from university which is included in *sabbatical* but emphasized by *leave* (in M1g). Other cases of 'expressing the same thing twice' would be *include* and *and so on*, which both convey the idea of incompleteness (in M1h), and *reason* and *because*, which can semantically be seen as including the elements 'reason' and a subordinator *that* (in M1i). The latter word combination can also be interpreted as a take-over from American theses, where it occurs frequently. Although redundancy is an important element in language in general and it is often – even in first languages – a matter of usage, convention and norm whether elements are regarded as 'necessary' or 'superfluous', these examples illustrate a second-language strategy of playing safe and saying rather too much than too little. This can be seen from (M1j), where the verb *write down* is usually seen as containing too many elements of *black and white*, whereas *put down* would be sufficiently empty to tolerate such an addition.

(M1a) The fire incident can be traceable to a live cigarette end . . .
(M1b) The election of officers was by secret ballot.
(M1c) We shall succeed if we pool our resources together.
(M1d) This perhaps may be so.
(M1e) When did you return back home?
(M1f) The teacher broke off for a few minutes during the course of his lecture.
(M1g) Where do you expect to spend your sabbatical leave?
(M1h) The articles in the drawer include books, pens, pencils, and so on.
(M1i) The reason why he came is because I invited him.
(M1j) If you really mean what you are saying, write it down in black and white.

M2: Idiomatic expressions are used in a slightly different form

Idiomatic expressions usually have a very fixed form as the idiomatic meaning consists of more than that of the single word elements involved. Thus variation in form is not common in Standard English, for instance, in terms of pluralization as it is in (M2a) and (M2b). Sometimes idiomatic expressions are mixed with similar ones (in M2c *with regard to* and *as regards* or in M2d *pick up* and *pick*, related to V4 above). There is also a tendency to make idioms more transparent and/or use more common synonyms (M2e and M2f).

(M2a) The manager had all facts at his fingers' tips.
(M2b) Was she speaking seriously or was she just pulling your legs?
(M2c) Nothing can be done with regards to your case.
(M2d) Moji is in a bad mood this morning, she is picking up a quarrel
      with everybody.
(M2e) Since they have said nothing, we can assume that they agree
      with us: silence, it is said, means [gives] consent.
(M2f) There was a deliberate attempt to drag my name in the mud
      [through the mire].

M3: English word forms are used in other reference contexts

In Africa English word forms occur in slightly different contexts
than in British Standard English, thus usually expanding their
referential meaning. The most striking examples of this are
kinship terms. Even the most casual visitor to Africa notices that
Africans seem to have very many 'brothers' and 'sisters' or even
'fathers'; this cannot only be attributed to the high birth rate and
the extended family structure. Kinship terms are expanded as
reference and address terms, because they go far beyond the
British core meanings related to the biological features of
consanguinity, generation and sex and are related to the social
features of seniority (age), solidarity, affection and role-relations
(cf. Alo 1989). Thus, all the mother's co-wives or sisters may be
addressed as 'mother', many elderly men as 'father' and people
from the same village without any blood relation as 'brothers and
sisters'. As it is very important to show respect to older people in
general, even older sisters may be ascribed the higher status of
'auntie'. This is supported by different kinship categorizations in
African languages, where seniority is often more important than
sex, which may occasionally in very basilectal English even lead
to sisters being introduced as 'brothers'.

Other common expansions occur, for instance, when *to book* is
used like Standard English *to hire*, *to forget* like *to lose*, *to refuse*
like *to deny*, *to see* like *to look*, *to reach* like *to arrive*, *arm* like
hand, *guest* like *stranger*, *strange* like *foreign*, and so on. In most
of these cases one can say that either the meanings have been
expanded or more specific features (selection restrictions) have
been dropped. *Escort* (in M3a) for instance originally implies a
special guard or act of courtesy, but by Africans it may be used in
the more general sense, without the narrower restrictions.
Similarly *students*, which originally refers to learners in higher
and in secondary institutions is also used for those in primary
schools (M3b). Only occasionally is the meaning restricted, as in
move with in the sense of 'go out with a boy-/girlfriend' (M3c).

Sometimes the semantic overlap between items accounts more (M3d) or less (M3e) clearly for the 'confusion' (*exchange* information has certainly a close relationship with *compare*, but its use in M3e usually implies that sheets of paper are swapped and not merely that both sheets are compared). Sometimes it seems to be relational restrictions (in terms of case grammar) rather than semantic ones that are broken (*clarify* in M3f means usually an effort by somebody who holds information and is in a position to make things clearer, not by somebody who needs this information). This is related, however, not to the meaning of particular lexical items but to the wider field of their usage in the syntactic context.

(M3a) Would you like to <u>escort</u> [accompany] me to a friend's house?

(M3b) The lecture is not intended for <u>students</u> [and pupils?] in the primary[!] and secondary schools.

(M3c) He has been <u>moving</u> [going out with] with the sister of my wife.

(M3d) I have to <u>convince</u> [persuade] the customs officials to release the car.

(M3e) Shall we wait and <u>exchange</u> [compare] notes after the meeting?

(M3f) I should <u>clarify</u> [seek clarification on] that point from the principal.

M4: Word collocations are used with different frequency

Collocations occur when certain words 'go together' particularly well or frequently, and are, in a way, associated with each other because they co-occur with unusual frequency. They may be less fixed than idioms, because their particular meaning occurs not only in the idiomatic context; but collocates still 'expect' each other to some extent. If similar words are used, the combination is less fixed or differs from what is expected in the context (M4a and M4b). Some fairly general terms are used instead of the more usual collocates (M4c and M4d), and some even develop specialized meanings in particular contexts (M4e). It is not always the case that collocations are stronger in British Standard English, because African English has developed its own specific ones (M4f).

(M4a) We had a lot of difficulties with the project at the beginning, but after some time it was all <u>smooth</u> [plain] sailing.

(M4b) They prepared the room in which the dance is <u>carried out</u> [performed].

(M4c) He never committed the action [crime] for which he is
       accused.
(M4d) The election cannot be done [conducted/held].
(M4e) Don't move [keep company, associate] with bad boys.
(M4f) He gave me a lift in his car, and I dropped [got out/down,
       alighted] near the hospital.

Many other innovative coinages forge new collocations, which
may mean little to the uninitiated. Thus *bottom power* refers to
'favours obtained by a woman through the use of her body',
national cake to 'rights, privileges, and items to be shared by the
state or citizens' and *to smell pepper* means 'to face a rough time
or be given a rough deal' (all from Adegbija 1989a).

Some of these examples show very clearly that a lot of these
differences are a matter of degree, and it is often only
impressionistically that differences of varieties in usage and
frequency are recorded; more precise statements would only be
possible on the basis of large-scale text comparisons.

Another way of expanding the meaning of words is to use them
metaphorically. This often reflects traditional African ways of
thinking (not naming certain things directly or talking euphemistically), as the following examples from literary English usage in
Zambia show (all again from Dominic Mulaisho, *The Tongue of
the Dumb*. London: Heinemann 1971):

She did not help the teacher [have sex with] (p. 106, l. 14)
The missionary coming here to insult our manhood (p. 100,
l. 9)
She still hasn't been purified (p. 48, l. 4)
Is the roof of the house well? (p. 59, l. 16).

A famous example of a different usage of a word, which may
cause some amazement, is *sorry*. Many visitors to Africa have
noticed that their African friends seem to apologize, for instance,
when someone stumbles, as if they had been responsible in some
way. When Africans say *sorry*, however, they merely use the
appropriate African form of expressing solidarity or sympathy,
because it is customary to express sympathy when someone has
an unfortunate experience. Thus the same word, which expresses
apology in Standard English, has expanded its meaning to
sympathy in African English, because a certain gap in the
vocabulary seems to have been felt by African users. Other
semantic incongruencies can be detected when the usage of
expressions of gratitude (*thank you*) and politeness (*please*), in

replies corresponding to American *You are welcome*, are examined carefully.

3.7 Discourse

Another important and rather neglected aspect of African English, the features which occur at the discourse level, is also intertwined with perceived cultural norms. By discourse we refer in this context to the use of more extended linguistic elements beyond single words or grammatical constructions, which are closely related to sociocultural usage and expectations in terms of the 'ethnography of speaking'. Many features at this level have been previously described under the more general heading of style (but in this context it may be worth distinguishing between general cultural style from individual style shifts, as explained in 3.1). The following examples illustrate some characteristic usages:

(D1) What can I do for you, chief?
(D2) Hallo, J. How are you doing? – How is your wife? – How are your children?
(D3) *When a handshake goes beyond the elbow we know it has turned to another thing. The sleep that lasts from one market day to another has become death. The man who likes the meat of the funeral ram, why does he recover when sickness visits him? The mighty tree falls and the little birds scatter in the bush.* . . . *The little bird which hops off the ground and lands on an ant-hill may not know it but is still on the ground.* . . . *A common snake which a man sees all alone may become a python in his eyes.* . . . *The very Thing which kills Mother Rat is always there to make sure that its young ones never open their eyes.* . . . *The boy who persists in asking what happened to his father before he has enough strength to avenge him is asking for his father's fate.* . . . *The man who belittles the sickness which Monkey has suffered should ask to see the eyes which his nurse got from blowing the sick fire.* . . . *When death wants to take a little dog it prevents it from smelling even excrement.* . . .
(Chinua Achebe *Arrow of God* (*Second Edition*). London: Heinemann
1974: 226, italics original)

The first example (D1) shows a form of address which may be very important: if the addressees or partners in communication have a title or are known by an honorary name it is often used even by close friends. If 'needed' even occupations can be used as titles, such as Dr, Pastor or Engineer, can be used as titles or even more neutral expressions occur, such as *chief* for an elderly or wise man or woman (which may occasionally be used very loosely and may even be applied to females in some areas), *mzee* ('old man' in East Africa), *agogo* ('old woman' in South Africa). This technique can also be used when a lecturer, for instance, has forgotten the name of a student, and thus addresses him or her as brother or sister. From an early age pupils at school learn that correct forms of address demonstrate respect for the human being, hence their usage is deeply rooted in behavioural norms. These forms of address may be strung together to heighten the politeness and the respect offered. They may then be combined with the discourse feature that follows.

The second example (D2) is the start of a longer conversation, which consists of several conventional sequences about the health, life and happiness of the addressee and his family. These questions are expected to be answered in short positive sentences; if the situation is not quite as positive, they may be qualified and specified later in the conversation. As it is customary for the speakers to show their respect for the hearers' personality before starting to discuss serious problems or even to criticize them, they must follow these conventions of polite discourse initiation. Such address forms and politeness rules depend, of course, on the age, sex, social class and personal relationship of the participants. It may however be the case that they still play a greater role in African than in Western societies. Whole ceremonies may be part of the traditional greeting formulae aimed at establishing a good basis for friendly communication. Such repetitions have been interpreted as typically African discourse markers in many narratives.

The third example is a firework of African proverbs. Although unusually condensed, even by Achebe's literary standards, the passage illustrates idiomatic phrases, not only semantic deviations of individual words, the meaning and importance of which are not easily evident from outside a particular African culture. Such proverbs or sayings (and even some discourse openings) are derived from common African experience and often carry a whole story with them. For one of the proverb's functions is to summarize matters that might be difficult to explain. Further-more, proverbs signify the speaker's wisdom and/or age, or they neutralize what may otherwise be unpleasant or dangerous truths for the hearer. Sometimes they may be pure rhetoric, sometimes they show love for traditional wit, irony or poetry. Achebe also emphasizes in *Things Fall Apart* (London: Heinemann 1958: 5) the value of culture-specific discourse in general and of proverbs in particular: 'Among the Ibo the art of conversation is regarded very highly, and proverbs are the palm-oil with which words are eaten.'

All three examples are related to politeness strategies, which are usually associated with power, distance and the extent of the threat to the 'face' of the communication partners in Western societies. 'Preserving face' is extremely important in many African cultures, and thus various strategies have to be developed to ensure it. Culture-specific differences in the interpretation of such conventions and strategies can lead to misunderstandings and can even generate negative cultural stereotypes, às for instance in English conversations between white South Africans and Zulus (cf. Chick 1985). Discourse behaviour, according to Western cultures, is said to follow the maxim 'short and to the point', whereas other cultures may value behaviour that proceeds at a measured, dignified pace (with vast possibilities of misinterpretation and negative stereotyping of the 'whites are hectic, Zulus are lazy' type).

Such cultural differences may also occur in the organization of stories or essays. Some studies (e.g. Kaplan 1966) suggest that the 'English' paragraph in written discourse shows linear development with every piece of information explicitly related to a topic stated at the beginning or end, that 'semitic' paragraphs show more parallelism, using appositional and comparative statements, and that 'oriental' paragraphs look at a topic from a number of different perspectives. Although it is impossible to generalize (Kaplan 1987) and although it is difficult to say how many stylistic features are carried over into the second-language structures of African English, some tendencies can be observed in certain text types, which may be seen as culture-specific discourse features. Some of these features are far from easy to interpret because they reflect underlying patterns of African thinking – a very difficult field in any case, and one that perhaps only African scholars can penetrate.

Sey (1973: 123) also explains some discourse features related to the nature of English as a second language:

> Style itself tends to be viewed as a purely decorative device rather than an aim to more effective exposition and fuller comprehension; and especially among the more naive speakers, it appears to be identified with the use of words and phrases that are presumed to be 'learned', and also with the impressive display of an extensive range of vocabulary. Since these two are not always matched by equally impressive command of varied and controlled use of sentence structures, a kind of prose results which is either monotonous or jerky

in rhythm – a string of loosely connected simple sentences interlarded with unexpected and ill-fitting preciosity. In some cases attempts at the use of more complex sentences only result in overinvolved syntax.

Thus if ENL speakers fail, for instance, to see the logic of certain conjunctions and sentence relaters in (D4a), it is important to remember that they are used as simple sentence connectors, when additional marking for reason, etc. is not always implied as strongly as in Standard English. This may also explain the use of some clichés, relatively meaningless formulaic expressions, such as the overemphatic *finally and in conclusion* in (D4b). Similar problems may also arise from simple semantic differences in the usage of discourse connectors, such as the conjoining of independent sentences without co- or subordinators (as in D4c):

(D4a) There is no agreement on what the concept of rural transformation means and <u>consequently</u> no attempt has been made to attain such agreement.
(D4b) Finally and in conclusion, I will just say this . . .
(D4c) Linguistic competence refers to a native speaker's language ability, __ how much he has grasped his own language.

The borderline to the 'general inadequacy in fluent self-expression' (Essilfie 1983: 129) is sometimes not easy to draw, as the following example from a formal welcome to freshmen at the University of Botswana written by an undergraduate illustrates (ibid.):

The social life at the University does sometimes overwhelm some students, so much so that they pay very little and in some cases no attention at all to their studies. Allocate your time properly so that you could accomodate [sic] each one of these activities without making any one of them suffer.
Nobody is ever or should ever be bullied into accepting any shade of believes [sic]. You have come here to grow and mature. The university's role is that of providing all it can to assist you grow, and this it does through provision of books in the library, staff from all walks of life. All these you will understand will be provided within the austerity measures currently in force throughout Botswana.
July 1st 1982 ushered in a new era in the history of this institution. Our parents have demonstrated their will and determination to provide education for their children. It remains for the University community through proper instruction by staff, serious studies by students and participation in the development struggle by all that their efforts were not in vain.

This takes us close to stylistic analyses of particular individuals and it is often difficult to draw the borderline between individual creativity and culture-specific deviation. The fact remains that the choice of *assist* instead of *help*, *carry out* instead of *do*, *undoubtedly* instead of *surely* and *a distant place* instead of *somewhere far away* is made more often by African than by British speakers of English in similar contexts. These style differences are linked to the problem of registers (mentioned above and examplified in sentences like D5 as opposed to D5'):

(D5)   I have come round to alleviate your loneliness.
(D5') I have come round to keep you from being lonely.

Here the different position of English in society may play a decisive role. Is it really true that the informal registers of African English are inadequately developed, or are they just developing, but independently from the British English model?

The decision to use English and not an African language in informal conversation, for instance, may be influenced by the topic, but it may also influence the topics dealt with in the discourse? Do Africans conversing in English, for instance, think more in academic categories? And this has formal repercussions. Thus the immediate situation may be avoided and this may account for a relatively low frequency of ambiguous demonstratives in colloquial English (Moody 1982). This may also be related to the lack of redundancy mentioned earlier: whereas demonstratives or other substitutes would be expected in native English the full noun would be mentioned repeatedly in African English.

Another interesting hypothesis in this context is that second-language speakers may need and receive more audial encouragement when they use English; that may be the reason why phatic words and sounds (*eeeh, ahaa*, etc.) appear to be more frequent in African than British English. They assure the speakers that they are still being understood, whereas native speakers do not need such encouragement and silence in their conversations is more acceptable as it is not taken as a signal of incomprehension so easily. But the issue is whether the same phatic encouragement is equally commonly used by the same speakers when they use African languages, because then it would be a cultural and not a second-language phenomenon.

These examples can only illustrate the complexity of such discourse and text studies. Much more work remains to be done in categorizing and analysing the various features, tendencies and strategies involved. Some linguists mention indirectness and circularity, repetition and wordiness (Chishimba 1984), others verbosity and preciosity (Sey 1973) as features of Africanness; but again it is not clear whether they are typical only of literary or scientific styles, or more widespread.

Notes

1. There is a certain controversy about lect rigidity and about the possibilities of determining their borderlines (Magura 1985 and Platt 1986), but the model can certainly be used as a descriptive basis for a dynamic speech continuum. These categories are similar to the categories of acrolang, mesolang and basilang, which are familiar in second-language acquisition research, both ranging from more sophisticated to more basic varieties. Schumann (e.g. 1978) even suggests that the early stages of any second-language acquisition are like pidginization and the later like creolization. In West Africa formal features between the two lect continua overlap only partly, but the problem of limited input of the target language is identical, although to a different degree (cf. 9.2).
2. Although the following examples stress the lack of phoneme differentiation as a distinct feature of most African varieties of English, there are also a few cases of overdifferentiation, such as vocalic nasalization by Yoruba speakers, who are said to distinguish *can* (be able to) and *can* (tin) by and nasalization, respectively, or the distinction between /w/ and /wh/ in words like *witch* and *which* made by Igbo speakers.
3. According to Lanham (1984: 223) this can have far-reaching consequences for comprehension, because listeners 'heard the text as a list of distractions' and this 'revealed an almost total failure to convey the coherence of the text and a loss of a good deal of its propositional content'.
4. An interesting alternative to our formal classification is offered by Williams (1987) for non-native varieties in general. She distinguishes between the principles derived from the four general charges of language, to be clear, quick and easy, processable and expressive. The principle of economy of production leads to regularization and selective production of redundant markers and the reduction of ambiguity to maximum transparency and maximum salience. As these principles have overlapping results in form and have to be complemented by others to explain all phenomena, the categorization of deviations is not always easy. Other lists of African features can be found in Bokamba 1982 and 1991 and in various 'common error' collections (e.g. Jowitt/Nnamonu 1985, Lewis/Masters 1987 or Hocking 1974).
5. An interesting complementary formal analysis would be to compile a list of features that do not occur in African English, although they

occur in first-language varieties or other second-language varieties (e.g. double negation only seems to occur in restricted cases of semantic implication, e.g. *avoid + not to do something*). This could be expanded into an even larger comparison of variety overlap, which would show that although African English overlaps with Standard English and other New Englishes to a large extent, it overuses some and underuses other structures.

6. As in all non-standard speech several factor groups appear to be involved in plural marking: semantic ones, when plurality is not marked overtly because it is expressed elsewhere, phonetic ones, when certain vowels or consonants precede and make pronunciation difficult or redundant (as in Standard English), and even phonotactic ones, when the preferred CV syllable structure is violated or when consonant clusters occur through the added plural markers.

7. The relative construction with *which* is not uncommon in non-standard British English. Here *which* is not really used as a pronoun because the pronoun *which + its* would be *whose* or *of which*, but rather as a conjunction or subordinator marking the beginning of a relative clause. *Which* then is used as a neutral relative conjunction able, together with the respective personal pronoun, to replace all other relative pronouns (this interpretation also explains the 'double marking' in example S1b below).

The opposite tendency, to maintain the pronominal meaning, but delete the conjunct, occurs in: *The plantations had a lot of people and most of which came from the interior.*

8. The problem with the interpretation of determiner usage in Africa according to the specific/non-specific system appears to be that it is not balanced: whereas the 'omission' of articles is very common, even in African news broadcasts, the 'superfluous' insertion of demonstrative pronouns is far less often observed. Even if the definite/indefinite and the specific/unspecific systems interfere, the question remains why they interfere with different strength on the two wings, which does not seem to be the case in South-East Asia.

9. Whereas the referential meaning may be the same in African and in Standard English, the register value is quite different; the imperative and the missing determiner make the expression rather impolite in Standard English, which need not be implied in African English.

10. The opposite tendency, to omit semantically empty pronouns, also occurs. Here phonetic perception of these meaningless, purely syntactic items, which are obvious from the context, may play a major role, as in: *I'll give ['t] to you.*

11. Studies of learner language that emphasize the contrastive perspective, e.g. Swan/Smith (eds) 1987, often give long lists of stigmatized interference features and tend to neglect the intralinguistic variation in the African as well as in the target language.

12. Whereas J. Branford's dictionary is exclusive, i.e. it lists only the approximately 3,500 words and expressions considered typical of and exclusive to the variety, W. Branford's (1987) is inclusive, i.e. it

contains almost 30,000 normal general English headwords from the Oxford English dictionary plus about 1,500 typically South African headwords (mainly from J. Branford's exclusive dictionary), about 570 compounds and diminutives, over 300 established English words with specialized meanings and about seventy acronyms (ibid.: xliii). The figures illustrate the statistical relation of regional to general entries in regional dictionaries of established varieties.

13. Student jargon at African universities is a well-known example of a variety with a limited range of topics (cf. Hancock/Angogo 1982 for Kenya and Anasiudu 1987 for Nigeria). At the University of Zambia (Lusaka), for instance, widows are female students whose boyfriends have graduated and mercenaries are 'soldiers of fortune' who are after them, academic poachers only copy from other students' assignments but do not read and may still get only a Gentleman's pass (grade C).

   Other well-known examples are the youth languages in the major urban centres (citytalk), which may be highly multilingual contact phenomena with varying degrees of English involved, such as Sheng in Nairobi or tsotsi language (isitsotsi, setsotsi or tsotsitaal) in South Africa.

14. An alternative approach is Sey's 'classification of Ghanaianisms' (1973: 70–2), which distinguishes coinages (African ≠ English word), extension (African > European meaning), restriction (European < African meaning), restriction + expansion, transfer (African ≠ European meaning) and shift ('rearrangement of characteristic patterns within the field'). The last category shows particularly clearly that Sey's word-based approach, which can be seen as a subcategorization of our category M3, must be complemented by frequency and context analyses.

Chapter 4

English in Education

The role of languages in education is crucial for the sociolinguistic situation of a country; it is in fact the major criterion of our classification of countries in the ENL–ESL–EIL continuum. The role of English as a subject must be distinguished from its role as a medium of instruction, and it is usually this second aspect that is hotly debated. Within the scope of this introductory book it is impossible to cover all the problems, techniques and methods of English language teaching in African countries. It may suffice to emphasize the sociolinguistic perspective again, including the problems arising from switching to English as a medium of instruction and the issue of falling standards. This leads to an analysis of the network of factors affecting English language teaching in Africa and the question of how these factors can be improved with the help of development aid.

4.1 The position of English in the education system

The position of English in a nation-state depends on the development of the government's national language policy (cf. 8.1). Besides administration, government and law, education has always been considered the most important sector of public life for language policy implementation. Therefore, English in schools does not only reflect the national sociolinguistic situation, including language policy and attitudes, it is at the same time an important factor in shaping that situation.

As English is, with few exceptions, still an additional, i.e. a second, third or even fourth language for those who use it in Africa, there are several levels at which African children may be affected by it; in general it is true that the stronger the position of English in the country the earlier and deeper the impact on its schoolchildren. African children can be affected by English in two ways. The first time they meet English is when it is introduced as a subject in the school curriculum, the second is when it is used as a medium of instruction.

Normally English must be taught as a subject for several years before it can be used as a medium, because in many African states exposure to reasonably proficient English is not available outside the classroom. However, the choice of a medium of instruction in African primary schools is far from easy. Some states or regions in Africa have to use English from the very first school year onward because they find it impossible to use an indigenous African language; either they cannot agree on which language to choose or they think the African languages available have not yet acquired the technical vocabulary they need. Even on a small scale the choice may be difficult: some school catchment areas (urban areas, for example) are linguistically heterogeneous and no language group wants to accept the other's mother tongue as a medium. If no African lingua franca is available the only possibility is a 'straight-for-English' approach, especially when parents see English as a means or prerequisite to socio-economic advancement for their children and press the school authorities to start English-medium education as early as possible. The same parental attitudes cause some private schools to use this approach, if allowed to do so by the Ministry of Education. Nevertheless, according to most UNESCO recommendations since 1953 (cf. UNESCO 1953), this approach is best avoided, since 'every child has a right of instruction in his own mother tongue'.

The 'straight-for-English' approach is practised today, especially in ethnically mixed areas, in (some) primary schools in Zambia, Kenya, the Republic of South Africa, Namibia, West Cameroon, Liberia, Sierra Leone and Gambia. It is also adopted in most private fee-paying primary schools, as in Nigeria for instance. It is understandable that this approach is extremely difficult for teachers and pupils (and sometimes parents, too); the actual practice in the classroom may vary, although a great deal of code mixing and unofficial use of mother tongues must take place until the pupils have acquired the minimum level of English that enables them to follow the lessons.

Another approach is to teach English as a subject in lower primary education and to use it as a medium in upper primary education, with the change-over usually between Standard 4 and

6. This has the advantage that all pupils can acquire a reasonable level of English before it takes up the burden of supporting the content of other subjects. As a result, this approach seems to be the most favoured in African countries today. It is practised generally in Nigeria, Ghana, Uganda, Malawi, Zimbabwe, Botswana, Lesotho and Swaziland.

A third group of nations uses not English but the local African languages, especially the national language(s), throughout primary education. These national languages are not only sufficiently developed and extensively used, but are also supported by national language policies. English remains an important subject, however, because it will be needed as a medium in all or some secondary schools. Sometimes English may be used only in natural science subjects, with an African language used in arts. This approach is followed by Tanzania, Somalia, Ethiopia and Southern Sudan.[1]

The other African nation-states use English more or less as a language for international communication, which is why they teach the language extensively at secondary school level but use other languages specifically, i.e. Arabic, French, or Portuguese, as languages of instruction. In most francophone West African states, for instance, all secondary school students have to learn English, because their nations are closely interrelated with their anglophone neighbours (cf. Treffgarne 1975).

At tertiary level, in addition to the nations mentioned before, English is the medium even at the universities of some Arabic-speaking countries, such as Egypt, Libya or the Sudan, in specialist fields such as medicine, pharmacy, engineering, architecture, natural science, computing or management. Sometimes even nurses are taught in English.

Finally, it is remarkable that English is taught in adult education programmes. Although it is usually not the language of initial literacy many adults take advantage of the English courses, either because they think that it provides them with economic or occupational advantages or because they want to be able to help and understand their English learning school-children.

Again it must be pointed out that this picture is not static. As educational language policy partly depends on general policy internally, and even externally, the emphasis may change. In the case of Libya in 1986, turmoil in its international relations caused the abrupt official banishment of foreign languages, especially English, from teaching schedules and publishing lists (but in practice this had little effect). Many countries are proceeding with experiments to determine which language provides more favourable results as a medium in certain classes – the debate about educational language policies is a never-ending one.

4.2 Arguments for and against English as a medium of instruction

Although the position of English in education may vary considerably in different African states there have been attempts to strengthen or to weaken it in most of them. As the arguments used by supporters and critics are relatively similar in most nations, they can be summarized in the following general discussion. First, four arguments (E1–E4) in favour of English will be presented and then four arguments (A1–A4) in favour of African languages (cf. Ansre 1977 or Adegbija 1989b). Each argument will not only be presented but also scrutinized and challenged by counter-arguments.

E1: The 'high cost' argument
As the young nations of the Third World have been under heavy strain with respect to manpower and financial resources since independence, all major changes in the educational system (as the change to another medium of instruction would be), have tended to be avoided. Any such change implies not only changing the curriculum, but also teacher training programmes and the production (writing and printing) of textbooks and teaching aids – all at enormous additional cost to an expanding education system. This has led to the continued use of old (often still British) textbooks, teaching methods and curricula. Opponents of the status quo counter the high cost argument by saying that changes will have to come anyway or are – with the help of national school book foundations, etc. – already under way. Since books, methods and curricula must in any case be modified and adapted to the changing African environment, would it not be possible to change the language together with the content?

E2: The 'anti-tribal' argument
Since the process of nation-building is crucial for African nation-states, as many aspects of public life as possible should contribute towards this aim. The selection of an African language would threaten the unity of the nation-state, because only in rare cases (e.g. in Somalia) do all citizens share a common mother tongue. Thus supporters of this argument maintain that English is the only ethnically neutral language. Nevertheless, even if this argument is strong, its critics argue, this does not exclude the use

of African lingue franche (such as Swahili), especially if they are spoken by more Africans as a second language than as a mother tongue.

E3: The technological argument

As modern terminology in African languages is still being developed, especially in the scientific and technical fields, it is held to be impossible to use these languages now and even doubtful whether conscious vocabulary expansion and propagation would improve their chances in the near future, since the efforts and costs involved would be enormous. The critics of this argument, who advocate the modernization of African languages, usually point out how much has already been achieved in certain cases. They claim that the case of Swahili, for instance, proves that African languages can speedily acquire a technical and scientific vocabulary.

E4: The 'international communication' argument

Supporters of this argument say that the world is shrinking because of world-wide communication, and that people need a common language more than ever before. As English has – through whatever historical and political processes – gained a unique status in the modern world, it would be foolish not to take advantage of this. As all attempts during the last hundred years to create an artificial world language have failed, a natural language might be more successful. On the other hand, supporters of African languages ask how many Africans are really involved in international communication and whether the small group that is would not better be catered for in special courses. Besides, they argue convincingly that this is rather an EIL than an ESL argument; in other words, it is not an argument for using English as a medium, but rather for teaching English and even for teaching it as thoroughly as possible. Furthermore, it is doubtful whether it really is an advantage for students when badly taught English is used as a medium of instruction.

A1: The psycholinguistic argument

Because psycholinguistic studies have shown that mother-tongue education is better for a child's cognitive development,[2], numerous recommendations have been made for giving African children this chance of fuller development. However, as these studies mostly refer to early educational development, and since other studies seem to show that multilingual education triggers otherwise latent mental capacities, opponents of this argument maintain that there is no reason to believe that English in education is harmful, provided that early education (possibly including literacy) has been carried out in the mother tongue.

A2: The 'élitist' argument

Because English is only spoken by an educated élite in Africa, using English in education provides children from an English-speaking home with an initial advantage, which is unfair to the other pupils, who are disadvantaged anyway. It is, however, a fact that in at least some African countries it was the parents who demanded the early introduction of English-medium education on the grounds that this was the only way to compensate for initial disadvantages by the time the pupils competed for places in further education. Furthermore, as English is still the stepping stone to well-paid employment in many anglophone countries the expansion of English language teaching may be the only way to undermine its élitist character. Again, this is rather an argument for the efficient teaching of English as a subject than for its use as a medium.

A3: The 'linguistic imperialism' argument

Because the European languages were imposed on Africa by the colonial powers, adherents of this argument say that, the colonial powers having been driven out, it is high time for Africans to fight for complete independence and rid themselves of all remnants of colonialism, including the European languages. Opponents argue that the English language today cannot any longer be seen as the property of one or two imperialistic nations, but has, in its various forms, developed into a true world language, or at least a language which is the property of the world as a whole.

A4: The 'cultural alienation' argument

Because English is the language of a European nation and a Western culture it cannot carry the associations and connotations of an African identity. Education in English may therefore deracinate the African child and alienate it from its own cultural background. This argument can be countered by pointing out that modern African life has already incorporated so many features of modern 'Western', international life that English is only one of them. Furthermore, African writers have already proved that it *is* possible to convey African culture, life and even traditions in the English language if this language is appropriately 'adapted' (cf. chapter 5).

This brief review of some of the main arguments suggests that none of them is adequately backed up by research, and that either side can refute the arguments of the other, most of these being opinions and attitudes, though nonetheless important for that (cf. chapter 7). There have even been some practical experiments to find out which approach yields better results in terms of subject skills, verbal skills in English or in general or academic performance as a whole, but none of them is absolutely conclusive, either because they could not control certain variables (e.g. parents' use of English) or because they had much more favourable input conditions than usual (e.g. in terms of schoolbooks and dedicated teachers). The most famous one was the 'six-year primary project' at Ife in Nigeria (cf. Afolayan 1978), in which the use of the mother tongue proved superior, but there were also others with different results (e.g. MacAdam 1978 in Zambia).

It goes without saying that there are many more arguments on either side, both sound and unsound, but the four main lines of argumentation presented by each group should now be clear. If there is any realistic solution to the problem of choosing a linguistic medium for African education today at all, it is likely to be a compromise. This would be in accordance with a long African tradition of multilingualism, which language specialists from predominantly monolingual European nation-states tend to forget. One possibility, which is in fact practised in most African nations, is to start education in the mother tongue, or the 'language of the immediate environment', and switch to English at a certain level afterwards. This may allow the children some advantages of both approaches: it can ensure basic literacy and fluency in an African language before adding another dimension, English, in order to provide them with the advantages of multilingualism.

4.3 Basic problems of using English as a medium: switching and standards

Since anglophone African nations still use English as the medium of instruction at some stage in their educational system, it is worth examining some of the educational problems involved. The first serious problem arises when English is introduced as a medium, even after students have learnt English as a subject for several years. The problem of switching the medium of instruction, particularly when it occurs more than once, was often

TABLE 4.1   Language use in primary education in Northern Rhodesia (Zambia) before independence

Year	Mother tongue	Official language	English
1	M	S	–
2	M	S	S
3	–	M	S
4	–	M	S
5	–	M	S
6	–	M	M
7	–	M	M
8	–	M	M

Key
M = medium
S = subject

given as a major justification for introducing English-medium education very early, such as in the following report for Northern Rhodesia/Zambia, which may sound unusual for a UNESCO statement:

> A child, therefore, may have begun in his mother tongue; changed to a main official vernacular, if that is not his mother tongue, after two years; changed to English as a medium of instruction two years later. . . . We [therefore] recommend that a policy decision be made to introduce English as the universal medium of instruction from the beginning of schooling.
>
> (UNESCO 1964: 25)

This report exemplifies the problem for areas where the child's mother tongue is not an official language and the child has to switch to another language twice. This is often neglected or entirely ignored nowadays, which is why the above example (Table 4.1) is historic (from the mid-1950s). In pre-independence Zambia the language time-table was much more complex than today – and based more on the four official African languages than on English, although urban areas switched rather earlier to English as a medium than is indicated here. It is interesting to note that even today language choice in education may be a hot issue, as can be seen from the disputes between Lozi and Tonga supporters, who could not agree which zone the mixed city of Livingstone (Zambia) was to belong to.

The 'solution' found in Zambia after independence was the straight-for-English approach discussed above. As this has other serious drawbacks and as it implies some sort of switching from

TABLE 4.2   English in primary education in Malawi

Standard	English as subject	English as medium
1	5 x 25 min	physical education
2	7 x 30 min	physical education
3	9 x 35 min	physical education
4	9 x 35 min	+ arithmetic
5	9 x 35 min	+ general science, geography
6	9 x 35 min	+ history, civics and others
7	9 x 35 min	+ history, civics and others
8	9 x 35 min	+ history, civics and others

the African language(s) of the immediate environment to the
European medium of instruction in any case, switching simply
cannot be avoided in the present educational situation in Africa.
But because the switch-over from an African to a European
language must come as a shock to many pupils, it needs careful
planning and preparation.

One method that has been attempted to prepare pupils
gradually for a different medium of instruction is to use the new
language in certain lessons, especially in those where more
stereotyped expressions are sufficient, such as physical education
or arithmetic. Table 4.2 shows the increasing importance of
English as a subject (measured in length of instruction) and as a
medium (measured in number of subjects) prescribed in primary
education in Malawi; it is characterized by a staggered introduction as a medium 'as far as possible'.

Another method attempted is to present a complete intensive
English-using course before the actual subject teaching in English
begins. As the teachers' talk and the textbooks are normally too
difficult, special emphasis has to be placed on systematic training
in listening and reading skills.

An example of an English-medium preparation course is
Learning Through Language (Dar es Salaam: Tanzania Publishing House), which consists of a pupil's book and a teachers' book
(by R.H. Isaacs), which was introduced into Tanzania in 1968
and is also used in other countries (e.g. Zambia) nowadays. As it
is self-contained and not written for a particular school level it
can be used profitably as a course preparing students for English
as a medium of instruction after some five years of English as a
subject, i.e. at the beginning of secondary school. It provides
graded reading passages with multiple-choice questions about the
content, and small tasks and summaries. As the texts are adapted

not only to the African child's language skills but also to his or her sociocultural environment, they have always been very popular in Tanzania. In many other areas, suitable materials have still to be produced. Even when appropriate teaching materials are available, special problems arise: Is the course integrated into the normal school-day or is it a full-day intensive course? Do only the English teachers or all the subject teachers take part in the course? Should specific subject-related lessons be taught in addition to the English textbook? How these problems are solved will always depend on local circumstances, and especially on the availability of teachers and teaching materials.

But even if the English-medium preparation course is taken seriously and carried through systematically, there will always be a mixture of African languages and English in the classroom. Often, it takes several years for English to be fully established as the only medium in class. Even then the teacher must always consider how difficult it might be for the pupils to follow his explanations of complicated subject-matter in a language with which they are not yet familiar. Unfortunately, this problem seems to have increased during the last thirty years.

In most anglophone African nations there have been constant complaints about the 'standard of English' since independence (and sometimes even before). Older civil servants and teachers particularly can be heard to observe that in their school-days primary school leavers were able to read and write English with reasonable fluency, but nowadays English has gone badly downhill.[3] 'A matter of some concern is the current performance of our students in the West African School Certificate Examinations. Teachers of English are particularly disturbed by the poor performance in English Language (Ndahi 1975: 18 as quoted in Odumuh 1987: 68). To make matters worse, as English is the general medium of instruction a drop in the pupils' competence in English may seriously affect their performance in other subjects.[4] This mutual dependence of English language teaching and teaching of other subjects in English makes it necessary for English language teachers to adapt their courses to the needs of the subject teachers and for these in turn to adapt their language to the pupils' level. But the teachers' competence in English may be relatively low and not very flexible, because many are still insufficiently trained. Thus, in order to convey their subject matter, some take refuge in African languages, others venture upon a special English 'interlanguage' to bridge the gap between the subject's language requirements and the students' language competence. Such an interlanguage is an approximative system used by learners in the process of learning the standard language. Unfortunately, the students are exposed to this English interlanguage more often than to a reasonably normative English. Many forms that are considered incorrect in Standard English and in the textbooks become fossilized and impede development towards higher proficiency. It has even been concluded that using this type of English as a medium of instruction is not necessarily an advantage in learning English.

Although most of these complaints are based on random observation, there are a few systematic studies. One of the latest documents is the Criper/Dodd Report on the situation in Tanzania. It reveals that the level of English, estimated on the basis of a nation-wide proficiency test, is far below the minimum English-medium requirements in all types of school up to university (Criper/Dodd 1984: 13). It must be remembered, however, that Tanzania is a somewhat special case because of its successful language policy of introducing Swahili as a truly national medium of communication. The greatest concern about English standards is the fear that a vicious circle may develop: when the pupils' English deteriorates, some of them are still trained to be teachers and their 'bad English' results in their pupils learning even worse English. Thus the problem may constantly be aggravated as education expands and not enough qualified teachers are available. Paradoxically, there is a danger here that the more English you have in a country the less it may be internationally comprehensible.[5] The problem may be compounded from primary school to higher levels and jeopardize the whole educational system. If teachers are constantly using books that are beyond the student's grasp, the whole teaching and learning process is slowed down intolerably.

It is interesting to see that even in a country like Nigeria, where English plays a very important role in national and international contexts, the quest for English language proficiency became the central issue during the British Council Conference on 'English Language Studies in Nigerian Higher Education' as among teachers generally (cf. Freeman/Jibril (eds) 1984). Even at the higher level in education special remedial courses, mainly in the field of English for Academic Purposes, seem necessary. In Lesotho, Botswana and Tanzania, for instance, all students must take and pass classes in 'communication skills' as part of their first-year programme. Some type of English language service unit (as it is called at the University of Botswana in Gabarone) had to be established in most universities. Such a unit must be faculty-specific as far as the teaching of specialized vocabulary is concerned but general with regards to basic study and writing techniques in the academic language English. Even when English serves only as a library language, because the dominant academic language is French, as in Yaoundé (Cameroon), there may still be a need for such a service unit.

The falling standard of English in schools must not be shrugged off as a minor problem, although it was to be expected in view of the rapid expansion of the educational systems in African nations during the past thirty years. Several accelerated development plans for education were geared more towards quantity than quality, and due to manifold economic short-comings the rural schools in particular were bound to suffer.

Another factor in the decline may have been the departure of many British ENL-speakers, including teachers, from independent Africa. As their native model of English disappeared, so 'Africanization' began to increase in the language as well as in the staffing. It is certainly not surprising that English standards have become a major issue just when the Africanization of the staff is almost complete. In Zambia, for instance, over 85 per cent of secondary school teachers were expatriates up to the 1970s, most of whom were native speakers of British origin (Africa 1983: 8), nowadays there are few left.

Looking at the overall picture quantitatively, however, it seems clear that there are many more Africans learning and speaking English than ever before (in absolute numbers and, in many countries, even as a percentage of the total population). But the quality of the English they speak has changed, too, and in the various plans to improve it many factors must be taken into account.

4.4 Factors affecting English language teaching in Africa

The quality of English language teaching in Africa is decidedly influenced by factors outside both the language and the educational system. In order to compare different countries it is useful to differentiate between two groups of factors: those relating to problems of development in the Third World generally and those relating to the specific sociolinguistic situation.

As almost all anglophone African countries belong to the less – or even the least – developed countries in the world, education like many other spheres of life is affected by, for instance, the shortage of books, paper, pens and pencils, blackboards, chairs, tables and desks, etc. Although some countries may be more affected by austerity than others, and although some may attribute a higher development priority to education than others, the general problems of development are fairly similar throughout Africa (cf. Blakemore/Cooksey 1981). The sociolinguistic situation, as has been mentioned earlier (chapter 2), is nation-specific. Knowledge and use of English depend on original colonial penetration and subsequent postcolonial change. Both cause a more or less strongly felt general language pressure on Africans, a need to be able to speak the language, which is obviously much greater in ENL–ESL nations than in EIL nations. This affects the motivation for learning English. The motivation in turn depends on attitudes towards English among teachers and learners, as well as on the place and role of English in the curriculum, especially perhaps in examinations, and this constitutes the educational language pressure. Many students tend to think that it does not really matter which language structures they use, what matters is managing to get the relevant ideas across. It suffices here to emphasize once again that all the factors mentioned are interdependent and influence the quality of English language teaching (Figure 4.1).

Of the many factors which derive from general problems of national development, only those which are specifically detrimental to the educational sector can be discussed here. They may also be particularly relevant because education is sometimes seen, notably by Africans, as one way out of underdevelopment. Unfortunately, however, it can also be demonstrated that the logical consequence of this argument, the rapid expansion of the education system, can aggravate some problems dramatically. Two factors have always been seen as crucial: the quality and quantity of teaching materials on the one hand and those of teachers on the other.

In many African countries school-books are a scarce and precious commodity and the ratio of books to students tends to range between 1:4 and 1:10 even for the most essential textbooks. This makes it impossible for students to study their texts or reading programme individually after class and thus to practise or repeat school lessons and exercises. It is, however, not only the quantity but also the quality of books which matters. Besides Africanizing the content, an adaptation to specific African grammatical 'problem areas' is necessary (as outlined in chapter 3). Besides textbooks, simplified readers are crucial, in which the language used is based on a learner-specific grading scheme; such grading should be based on considerations of practical use in the learners' environment as well as on the natural developmental order in the learner's interlanguage as

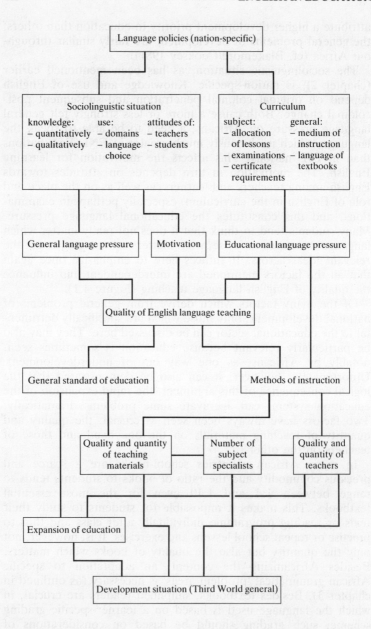

FIGURE 4.1   Factors affecting the quality of English language teaching in Africa

observed in second-language acquisition research. Making school-books relevant by including the sociolinguistic complexity of the African language environment is an enormous task. Many textbooks focus on achieving pronunciation contrasts which do not exist in the speech of millions of educated English native speakers nor in that of virtually all English users the African learners hear in their environment.

Publishing school-books is, however, not only a matter of writing them, but even more of securing printing facilities, and ink and paper. Foreign publishing houses will only print books that are expected to find an immediate and large market. The problem of teachers must also be considered qualitatively and quantitatively. As the prestige of teachers is no longer what it used to be – at the end of the colonial period they were the national élite – few secondary school students dream of becoming teachers nowadays. The best students want to attend universities or technical colleges (they often have higher admission terms as to quality and quantity of A-level passes) and the lower ranks go to teacher training colleges, whose best students leave for careers in administration, business or politics. Although there are certainly vast differences among English teachers, the standard of their English and of their teaching is often disappointing these days. Besides their own proficiency they have to cope with a great number of practical and methodological problems. This pedagogical side cannot be explored in depth here; suffice it to say that many problems are related to the teachers' role in the educational process. More often than not teachers act more as dispensers of information than as communicators who help students to digest information. In this process of digestion language obviously plays a central part. On the linguistic side, some knowledge about English in its African context is essential. English cannot be taught efficiently unless the teacher has some understanding of the systematic differences in English use and usage between Standard English and the local performance norm.

This outline of problems demonstrates that it is an illusion to demand absolute efficiency in English language teaching in Africa. In the rural areas especially it is often impossible to maintain a reasonable standard of teaching. Under these circumstances, achieving adequate efficiency in English language teaching to maintain the level of English in African schools may even be considered a success. In conclusion, it may be helpful to point out that English language teaching today can also be influenced positively by improving some of the factors analysed.

Although it is, of course, the responsibility of national governments to allocate enough financial, material and manpower
resources to English language teaching to secure a satisfactory
level of education in general, international development aid has
to play a major role in improving the situation.

4.5 English language teaching and possibilities of interna-tional development aid

As language teaching and education are not only severely hit by
development problems, but also often seen as one way of
improving the dismal situation of ELT, it is not surprising that
international development agencies 'invest' in English language
teaching in many ways. Not only the ENL nations, such as
Britain, the USA or Canada, but even EIL nations, such as the
Scandinavian countries or Germany, and their aid organizations
support English language teaching directly and indirectly by
financing lecture tours and scholarships, by helping with book
publishing and improving teacher training through provision of
subject specialists. The leading agency is usually the British
Council, as it has representatives or even English Language
Officers in most 'anglophone' African countries and in many
others. The British Council is funded by the Overseas Development Agency (ODA), which handles part of Britain's general
development aid, and from a British government grant, and has
two hundred English language specialists working as advisers and
teachers, most of whom are in Africa. Teaching, and encouraging
the use of, the English language is one of the Council's highest
priorities because, as its Director-General put it: 'Britain's real
black gold is not North Sea oil, but the English language. It has
long been the root of our culture and now is fast becoming the
global language of business and information. The challenge
facing us is to exploit it to the full.' (Richard Francis, 'The British
Council Report 1987/88', 1988: 8.) As it is only possible to give
some examples from the vast involvement of development
agencies in the educational sector in general and language
teaching in particular the following sections will concentrate on
the areas that have already been identified as crucial, i.e.
textbooks and teaching materials, and teachers and teacher
training.

The ODA Book Presentation Programme has proved very
important in many countries. It has often been used to
reintroduce extensive reading in the syllabuses. On 21 April 1988
the British Minister for Overseas Development announced the

Textbooks for Africa Project, designed to pass surplus British textbooks to African schools. The British Council plays, together with other agencies, a central role in organizing such projects. Other agencies have also supplied textbooks for schools. The World Bank funded a scheme that provided enough copies of the Longman *Primary English for Lesotho* at very low cost for all pupils in Standards 1–4 in the country, plus sufficient annual replacement copies.

In order to ensure that school-books are realistic and adapted to the sociolinguistic environment writing cannot be done by outside specialists (alone); African authors have to be encouraged to write textbooks and readers that are on the one hand attractive to students and on the other adapted to their language specific problems.

Another type of ELT programme, which reaches a much wider audience, is the provision of ELT television programmes. Thus the well-known series *Follow Me* was presented to *Radio Télévision Marocaine* and broadcast in 1987, while *Radio Télévision Algérienne* showed *Follow Me* and *On We Go* at prime time on several occasions.

As far as teachers are concerned development agencies prefer to work in teacher-training institutions, because of the multiplier effect. ELT specialists are sent to train young African teachers in English grammar, syllabus design, new methodologies and even adapted teaching techniques. The British have worked under the KELT scheme since 1977 (KELT = Key English Language Teaching, in development jargon). In Sierra Leone, for instance, KELT officers have been allocated to each of the country's four teachers' colleges in an attempt to revitalize primary-level English teaching throughout the country. In many other countries KELTs work in the Ministries of Education, particularly in the departments for curriculum development, textbook writing or the inspectorate. In some countries specialist English resources (teaching equipment and national and international manpower) are concentrated in one or a few institutions. The Sudanese English Language Teaching Institute (SELTI), which was set up in 1975 and has been supported by foreign aid money and ELT specialists, is a good example of the way in which resources can be pooled in one national institution.[6] It offers not only remedial ELT in-service seminars to English teachers, but also a one-year TEFL diploma course for intermediate school teachers. Its syllabus is more practically oriented than the comparable degree course at the university in Khartoum (Sandell 1982, chapter 6).

In general, nation-wide networks of teacher centres are

necessary to help overcome practical difficulties by providing resources and consultation. No substantial improvement of English teaching will be achieved unless themes and reading materials are directly related to the students' practical language needs. This implies that, under the prevailing economic situation, English teachers will have to devise (part of) their teaching material themselves. Teacher centres have to fulfil a central function in this situation.

Particularly important institutions are the respective national examinations councils, which have been or will be set up in almost all 'anglophone' African countries. For many years the tests for the Cambridge Overseas School Certificates have been set and marked by the University of Cambridge Local Examinations Syndicate. Not until the 1980s did some nations manage to complete (Zambia) or even to start (Zimbabwe) a training programme aimed at having all school certificate examinations marked in the respective country or region. The fact that exam papers are marked in Africa by African examiners obviously raises the question of standards and underlines the need for micro-policy decisions necessary concerning the acceptability of local forms as local norms. Only national examiners can apply national norms in marking practice consciously or unconsciously. This makes decisions in the examination councils concerning acceptability crucial for the entire educational system.

A certain sign of the growing American influence (and with it their language forms and standards) is the number of Peace Corps volunteers engaged in ELT. In Morocco there were over sixty in *lycées* and universities in 1986/87. And, as in most other English teaching institutions in North Africa, many Moroccan schools use American textbooks. As Morocco maintains French as its international language (despite attempts at an intranational Arabization policy) English is taught mainly for special purposes. In Botswana the US Agency for International Development provided most of the funds, equipment and specialists for the Primary Education Improvement Project and the Junior Secondary Education Improvement Project in the 1980s. In other countries the US recruit university teachers under the Fulbright scheme. The Canadians have been involved with ELT through their CUSO (Canadian University Service Overseas) TESL programme.

It must be emphasized that most of these measures are seen as temporary projects. Most aid is now project-related and KELT officers have African counterparts who will take over once the project has been completed. It is therefore a good sign when the aid programmes for ELT in secondary schools (e.g. by Peace Corps volunteers in Senegal in 1983) are phased out or when states in Nigeria announce that CUSO and VSO TESL programmes are no longer needed, although the authorities must, of course, make sure that English courses are run by qualified teachers, either by national staff or by locally recruited Asians and other Europeans with (near-)native competence. Several countries, such as Zimbabwe and Botswana, had to ask European development agencies in Britain, Germany and Scandinavia to recruit a great number of qualified (mainly mathematics, science and English) teachers for them in the 1980s. This is a further indication of the close link between English and the expansion of education in general.

Notes

1. There are few exceptions to these group patterns. In Cameroon, for instance, English is taught in all primary schools for nation-building purposes to link francophone East to anglophone West Cameroon, but it is not used as a medium in the East.
2. Unfortunately the development of higher order cognitive skills, such as interpreting, analysing, synthesizing and constructive criticism, does not rank very high on many African syllabuses. In any case, active student participation in classroom work is usually very limited. Even English language teaching is more concerned with teaching about the language than with language in use. The role of language in shaping the students' general cognitive skills should be examined more closely in the African context, irrespective of whether the medium is English or an African language.
3. There is plenty of evidence, if usually subjective and not empirically founded, for this development, such as the preface to McGregor 1971 for Africa in general; Boadi 1971 for Ghana; Freeman/Jibril (eds) 1984 for Nigeria; Schmied 1986 for Tanzania, and many other official and unofficial reports, e.g. in the British Council 'English Teaching Profiles' on most African countries.
4. Many educationalists use linguistic data as 'indicators' or 'evidence' for social–psychological statements about educational development. The more theoretical problems of such approaches are discussed in Stubbs (1986: 233–45). The fact that educational underachievement can be caused by linguistic differences and the lack of public and professional awareness of them became well-known through the 'Black English Trial' in the United States (cf. Labov 1982).
5. This is in line with our ESL–EIL categorization, which also implies that the more the language is used for intranational purposes the more a nation is free to and must set its own standards.
6. The continuous political and economic crisis in the Sudan (and many

other African countries) together with the attraction of specialists to
other teaching institutions in more stable African countries (e.g.
Kenya) or even to office jobs in Saudi Arabia makes it often
impossible to assess the value of such institutions. The fact that they
can give courses that would have to be attended abroad saves money,
however, that can be invested in other activities.

Chapter 5

English in African Literature

No attempt can be made here to explore literary works in any depth from the perspective of literary stylistics. For the purposes of this study, language in literary texts is simply regarded as discourse within one category or type of text, the usage to be described having particular functions. The opinions of the writers, as linguistic decision-makers – at least in their own works, and often beyond[1] – are important here, as well as that of the linguists, or text analysers.

5.1 English – an African means of literary expression

As in other spheres of African life (cf. 4.2 for education and chapter 7 generally), since independence the use of English in creative literature has been seriously questioned, most forcefully by Ngugi wa Thiong'o (1986: 153):

> An African writer should write in a language that will allow him to communicate effectively with the peasants and workers in Africa – in other words, he should write in an African language. As far as publishing is concerned, I have no doubt that writing in an African language is as commercially viable as writing in any language. Market forces might even have the added advantage of forcing those who express themselves in African languages to strive for local relevance in their writing because no peasant or worker is going to buy novels, plays, or books of poetry that are totally irrelevant to his situation. Literature published in African languages will have to be meaningful to the masses and therefore much closer to the realities of their situation.

Despite these arguments Ngugi has found few followers in practice; possibly because he forgot that peasants and workers

may be no more literate in an African than in a European
language (depending on the educational system). He may also
have overlooked the fact that English is now an African language
in some sense, and accepted as such by many Africans. And he
may have failed to recollect that realism is not necessarily directly
reflected in literary language. On the other hand, it is also
important to remember that English has served as a medium of
African expression since it first found its way into the continent,
and won international recognition with the Nobel Prize award to
Wole Soyinka in 1986. For at least two centuries English has
been used for letters and diaries, for journalistic reports and
accounts of travel, for literary comment and political tracts, for
sermons and public speeches and fiction of all types (cf. L.
Brown's anthology 1973). Some of these are very interesting from
a linguistic point of view. This is borne out in the following
excerpts from two of the earliest African writings in English:
Antera Duke's diary, published in 1786, and an autobiography
*The Interesting Narrative of the life of Olaudah Equiano, or
Gustavus Vassa the African, written by himself*, published in 1789:

> . . . about 6 am in aqua Landing with small Rain morning so I walk
> up to see Esim and Egbo Young so I see Jimmy Henshaw com to see
> wee and wee tell him for go on bord Rogers for all Henshaw family
> coomy and wee have go on bord Rogers for mak Jimmy Henshaw
> name to King Egbo in Coomy Book so hear all Captin meet on bord
> Captin ford about ogan Captin Duk was fight with ford soon after 2
> clock time wee com ashor and I hear one my Ephrim abashey Egbo
> Sherry women have Brun two son one Day in plower andam Duke
> wife Brun young girl in aqua town.
>
> (Antera Duke, ed. Forde 1956: 112)

> I have before remarked that the natives of this part of Africa are
> extremely cleanly. This necessary habit of decency was with us a part
> of religion, and therefore we had many purifications and washings;
> indeed almost as many and used on the same occasions, if my
> recollection does not fail me, as the Jews. Those that touched the
> dead at any time were obliged to wash and purify themselves before
> they could enter a dwelling-house.
>
> (Equiano as edited by Edwards 1967: 12)

These two paragraphs suggest that there has always been a
wide range of forms of English in Africa, from the basilectal to
the acrolectal end of the continuum (with forms similar to those
described in chapter 3). If these texts were to serve as data for a
scholarly analysis of Early African English it would be vital to

know whether they had been 'improved' by another hand to embellish too plain a style (some people see even Antera Duke's diary as an Anglicized version of the pidgin English used around Calabar in the late eighteenth century), or whether they were really written in the broken English of the pre-pidgin era. But this would be difficult to prove.

Despite numerous documents and books written by Africans, English has been accused of being élitist, of being European and culture-bound, of being a remnant of colonialism and a cause of cultural alienation, and of cutting Africans off from their own traditions (the so-called psychological amputation). The abolitionists have proposed the promotion of African languages instead, be they ethnic languages (e.g. Ngugi has written all his works first in Gikuyu during the past ten years) or a unifying African lingua franca (e.g. even the Nigerian writer Soyinka has advocated the use of Swahili!). As early as 1959 the Second Congress of Negro Writers and Artists in Rome passed the following resolutions (cf. P. Young 1969/70):

(a)   that independent African countries should not adopt European languages as national languages;
(b)   that a pan-African language be chosen and fostered;
(c)   that a team of linguists be selected to modernize that language.

In the words of the African writers themselves the two positions in favour and against English can be exemplified by the quotations which follow. The first represents the call to use a pan-African medium: 'We exhort all writers to apply every strategy, individually and collectively on both national and continental levels to promote the use and the enrichment of Swahili for the present and future needs of the continent (report on the Inaugural meeting of the Union of writers of the African peoples in Accra 1974 by Soyinka 1977: 48). The problem with this recommendation is that even if African writers were to agree on a pan-African language it seems highly unlikely that they would find the necessary support from African politicians or educationalists over the next few decades.

The pro-English group, the adaptationists, have emphasized practical considerations, such as publishing difficulties and the role of an international readership. They suggest that it is impossible to avoid modern realities, that English is part of the African experience and the medium of an emerging African literary tradition. They even praise English as the language of the pan-African movement and the language of liberation (which is still true for South Africa today), and they quote Shakespeare:

> You taught me language; and my profit on't
> Is, I know how to curse: the red plague rid you
> for learning me your language.
>
> (Caliban in *The Tempest* I, ii, 363ff.)

They thus accept English in Africa as an historical fact. 'I have been given this language, and I intend to use it' (Achebe 1977: 55). In Armah's words the argument against African languages (other than English) runs as follows: 'Those who want Africans to write in those microlanguages (each little language on the continent from Akan, through Kikuyu to Zulu) are staring into a rearview mirror. The way forward lies through a common African language (Ayi Kwei Armah, *West Africa* 11 February 1985: 263). Although the two approaches seem to be contradictory there may be enough room in the broad developing stream of African literature for both, possibly as 'national' and 'ethnic' tributaries (cf. Achebe 1965: 23). Here we can follow only the first tributary.

The conscious creative African writer who wishes to use English as a literary medium has to struggle to adapt this medium to the sociocultural environment. The problems for him are that English has, for his purposes, some undesirable elements in it on the one hand, while lacking some important elements on the other (cf. 3.5). As for the former, Mazrui (1974: 98) gives us a vivid indication: 'If the English language were now to mature into an indigenous language to its place [sic], the black users of the language cannot afford to be complacent about the cumulative negativeness of the concept of blackness in English imagery.' Mazrui mentions the unfavourable or even derogatory collocations *black market*, *blackmail*, *blackleg* and *The Black Hole of Calcutta,* and it is easy to find many others (*blacklist*, *black sheep*, or even *black magic* as opposed to *white magic*). The problem of such undesirable elements can be solved by cultural translation, but how can an African writer express the missing elements? Can he render *chi* as 'personal god' or *ozo* as 'title' without losing too much of the Igbo cultural background? He is forced to look for compromises and to 'aim at fashioning out an English which is at once universal and able to carry his particular experience' (Achebe 1965: 29). Although the examples presented here are African, the problem is certainly not restricted to Africa – and as their Indian colleagues, for example, choose English to address a national and an international audience an African writer can readily do the same. This brief discussion from the writers' perspective demonstrates that adapted African forms of English can be a powerful African means of literary expression. If this discussion focused more on the novelists than on the dramatists this may be due to two reasons. First, on stage the polyglot nature of the African linguistic scene is often portrayed more realistically,[2] because on the one hand the dramatist has to use language more directly to create a realistic atmosphere and on the other he shares more linguistic background with his immediate audience. This implies the possibility of using different languages in one play. Ngugi wa Thiong'o (Kenya), for instance, used English, Swahili and Gikuyu, Athol Fugard (South Africa) uses Standard South African English as a base language and various other forms according to the social environment (cf. Hauptfleisch 1989). Secondly, the wide scope of dramatic performance between various forms of national and street theatres has to be taken into consideration. Particularly, forms of popular development or activist theatre have to use 'grass-root languages' (including Krio and Pidgin in West Africa) to reach the masses. The choice of English is, of course, only reasonable when the wider national or even international audience is addressed.

Yet, despite numerous attacks, African literature in English has flourished since independence and contributed a great deal to the wider stream of Commonwealth literature. This development may partly be attributed to a growing interest in and awareness of African literature in Africa and elsewhere, and to new publishing outlets in (e.g. the small Onitsha printing presses or the former East African Literature Bureau) and outside of Africa (e.g. the famous African Writer Series of several British publishing houses). But fundamentally it has been achieved through the fresh and vigorous approach of African writers to the use of English in creative literature.

5.2 Linguistic types[3] of African literature in English

From a linguistic perspective African literature can be analysed in various ways. From the aspect of language variation the following questions are interesting: Does the writer accept the English language as a medium or reject it? If he accepts it – and only this group concerns us here – does he deliberately deviate from (British) Standard English or not? He may want to deviate in order to remind his readers that the scene is not set in an English

native-speaker context but in Africa. Thus he may want to use
African forms of English, possibly not only educated African
English but the entire continuum down to broken and pidginized
forms: if, that is, he is able to. For such writers the rejection of
(British) Standard English, i.e. the former colonial norm, may be
a decisive motive. Although they do not reject the language as a
whole, they may experiment with African forms – realistic or not.
Some writers may achieve this by a more or less literal translation
from an African mother tongue. Naturally, if an author
consciously uses the translation procedure the syntax of his
English sentences may be seriously 'distorted', which is why this
method is rejected by most writers and critics. When literary
texts are selected for teaching purposes, deviant syntax may be a
disincentive. If an author does not deviate deliberately, he is
likely nevertheless to deviate to some extent (depending on his
educational background and literary purposes); but he will have
less creativity or variability in his use of the language. Although a
writer of this type may not have sufficient command of English to
deviate consciously, he may still be aware of his 'African' style
and accept influences from African languages as a specific literary
value; or he may be quite unaware of this in an unsuccessful
attempt to write Standard English. It is, of course, always a
question of degree as *to what extent* the writer deliberately wishes
to deviate and *to what extent* he is consciously aware of deviation.
These distinctions cannot be seen as separate categories but
rather as predominant tendencies. Since the borderlines are
flexible and some authors' works fall into more than one
category, Figure 5.1 is certainly an oversimplification; but it does
summarize the possibilities and exemplifies them by giving a
famous writer for each category.

In the following sections sample passages illustrate these types.
They are taken from Nigerian writers because the literary scene
in Nigeria has always been the most fruitful and inventive,
possibly because the sheer size of the population offers a greater
reservoir of readers. The fact that its people are more aware of a
wider range of stylistic variation within English through their
familiarity with pidgin may also be significant. A similar analysis
could probably be made of writers from Kenya (e.g. Ngugi wa
Thiong'o) or South Africa (e.g. Alex la Guma, Ezekiel
Mphahlele);[4] although in most other countries writers have
always tried to stay closer to Standard English. In other countries
there are only few examples of such linguistically broad creativity
in the novel. In Zambia, for instance, *Sofiya* (1979) by Storm
Bayamoyo (Lusaka: National Company of Zambia) can be seen

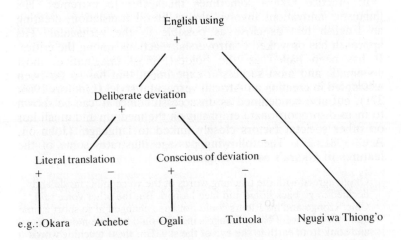

FIGURE 5.1 Linguistic types of African literature in English

as the first attempt to use urban vernacular Zambian English speech consistently as a medium of adopted literary creativity. But as in most anglophone African nations this is only a beginning.

The first type rarely occurs but is most distinctively exemplified in Gabriel Okara's *The Voice* (London: Heinemann 1964). Okara (1963: 137) justified his approach as follows:

> As a writer who believes in the utilization of African ideas, African philosophy and African folk-lore and imagery to the fullest extent possible, I am of the opinion the only way to use them efficiently is to translate them almost literally from the African language native to the writer into whatever European language he is using as his medium of expression. I have endeavoured in my words to keep as close as possible to vernacular expressions. For, from a word, a group of words, a sentence and even a name in any African language, one can glean the social life of a people.

> . . . a writer can use the idioms of his own language in a way that is understandable in English. If he uses their English equivalents, he would not be expressing African ideas and thoughts, but English ones.

> Some may regard this way of writing in English as a desecration of the language. This is of course not true. Living languages grow like living things, and English is far from a dead language.

In practice Okara sometimes takes this to extremes. His linguistic innovations involve almost literal translation, creating an English text as close as possible to the vernacular. His approach has provoked controversial reactions among the critics. It has been hailed as 'the boldest, most imaginative, most systematic and most successful experiment that has so far been attempted in creating an African vernacular style' (Lindfors 1966: 271), but also condemned as unsuccessful since it 'can be shown to focus disproportionate emphasis on the medium and much less on other societal factors closely linked to language' (Johnson, A.C. 1981: 27). The following passage illustrates some of the features of Okara's use of English:

> Okolo agreed with the teaching words of the voice in his inside and decided to go back home and face Izongo. But the other voice said Chief Izongo and his Elders could not have changed in so short a time and that if he went back, Izongo's inside would become more septic and stink from earth to the eye of the sky. But these teaching words filed in through one of Okolo's ears and filed out through the other like canoes going one by one through a canal. So, in the end, Okolo said he must to his village return, if he could. But this time he would the masses ask and not Izongo and his Elders. If the masses haven't got *it*, he will create *it* in their insides. He will plant *it*, make *it* grow in spite of Izongo's destroying words. He will uproot the fear in their insides, kill the fear in their insides and plant *it*. He will all these do, if only . . . if only what? Okolo asked, speaking out, but his inside did not answer.
>
> (Okara 1964: 90)

The particular linguistic quality of the work seems to involve a combination of deliberately ambiguous lexis (*his inside* = soul, mind, heart, essence; *it* = life?) and quaint syntax, including a frequent use of object-before-verb inversions (*he must to his village return* and *he would the masses ask*), frequent pre-nominal positions of modifying phrases (e.g. *a fear-and-surprised-mixed voice*, p. 66), and even an idiosyncratic clause-final *be* (*I could have been a big rich man be*, p. 105). Interestingly, Okara did not repeat this experiment.

The second type is represented in the classic African novels of Ekwensi, Soyinka and Achebe, who justify their approach by such statements as:

> When we borrow an alien language to sculpt or paint in, we must begin by co-opting the entire properties of that language as correspondences to properties in our matrix of thought and expression. We must stress . . . stretch it, impact and compact it, fragment and reassemble it. . . .
>
> (Soyinka 1975: 67)

For an African, writing in English is not without its serious set-backs.
He often finds himself describing situations or modes of thought
which have no direct equivalent in the English way of life. Caught in
that situation he can do one of two things. He can try and contain
what he wants to say within the limits of conventional English or he
can try to push back those limits to accommodate his ideas. The first
method produced competent, uninspired and rather flat works. The
second method can produce something new and valuable to the
English language as well as to the material he is trying to put over.
But it can also get out of hand. It can lead to simply bad English
being accepted and defended as African or Nigerian. I submit that
those who can do the work of extending the frontiers of English so as
to accommodate African thought patterns must do it through their
mastery of English and not out of innocence.

(Achebe (second edition), 1973: 12)

In this connection, Achebe provided a very good example of the
way in which he transforms English into an African medium in
his fiction:

Allow me to quote a small example, from *Arrow of God* which may
give some idea of how I approach the use of English. The Chief Priest
is telling one of his sons why it is necessary to send him to church:

'I want one of my sons to join these people and be my eyes there.
If there is nothing in it you will come back. But if there is something
there you will bring home my share. The world is like a Mask,
dancing. If you want to see it well you do not stand in one place. My
spirit tells me that those who do not befriend the white man today
will by saying *had we known* tomorrow.'

Now supposing I had put it another way. Like this for instance:

'I am sending you as my representative among those people – just
to be on the safe side in case the new religion develops. One has to
move with the times or else one is left behind. I have a hunch that
those who fail to come to terms with the white man may well regret
their lack of foresight.'

The material is the same. But the form of the one is *in character*
and the other is not.

(Achebe 1965: 29)

Achebe's approach leaves the writer ample space within the
total range of English to use language as a creative literary
device, e.g. for characterization (see chapter 5.3). In general,
Achebe tries to capture the rhythm and cadence of his mother
tongue Igbo. This is particularly obvious in *Arrow of God*
(London: Heinemann 1965), in which he also uses African
proverbs extensively as an important cultural value marker (cf.
3.6). Although Achebe incorporates African elements quite

freely into his English, he does not want to impose the syntactical structure of his mother tongue on the second language.

In contrast to the deliberate, 'rule-bending creativity' (Spencer 1971a: 3) of the most famous, sophisticated writers, some writers do not have a sufficient command of English to follow their example, because of their limited educational background. The group of writers who produced the so-called Onitsha (or Igbo) market literature belong to the third type, although among them there is necessarily a wide range of style as well as topic. This type of literature catered for a special market and is thus of particular importance from the point of view of literary sociology. The slim pamphlets of about forty to sixty pages were usually produced in the town of Onitsha in Nigeria. They were written for a moderately educated readership, like office workers or secondary school students, and illustrate widely popular varieties of broken and pidginized English. The following passages from *Life Turns a Man up and down* (Onitsha, n.d.) by N.O. Njoku and Co. ('the strong man of the pen', p. 1) illustrate some characteristic features (pp. 2, 8, 9):

> This man is a womanizer and a smoker. He can finish ten packets of C.G. a day and cannot pass a night without a lady. He does not care for any body. He dosen't [sic] know his home town again. He does not care for his parents. What he knows is to take C.G. and chase girls about.

> He hasen't [sic] known that C.G. is dangerous to human beings and girls are poisonous to boys. He will one day suffer them.

> A poor man thinks every now and then. He is not happy. Himself and his family are not enjoying life. They buy and use secondhand dresses and shoes. A soup cooked with 20 kobo lasts one week for the poor man and his family.

> A poor man wears 'Patch-Patch' dresses not because he does not know that it is not all that good, but because he cannot afford to by [sic] new clothes.

> A poor man suffers inferiority complex. He cannot be offered a honourable seat at any occasion.

The purpose of this type of literature is obvious: it must be educational, moralistic and entertaining (which explains the great number of '*How-to* books'). The writers often present a strongly didactic moral at the end: 'So, my advise [sic] to boys of your youth, "Beware of ladies" mostly school ones otherwise they buy

you cheap' (C. Umunnah, *They Died in the Game of Love*.
Onitsha, n.d.). They often show an over-zealous preference for
Western values and try to orientate their language towards the
commonly accessible models of Shakespeare, the Bible, films and
newspapers. Influences from widely different stylistic models
often lead to an inappropriate mixture of registers or varieties
and stylistic underdifferentiation.

Although the heyday of Onitsha market literature was before
the destruction of the town in the Nigerian civil war, a similar
type can still be found there and in other places in Nigeria, as
well as in other countries where printing facilities are available.
In Nigeria Segun Oyekunle (*Katakata for Sofahead*. London
1983), Tunde Fatunde (*No Food no Country*. Benin 1985) and
Ken Saro-Wira (*Sozaboy*. Port Harcourt 1985) have developed
similar genres.

Whereas the Onitsha writers and their followers normally
exhibit little enthusiasm for the indigenous cultures, writers who
also lack the education to be able to use deviations from
Standard English deliberately and skilfully may still be conscious
of the fact that their writing is soaked with Africanisms,
linguistically as well as culturally. The most famous example of
this fourth type is Amos Tutuola's *The Palm-Wine Drinkard* [sic]
(London: Faber 1952). Although this was one of the first African
novels to receive Western critical acclaim, Tutuola's 'uneducated'
English was negatively received by his fellow-countrymen while
being hailed by some European critics as a splendid synthesis of
oral and literary traditions. This may be one reason why Tutuola
did not attract many African followers (unlike Achebe); another
reason may be that the harsh realities of Africa's development
problems dominated the later scene so much that no writer could
afford to create Tutuola's mythological fantasy worlds again.
Tutuola's distinctive style may be glimpsed in the following
passage (p. 9):

> But in those days, there were many wild animals and every place was
> covered by thick bushes and forests; again, towns and villages were
> not near each other as nowadays, and as I was travelling from bushes
> to bushes and from forests to forests and sleeping inside it for many
> days and months, I was sleeping on the branches of trees, because
> spirits etc. were just like partners, and to save my life from them; and
> again I could spend two or three months before reaching a town or a
> village. Whenever I reached a town or a village, I would spend almost
> four months there, to find out my palm-wine tapster from the
> inhabitants of that town or village. . . .

It is often of course impossible to judge from the text whether
certain forms are used consciously or not. It is, however,
important to recognize that some authors are obviously masters
of a full range of English linguistic variation and can use this
creatively in their writing.

5.3 Variation in English as a creative literary device

In Achebe's work many examples can be found where conscious
stylistic variation is used, mainly in the presentation of speech in
order to suggest the speaker's character and personality, or even
to demonstrate how a speaker may deliberately change his
language to emphasize different aspects of his personality.
Christopher in *No Longer at Ease* (London: Heinemann 1960:
99f.) is one of the most explicit examples: at first he shows that
he is not a rich man by speaking pidgin English and later that he
knows how to move in élitist circles by speaking Standard
English:

'. . . What can I offer you?'
'Champagne.'
'Ah? Na Obi go buy you that-o. Me never reach that grade yet. Na
squash me get-o.'
They laughed.
'Obi, what about some beer?'
'If you'll split a bottle with me.'
'Fine. What are you people doing this evening? Make we go dance
somewhere?'
Obi tried to make excuses, but Clara cut him short. They would go,
she said.
'Na film I wan' go', said Bisi.
'Look here, Bisi, we are not interested in what you want to do. It's
for Obi and me to decide. This na Africa, you know.'

Whether Christopher spoke good or 'broken' English depended on
what he was saying, where he was saying it, and how he wanted to say
it. Of course that was to some extent true of most educated people,
especially on Saturday nights. But Christopher was rather outstanding
in thus coming to terms with a double heritage.
Obi borrowed a tie from him. Not that it mattered at the Imperial,
where they had chosen to go. But one didn't want to look like a
boma-boy.

'Shall we all come into your car, Obi? It's a long time since I had a
chauffeur.'
'Yes, let's all go together. Although it's going to be difficult after

the dance to take Bisi home, then Clara, then you. But it doesn't matter.'
'No. I had better bring my car', said Christopher.

Non-standard language has always been used in English fiction and drama as a speech marker to suggest the social background or class, especially with minor or comic characters. So it is not surprising when Chinua Achebe uses such devices in *Anthills of the Savanna* (London: Heinemann 1987), for instance, in presenting the speech of taxi-drivers, policemen, market-mammies and girl-friends. When a superintendent of police, a newspaper editor or other intellectuals speak pidgin or simplified English they are talking 'down' to less educated people, not necessarily derogatorily, but also (as an unmarked choice) in order to make themselves understood or (as a marked choice) to create solidarity with fellow citizens. They switch back to more standard speech when they talk normally among themselves. Thus pidgin is a bridge between two worlds.

This variation in English within a literary work is, however, not used only by world-famous, established and educated writers but even by some exponents of Onitsha market literature. Ogali A. Ogali offers a similar example by contrasting the language use of the uneducated chief Jombo and the educated school teacher Mark Johnson (note the traditional versus the modern name) in his play *Veronica My Daughter* (Washington: Three Continents Press 1980: 162):

Chief Jombo   Come in my good friends and neighbours. Na me say make dem call you all for cam settle small palaba wey dey for my house. Na bout Veronica my daughter and dem man (*Pointing to Mike*) wey siddon there him name be Mikere. I say make Veronica my daughter marry Chief Bassey – na him be dis man wey siddon me for side – but Veronica say him go marry Mikere wey him like. Me, I don talk alone tire. I no sabi grammarian and politician and logician as dem sabi, na him make dem call una wey sabi like dem. Anything wey una talk, I dey inside.
Chief Bassey   Na true you talk my friend. I still ready for marry your daughter. My money dey too much.
Mark Johnson   Well Chief, friends and all, I think am an interested member in this matter by the virtue of my being the Headmaster of the Public School, besides being Vero's Class Teacher. Chief! You could remember what I told you when you first reported this matter to me. I told you that Vero was right to choose her own husband. It is illegal if you force her to marry contrary to her wish. On the other hand, I promised speaking to Veronica privately on this matter. I assure you all, that I did. Vero confirmed her promise three times

before me. After all, the school closes next week Friday and I am
sure Vero is passing her examination for she has been very studious.
That is just what I have to say.

Another of Ogali's characters who is even more extravagantly
illuminated by the language he uses is Bomber Billy, who loves
stilted, latinized English (ibid.: 148):

Tom Why are you moving with a walking stick – is anything wrong
with your leg?
Bomber Billy As I was descending from a declivity yesterday, with
such an excessive velocity, I suddenly lost the centre of my gravity
and was precipitated on the macadamised thoroughfare.
John (*Whispering to Tom*) I told you he is fond of big words. Do
you understand him?
Tom Am sure, Billy, your bones are hopelessly broken.
Bomber Billy Oh no! Don't put my mind under perturbation. But
after my precipitation whereby my incunabula got soaked, it was
made incumbent on me to divest myself of all my habiliments which
were saturated as a result of my immersion in the rivulet.

This excerpt shows how effectively a character can be (mis-)
represented by his language. It also makes clear that language in
literature is not a direct reflection of actual language use. Rather,
it exaggerates a stylistic tendency of some Africans, to use high-
flown words, for humorous purposes and, in this case, to convey
the simple message that this character is too pompous and thus
quite unfit to marry a girl like Veronica.

Here it becomes clear that language and style serve more than
one purpose; in addition to the obvious necessity of reporting the
message of the story including actual verbal communication, they
may signal traits of character and symbolic overtones that serve
to help interpret the writer's message beyond the realistic
surface.

5.4 Linguistic realism and literary representation

A major problem for linguists is to determine the extent to which
the language used in literary works can be judged to be
representative of the linguistic realities in which they are set.
Literary works are after all a special category of text written with
a particular aim, within a certain tradition, and according to
certain literary, sociological (and even marketing) conventions.
To what extent does literary African English then truly reflect

everyday language use and language variation? To what extent does it reflect the author's impressions of this linguistic reality? And to what extent is it a creative form that serves other literary purposes? Of course, writers are usually not linguists and their view of the world and communicative processes is not based on scientific analysis but on participant observation, allied with linguistic creativity. That is why it would clearly be a fallacy to treat literary language as an authentic representation of sociolinguistic reality. A 'linguistic description', as in the following passage, which also exhibits a few lexical Africanisms discussed earlier (in 3.6), is certainly the exception.

> The next concern, food was more rapidly available. Scores of little huts with grand names competed for the travellers' custom with colourful signboards backed up with verbal appeals: *Goat meat here! Egusi soup here! Bushmeat here! Come here for Rice! Fine Fine Pounded Yam!*
>
> The word *decent*, variously spelt, occurred on most of the signboards. Chris and his companions settled for Very Desent Restorant for no better reason than its fairly clean, yellow door-blind.
> (Achebe, Chinua. *Anthills in the Savanna*. London: Heinemann 1987: 207)

Although the literary texts quoted here may be regarded as illustrating African varieties of English, literary texts are unreliable sources of linguistic or sociolinguistic data. Nobody takes it at face value when farmers speak Standard English in African novels. The problem usually arises with the representation of the non-standard, or basilectal varieties of English along a social continuum. In such cases it can be a controversial issue whether 'the lower characters' speak authentic pidgin or some genuine form of broken English or some unrealistic mixture. Although there is not yet a generally accepted and codified variety of pidgin, mixtures can be found in the lexicon as in the grammar. There are numerous examples in Saro-Wira's *Sozaboy* (Port Harcourt 1985). Pronouns like *you* or *they* instead of *una* and *them*, nouns like *mother* for *mama*, prepositions *at* and *to* instead of only *for*, constructions with *of* genitives (*sister of yours* instead of *yo sista*) or plural *-s* or, in general, the use of too many synthetic forms obviously deduced from Standard English are often objected to as showing lack of authenticity and consistency.

These features are only realistic when they serve the obvious purpose of characterizing certain figures through their language, when they occur in direct or indirect speech, including various stream-of-consciousness techniques. Here linguistic stereotypes play a decisive role: an uneducated African 'has to' mispronounce or misspell 'The expats live the country', and such problem words as 'desent' and 'restorant' above.

Even more exotic is the style in Okara's *The Voice* (London: Heinemann 1964). This is characterized by *-(e)th* endings instead of Standard English *-s* or unmarked forms for verbs (*things changeth*, p. 25), the varying use of *as* and *like* in the same construction on the same page (*a person can his insides change like you change a loin cloth* as opposed to *They cannot their insides change as you change a loin cloth*, p. 50) or the mismatches of tone and register (*She was struck with the name of witch and was ostracised*, p. 32). In such cases it may be impossible to decide to what extent these inconsistencies are part of regular learner language (if that is what the writer aims at representing) and to what extent they are simply creative and experimentally idiosyncratic.

All unusual forms of (written) English must be seen in relation to the audience and readership an author has in mind. In Nigeria educated readers are literate, or at least most fluent, in Standard English; and even less educated ones, whom some authors want to address explicitly, may be more familiar with the anglicized written form of non-standard speech than with any phonemic alternative. International readers might be excluded altogether. It is, however, worth bearing in mind that in extreme cases, like the examples from Okara's Ijaw-English above, interpretation may not be easier for a Zulu or even a Hausa reader than for a European. Thus all literary production is a compromise between realism and the readers' comfort. These two aims are to some extent opposed. According to Smith and Nelson (1985) the problem an African author faces in conveying his thoughts and feelings to his readers can be seen on three successive levels: intelligibility involves word/utterance recognition, comprehensibility denotative meaning and interpretability the contextual sense of the text. If a writer attempted to emphasize deviant pronunciation, as reflected in his spellings (closely associated with intelligibility), deviant lexicon (related to comprehensibility) and deviant syntax (often the decisive stumbling block to interpretability) all at the same time, his work would be much more difficult to read – if it was read at all. And of course, it might not gain the support of the educational authorities for fear that learners would be exposed to 'corrupt' English.

Another example of inconsistent usage occurs in the following passages:

But they don't know what to do because Bullet himself said nothing. Even the boys do not know that it is urine that the **soza captain** gave him to drink. **Na me one wey è tell.** But all the boys are sympathising with him. And although the **soza captain** removed him from **san mazor** and took away all his ropes, all the boys still respect him and they will do anything that **he tell** them to do. So when the new **san mazor** is there, they will all keep quiet and you will think they are **mumu.** But if **Bullet talk** to them, they will do exactly as **he tell** them. **Even sef,** they cannot respect the **soza captain** as they respect Bullet. Then **the soza captain begin** to march from his tent to where we were all sitting in the speed boat. Before he **reach** where we were staying, Bullet turned to the boys who were sitting like **mumu** and said 'No be everything **wey eye see** that mouth **dey talk.** I think **una understand?'** All the boys together answer '**Ya**' and then they continue to sit like **mumu.** By this time the **soza captain have** reached the speed boat. Then he entered the boat, sat down, and gave order for the boat to move. The boat **man start** the engine and the boat just **shoot for front quick quick** with plenty noise. We passed the mangrove swamp, bend through the creek with plenty mudskippers and crabs and the birds singing in the tree. Soon we **come reach river.**

During an enemy attack Bullet shoots the captain in revenge for past humiliations and turns to his fellow-soldiers saying: 'You will remember what I said before. It is not everything that your eye see that your mouth will talk. Come on, Sozaboy, help me carry that anmal into the boat.

(Saro-Wira *Sozaboy.* Port Harcourt 1985: 106–8)

In this excerpt we have the authentic pidgin flavour conveyed through uninflected verbs, the extension of the preposition *for*, serial verbs and the use of the pronouns *wey* (relative) and *una* (second person plural) or *na* for forms of *to be.* At the same time complex tenses, progressive forms and subordinated clauses are used and there is even an abrupt transition to the documentary variety of Standard English, as in an army report.

But in this case the author has made it clear from the beginning that he does not aim at an authentic representation of language, for he writes in the 'Author's Note' (ibid.: n.p.): 'Sozaboy's language is what I call "rotten English", a mixture of Nigerian pidgin English and occasional flashes of good, even idiomatic English. This language is distorted and disorderly. . . . It thrives on lawlessness, amd is part of the dislocated and discordant society in which Sozaboy must live, move and have not his being.' This indicates that even if a writer were able to transfer authentic language into his fiction or drama this is not necessarily his intention. He would be a poor writer indeed, if he only tried to create a reflection of the 'real' world without any innovative 'breaking of rules'. As we have seen above, literary form serves a purpose, for instance character depiction or formation, and complete realism is not the aim. A traditional function of non-standard language is comic relief: when 'high politics' has been discussed for some time and a policeman intervenes with a pedestrian parking ticket (as in Achebe's *Anthills in the Savanna* 1987: 128) the level of the language switches together with the topic. Another purpose may be to symbolize a dislocated and discordant 'rotten society' in a distorted and disorderly 'rotten language', as in *Sozaboy*.

The writer can also indicate stereotypes and public notions about language forms and language use. Such stereotyped views are often held about the language used by certain ethnic groups or in certain professions and roles, which may be reflected in the speech presentation and narrative.

> The man with fine shirt stood up. And begin to talk in English. Fine fine English. Big big words. Grammar. 'Fantastic. Overwhelming. Generally. In particular and in general.' Haba, god no go vex. But he did not stop there. The big grammar continued. 'Odious. Destruction. Fighting.' I understand that one. 'Henceforth. General mobilization. All citizens. Able-bodied. Join the military. His Excellency. Powers conferred on us. Volunteers. Conscription.' Big big words. Long long grammar. 'Ten hens. Vandals. Enemy.' Everybody was silent. Everywhere was silent like burial ground. Then they begin to interpret all that long grammar plus big big words in Kana. In short what that man is saying is that all those who can fight will join the army.
>
> (Saro-Wira *Sozaboy*. Port Harcourt 1985: 47)

This symbolizes the plight of the little man in the big power game manipulated by those with the 'fine fine' English and the 'big big' words. Should an author really maintain standards of correctness in form when his content concerns a world that has lost all decent humane standards?

Finally it must be borne in mind that variation in literary language is to be found in all literary works and that it fulfils various functions; it may reflect the writer's own general style or serve as an indication of individual style and differences between characters and situations, or it may be used to symbolize dominant patterns of the author's message. Specific to Africa are only the particular cultural and linguistic values of these principles. Here the general sociolinguistic background, the usual formal variation and the common attitudes and stereotypes must be taken into consideration as far as possible; only then will the reader be able to evaluate precisely the stylistic features of the individual literary work of art.

Notes

1. Undoubtedly, African literature has a formative influence on the language of educated Africans, because literature still takes a prominent place in secondary education. Unfortunately the great overlap of English language and English literature in the field of literary stylistics is not utilized to expand the student's knowledge and perception of language in use (in this particular domain). The detailed discussion of creativity and realism in literature (see 5.3 and 5.4) could strengthen the literary as well as the linguistic side of English teaching in Africa. It might also attract the literary-minded students to closer linguistic analysis.

2. The possible tension between linguistic realism and literary conventions and representation is discussed in 5.4. In this context it may suffice to say that even on stage it is, of course, possible to write a play in a chosen language and plant deliberate linguistic indicators or stereotypes to suggest that the language used or perceived in a similar action in reality would be different from the one on stage. Such conventions seem to be used, however, more in narrative than in dramatic writing.

3. The linguistic text types identified here are in fact deductive prototypes, that is the types and the examples represent what is perceived as relatively 'typical' according to the decisions of language use explained. A really inductive linguistic categorization would analyse texts according to the frequency and (co-)occurrence of linguistic features (e.g. words of particular stylistic and associative value, grammatical and context features; cf. the checklist in Leech/ Short 1981: 75–80) and use statistical procedures to group together texts in several dimensions (e.g. narrative–non-narrative, elaborated versus situation-dependent; cf. Biber 1988). Then it would also be possible to classify texts empirically according to the position of texts or characters in the lect hierarchy, their 'Africanness', i.e. the density of African features, etc. But such corpus-based investigations have hardly begun.

4. Mphahlele (1964: 304f) predicted a particularly lively development for South African English, which seems to have been suppressed by the political developments, but indicates the direction rather early: 'South Africans began to be published in journals and in this way they could do violence to standard English and carry their audience with them, exploiting a popular kind of English. It is more likely here than anywhere else in Africa that we shall see one mode of English succeed another owing to the restlessness of the situation.'

Chapter 6

Influence on African Languages

In every multilingual situation, when large groups of speakers of several languages live side by side, their languages influence one another. Strictly speaking it is not quite correct to speak of the influence of languages on one other, because the latter come 'alive' only when used by human beings; it would be more accurate to say that speakers of language A incorporate elements of another language B into their rendering of language A. Thus, as has been shown in chapter 3, Africans incorporate African features into their English. On the other hand, they incorporate features of English into their African languages, when they find it convenient. The influence on the individual speech act must be distinguished from the impact made on the general language system. There is a sociolinguistic and a linguistic side to this influence; the sociolinguistic processes include the strength and circumstances of, and attitudes towards, English influence; this influence is particularly dominant in certain domains of language use and may cause various reactions. Linguistic analyses reveal that the influence of English is pervasive on all linguistic levels. The linguistic form also plays an important part in the acceptance of language influence; if loans are acceptably integrated phonetically and grammatically, they can make an important contribution towards the modernization of African languages.

6.1 Multilingualism and the penetration of English

The influence of the English language on African languages varies considerably. In general, the strength of English penetration into an African language depends on the position of English in the sociolinguistic environment, which in turn depends largely on the length and intensity of contact with English. Historically languages in coastal areas have been more deeply influenced than those inland. Whether a widespread African lingua franca (such as Hausa in Northern Nigeria and beyond) is used or not, and the linguistic complexity of the African languages available are further significant factors. Today the influence of English is pervasive everywhere particularly through educational bilingualism and the general modernization processes.

As English is used in Africa as a language of education, especially of higher and technical education, it is not surprising that African speakers are used to English in certain mental activities like abstractions, analogizing and discussing technical matters. They have been introduced to new ideas, objects, notions and concepts through English, thus many of these bilinguals have come to associate ideas learned at school with the use of the English language. Even when they leave school, their exposure to such concepts is mainly in English, as broadcasts about Western technology and science on the radio and television are exclusively in English. However this is not only a question of speech habits but also of language competence in technical registers of African languages. In certain domains it is quite natural to use English material to expand African languages in areas where they have not been used before. Thus decreasing English use may well result in increasing English influence on African languages.[1] Many technically oriented polyglots in planning and administrative offices adopt a very pragmatic view of European influence in general and on African languages in particular. They believe that in order to function effectively African languages must adapt or adopt certain features which make English so suitable for modern communication. Whatever helps African speakers to communicate clearly and effectively should be promoted.

On the speech act level of such multilingual speakers, this influence may range from thorough code-mixing (or alternation) to slight collocational preferences within the African language. The following examples from two very different text types, a more technical one and a more personal one, illustrate some sociolinguistic and linguistic factors involved. The first is from a newspaper advertisement, a technical description of a car, in Swahili, which is loaded with unadapted English words and even uses two expressions for the same thing (*injector pumps* and *pumpu za upepo*). The second is a private letter in a novel in Shona, which mixes set phrases or even clauses from English in the Shona context (see 7.5), because the writer wants to show his

social 'superiority' (in the novel this literary device is used to
ridicule his attitude, cf. 5.3); some loans from English are written
as a Shona pronounces them.

- Kuchonga Cylinder Head, kunoa Flywheels na kutengeneza upya
  Pressure Plate Discs za aina zote za magari.
- Kutengeneza Discs za Breki za magari ya aina zote ya abiria.
- Kufanya majaribio ya aina zote za Injector Pumps isipokuwa
  Rotative Pumps.
- Kufanya majaribio ya Breki zinazotumia upepo na Pampu za
  upepo.
- Kuchonga upya Drum za Breki kwa magari yote makubwa.

(*Mzalendo*, Dar es Salaam 9 February 1986)

Shamwari, ini ndaneta nokusevenza. **You see, fiend**, manje **you think**
munhu angasevenzere **seven sherengs** pa **one weeks**? Handisi srevi
yavarungu! Unotumwa somuranda; unijobheswa sedhongi; unotukwa
sembwa. **What for good** panyika yedu? Chirega tifire muno
muruzevha mwana waamai. **Godhi herep piporo of mayi nashen. Dhey
cry orr days! Dhey cry, cry every manzi. What for good**?

My friend, I am tired of working with White people. Tell me my
friend, do you think a man can work for seven shillings a week? I am
not the White man's slave! They send you on errands like a slave;
they make you labour like a donkey; they scold you like a dog. What
good is there in our country? Let us die out here in the Reserve,
brother. Oh God, please help the people of my nation. They cry
every day. They cry and cry every month. For what good?

(Chidzero, *Nzregnamutsvairo*, p. 6, quoted in Ngara 1982: 101)

The letter also shows that it is not necessary for speakers of the
influenced language to be (fluent) speakers of the influencing
language, too, even though the first use of influenced elements
may be either a conscious, creative effort or an unconscious slip
of the tongue by bilinguals. The process may gain momentum
and elements may be taken over more or less consciously by
others until finally the system of the African language is changed.
Whereas code-mixing and code-switching are bilingual phenomena, even the monolingual African can benefit from English,
particularly in certain domains.

6.2 Domains of English influence

Although it is obvious that in a multilingual situation languages in
contact interchange linguistic elements, the direction of the flow
can be either way. This depends on the domains of life these

linguistic elements belong to. Those domains associated with traditional culture, such as agriculture, food and rites, tend to find their expression in African languages (cf. 3.5), because English equivalents do not exist or are considered inappropriate by Africans. Domains associated with modern European life and inventions, such as technology, administration, education, sports and entertainments, tend to be expressed in English terms, even if that entails incorporating them as loans into an African language context.[2]

The following examples (Table 6.1) from Bemba, Hausa, Luo, Mina, Nyanja, Okpe, Shona, Swahili and Yoruba amply document that this development takes place in almost every African language in 'anglophone' Africa – albeit to a different degree. The spelling of lexemes usually reflects the English form as it is spoken rather than as it is written[3] (although spelling conventions between and within African languages vary considerably, particularly with borrowings), as well as slight naturalizing modifications (e.g. prefixes in languages with noun class systems; see 6.5) to incorporate the foreign elements better into the African language structure.

TABLE 6.1   English loan-words in Bemba, Hausa, Luo, Mina, Nyanja, Okpe, Shona, Swahili and Yoruba in modern spheres of life

BEMBA (Zambia)
Technology: ikolobo (bulb; < globe), akanensala (razor-blade), talaiva (driver), foni (phone), itanki (tank), lole (lorry), shimaini (miner), inkoloko (clock), ishitima (train; < steam)
Finance/business: banki (bank), cheke (cheque), chenji (change), akampani (company), lishiiti (receipt), penshoni (pension)
Education: isukulu (school), choko (chalk), ticha (teacher), ibuku (book), pensulo (pencil)
Administration: kafinala (governor), meneja (manager), pulisident (president)
European customs: itoloshi (trousers), icipatala (hospital), bafwa (bath), buleti (bread), impoto (pot), keke (cake)

HAUSA (Nigeria, Niger)
Technology: lori (lorry), injin (engine), wili (weel), redio (radio)
Finance/business: dala (dollar; currency), ofis/ofishi/ofishin (office)
Education: digiri (degree), satifiket (certificate), fensir (pencil), sakandare (secondary), ambulan (ambulance)
Administration: cif joji (chief judge), sakatori (secretary)
European customs: filim (film), sinema (cinema), bafu (bath), bandeji (bandage), kicin (kitchen), letas (lettuce)

TABLE 6.1 *cont.*

LUO (Kenya)
Technology: jet (jet [plane]), sipiring (spring), opena ([bottle] opener),
    betri (battery), reru (rail [way]), genereta (generator)
Finance/business: bengi (bank), akaont (account), risit (receipt), lon
    (loan)
Education: sikul (school), digri (degree), diploma, desk
Administration: namba (number), fis (fees), pakti (packet), laises
    (licence), kapten (captain)
European customs: gita (guitar), sinema (cinema), gol (goal), kabat
    (cupboard), sikaf (scarf), buskut (biscuit)

MINA (Togo, Ghana)
Technology: lɔri (car; < lorry), catarila (caterpillar), bɔs (bus), taya
    (tyre), rɔba (plastic; < rubber), mələ (ship; < mail), skeli (scale),
    stiya (steer[ing-wheel]), gɔta (gutter)
Finance/business: tchɛki (cheque), tchɛdji (change)
Education: sukulu (school), tchitcha (teacher), wɔchi (watch), chumeka
    (shoemaker)
European customs: chɔchi (church), cheti (shirt), bɛdi (matras; < bed),
    refri (referee), gol (goal), chimgɔm (chewing-gum)

NYANJA (Zambia)
Technology: injini (engine), waya (wire), lori (lorry), draiva (driver),
    kareza (razor-blade)
Finance/business: banki (bank), kampani (company), cheke (cheque)
Education: sukulu (school), buku (book), pepala (paper), bopeni
    (ballpen), winifomo (uniform)
Administration: ofisa (officer), ofesi (office), sekeletari (secretary),
    sitampa (stamp)
European customs: bendi (bend), buledi (bread), poleji (porridge),
    tebulo (table), poto (pot), koloko (clock)

OKPE (Nigeria)
Technology: íjini (engine), ijin(n)ía (engineer), imóto (motor[car/lorry]),
    ibosi (bus), itelívishoni (television)
Finance/business: ibánki (bank), akánti (account), ishéki (cheque),
    ifáktry (factory), ipenshoniani (pensioner)
Education: itísha (teacher), isukúru (school), ibréki (break[2]), ipénsuru
    (pencil), ipéni (pen), irula (ruler)
Administration: isékretri (secretary), ófisi (office), ófisa (officer), ikópul
    (corporal), ósipitu (hospital), ikánsuru (council)
European customs: isinima (cinema), idisiko (disco), ibórhu (football),
    ikeki (cake), ishóshi (church)

SHONA (Zimbabwe)
Technology: dhiraivha (driver), treni (train), rori (lorry), tangi (tank)
Finance/business: bhangi (bank), cheki (check), femu (firm), dhora/
    dhola (dollar), indastiri (industry)
Education: ticha (teacher), chikoro (school)

TABLE 6.1 *cont.*

Administration: garhumendi (government), inispekita (inspector), praiminista (prime minister), paramende (parliament), politikisi (politics), menisiparati (municipality)
European customs: poriji/parichi (porridge), siwiti/chiwitsi (switch), keke (cake), shati/sheti (shirt), mutirauzi (trousers), bhutsu (boots), bhora (football)

SWAHILI (Tanzania/Kenya)
Technology: breki[1] (break), beteri (battery), jenereta (generator), injini (engine), injinia (engineer), redio (radio), waya (wire), meli (ship; < mail)
Finance/business: benki/banki (bank), cheki (cheque), chenji (change), kampuni (company), risiti (receipt), pensheni (pension)
Education: breki[2] (break), jiografia (geography), fisikia (physics), diploma
Administration: afisa (officer), paspoti (passport), meneja (manager), kesi (case), reli (railway), hospitali (hospital)
European customs: densi (dance), keki/bisikuti (cake/biscuit), bendi (band), kilabu (club), kisosa (saucer)

YORUBA (Nigeria)
Technology: aláàmù (clock; < alarm), básíkùlù (bicycle), énjìnì (engine), gáréèjì (garage), mokáníìkì (mechanic), redió (radio)
Finance/business: àlùbànsì (advance [payment]), fáàmù (firm), háyápòséesì (hire-purchase), kasíyà (cashier), kómpìnì (company)
Education: désiki (desk), kíláàsì (class), lésìnì (lesson), pénsùlù (pencil), satífíkéètì (certificate)
Administration: ènkúwári ([official] enquiry), lánsénsì (licence)
European customs: bíà (bier), dànsí (dance), kómbóòdù (cupboard), kótènì (curtain), sinimá (cinema), sókà (soccer), sokoléètì (chocolate).

This shows in which domains English was the dominant language (and culture) in colonial Africa, importing objects and concepts together with the linguistic terms for them into Africa. In some domains, such as the army, language use is now even prescribed. If the language of command is English (as in Zambia, for instance), military terms are easily taken over into African languages, e.g. in Bemba *koopolo* from English *corporal*, *saacenti* from *serjeant*, *peleeti* from *parade*, *taputapu* from *double-double* (meaning 'fast'), *umu-nshinga* (plural *imi-*) from *machine gun*, *mantiini* (plural *ba-*) a 'rifle' from the brand name *Martini(-Henry)*, *i-bataalyeni* (plural *ama-*) from *battalion* (Kashoki 1975: 727).

Besides normal words, a large number of proper names and international standard expressions, such as the adjectives *-a kijerumani* (German), *-a kisoshalisti* (socialist), and the nouns *dola*, *maili*, and *mita* (meter) in Swahili, Djama (German) and *dola* in Mina or *pondo* (pound), *maminetsi* and *masekonzi* in Shona (minutes/seconds, each with plural prefix) found their way into the African languages.

From a semantic point of view it is important to separate the cases when an English word is taken over into an African language in its original English meaning from the others where the meaning in the African language differs. The meaning may be (as in the following examples from Mina and Lozi respectively) expanded (*pɛpa* includes single sheets of paper and complete notebooks; *pulanga* does not only refer to planks, but also to trees); it may be restricted to part of the English meaning (*airon* from *iron* means only 'the machine to iron shirts, etc.'; *msuti* is only used for a man's suit); it may be shifted to a related (*bɛdi* with the new meaning 'matras' is still closely related to the original 'bed'; *misitilesi* is a female counterpart, not a mistress) or a less-related object (*mɛlɛ* as 'boat' is obviously the short form of the original English *mail boat*; *melo* refers to a fast/passenger train (+mail), whereas *gusu* is a slow/goods train).

Some words undergo complex formal and semantic changes, which can hardly be reconstructed. The lexeme *kapenta*, which is widely used in Zambia and Zimbabwe for small fish (*dagaa* in East Africa), is said (Mudzi 1976: 68) to be derived from the English verb *paint*, which was taken over into Lozi and referred, at first in connection with *kupenta milomo* (to paint lips) and then separately as *kapenta*, to a loose woman or prostitute, later it was transferred to the dish that was an ideal meal for these women as they had no time to cook, and finally it lost the connection with prostitutes altogether and few people remember its complex etymological development.

6.3 Reactions to English influence

The reaction to the use of English elements in African languages differs greatly among Africans, depending on the social characteristics of the community or individual (how 'accommodating' they are) and the linguistic characteristics of the influence (see 6.5). This applies to the individual speech act level of creative borrowing as well as to the systematic level of relative general use and acceptability. Purists are resistant to foreign elements and object to their use because they feel their language is being adulterated. Adaptionists are said to be accommodating especially when the influencing language enjoys considerable prestige in the speech community. Interestingly, purists are often quite oblivious of foreign elements that came into the language in the past, because they are integrated into the (African) language system. Others, less purist in their outlook, try to draw a line between necessary foreign elements for non-African concepts, ideas and objects and unnecessary foreign elements for items that could be just as adequately expressed in the African language. Whereas the process is called integration in the first case, it is called intrusion, for a single word or phrase, or interlarding, for longer utterances, in the second. It is worth noting, however, that the strategy of code switching, which seems to be the more neutral expression for the same process, is often pursued by the most proficient bilingual speakers and obeys relatively strict grammatical rules. The strategy may be more or less consciously applied for stylistic or sociolinguistic reasons, i.e. because the speaker wants to express specific nuances of meaning or to symbolize a certain identity or particular values.

Another important factor influencing the development of African languages, especially of those chosen as national languages, are national language academies, councils or institutes. They are usually found in states with an active national language policy. Hence many of these institutions show some purist tendencies directed against the seemingly overwhelming English influence. Although they are actively trying to develop African languages to give them a wider vocabulary in new domains, and sometimes even to expand the grammar, they are also trying to regulate this development, and in particular the foreign linguistic influence. Normally a preference is shown for linguistic material of African origin. Thus a hierarchy of more or less desirable source languages for borrowings is established: only when language material cannot be found within the same language, do linguists look for material, often in the following order of preference:

(1) from other national languages (in the case of state institutions);
(2) from within the same language family (e.g. Bantu);
(3) from other African languages;
(4) from Arabic (especially in states with a sizeable Muslim population) and
(5) from the classical (international) languages Latin and Greek;

(6)   only as a last resort from other languages 'foreign to Africa' (i.e. English and French).

Some of these institutions even issue lists of approved lexical items or constructions in order to influence language development from above. This may lead to parallel developments from above and below, i.e. officially approved terms will coexist with creative *ad hoc* formations. Compare the following rival words in Swahili and how they coexist with different emphasis and frequency: *ripoti* is a more formal, mostly written report, whereas *taarifa* is rather a bulletin; similarly *mafuta* covers *diseli* and *petroli* as well as cooking-oil; *wiki* (week) is less frequently used than its Arabic equivalent *juma*; and *risiti* ('receipt') is limited by *stakubathi* which can also be used as a verb; *sayansi* means 'science' but so does *elimu* in Arabic, which is nowadays normally restricted to 'education' in Swahili; *elekrisiti* is only marginally used today (at least in Tanzania) instead of *umeme*, but sometimes *stima/sitima* (from *steam*) is used; similarly *motobaiki* and *motosaikeli* have lost ground compared to the onomatopoetic term *pikipiki*.

This shows that there often seems to be room for several expressions with slight differences in meaning. In Swahili, for instance, a *hoteli* of the European type, normally in East Africa also a restaurant, is differentiated from a *nyumba la kulala*, a 'house to sleep' of the African style, or a *shule* (from German) as it was introduced by missionaries and colonialists from a *chuo*, a Koranic school or, adopted from above, a place of higher learning up to university (= *chuo kikuu*). What annoys many language developers about the English influence is that widespread bilingualism facilitates transfer, but it also hinders standardization in the African language. When stylistic differences develop it is often the more informal styles that are anglicized to a greater extent than the more formal ones. Some purists only accept an English word when it is totally assimilated, i.e. in spelling, pronunciation, grammar and even intonation, whereas most educated speakers demand only partial assimilation, i.e. adjusting loans in such a way that they do not disturb the original structure of the African language but keeping them transparent by retaining some clue as to their origin.

This shows that processes of language influence, from the first more or less deliberate occurrence in the individual speech act to the final accepted use and integration in the African language,

depend on sociolinguistic variables as well as on linguistic ones.
That is why both sides of the coin have to be analysed.

6.4 Language influence at different linguistic levels

A comparison of the different linguistic sub-levels of phonology,
vocabulary, morphology, syntax, idiomaticity and style[4] shows
that influence is most protruding in vocabulary, especially when
the foreign form is retained, but this section will illustrate how
pervasive the process of language influence can be on all levels.

Although the phonological level generally seems to be more
resistant to foreign influence, the introduction of (standard)
written varieties of African languages exerts strong pressure
towards adopting a spelling pronunciation for some forms, since
more authority is often attributed to the written than to the
spoken language. Furthermore, English influence favours tendencies towards Europeanizing African languages which is often
deplored by African traditionalists (e.g. Khalid [1977: 155]
laments 'the false "standardization" of Swahili'). Thus, English
may, for example, have played a certain role in de-Arabicizing
some pronunciations of modern Standard Swahili (e.g. *h*, *gh*),
but the Bantu mother tongues exert pressure in the same
direction.

Although the influence on the sound system of African
languages usually does not go as far as adding new sounds
completely unknown before, some examples of system changes
can be found, for instance in Zulu (cf. Khumalo 1984). Like
other Bantu languages Zulu did not have an equivalent to the
English /r/. That is why in older loan-words from the times of the
initial language contact /r/ is interpreted as /l/, as in *ilula* for
'ruler' (as a leader/chief). But since then /r/ has been added to the
Zulu system and modern Zulu uses it in the loan-words, such as
irula (the drawing instrument), although there is still considerable
variation between /l/ and /r/, such as in *iroli* (from *lorry*).

This example shows that contrastive differences between
English and African languages which influence the English of
bilingual African speakers also influence the African languages.
Word stress and tone patterns are striking illustrations of the
consequences of this influence. Yoruba, for instance, is a tone
language in which stress is insignificant. Thus when English words
are transferred into Yoruba, English word stress is usually
realized as a high tone to reflect the original prominence of the
syllable. But as stress often falls on the first syllable in English
this results in a high–low tone sequence in words like *pánù*

(<*pan*) or *títì* (<*street*). This is however an unusual pattern in Yoruba and identifies these words as loans. Thus the tone patterns are changed at least proportionally. What is more dramatic is that some bilinguals are beginning to substitute stress for high tone in Yoruba creating certainly a major change of the language system (Banjo 1986: 537, 539).

Foreign language elements are usually most evident on the level of vocabulary. A word-class analysis of the loan-words reveals that nouns are by far the most frequently borrowed items into African languages, constituting normally more than 90 per cent. In Swahili, for instance, only very few special verbs, such as *-feli* ('fail') and *-wini* ('win') in sports, and even fewer adjectives, mostly denominatives such as *-a fisikia* (from 'physics'), can be found. Extreme cases of 'Western activities', such as *Umepata kuskii*? Have you ever skied? (Eastman 1981: 2), are naturally very rare. In Bemba *-feluka* ('fail') and *-wina* ('win') are also used, together with *-lusa* ('lose'), *-taipa* ('type') and *-saina* ('sign'), e.g. in *saina apa* 'sign here' or *alisaina* 'to be signed'. In Shona *-winha/wina* also exists, together with *-akita* ('act in a play'), *-maka* ('mark schoolwork), *-bhita* ('beat in music'), *-fota* ('take a photo') or *bhenga* ('deposit money in a bank').

With certain word classes, such as prepositions, which are more differentiated in English than in most African languages, problems are bound to arise. *Before* and *after* have a local and a temporal meaning. Sometimes the temporal meaning is better expressed verbally as in Shona (Ngara 1982: 88):

> pamberi pokudya > vanhu vasati vadya.
> before meals > before people ate.

> akasrika mushure matendai > akasvita Tendai asvika.
> he arrived after Tendai > he arrived after Tendai had arrived.

Sometimes other prepositions or local prefixes appear to be authentic:

> Siya chipo chako pamberi peatare > siya chipo choko paatare.
> Leave your gift before the altar > leave your gift at the altar.

> Musarakidze ururami hwenyu pamberi pavantu > musarakise ururami hwenyu paparantu.
> Don't show your goodness before people > don't show your goodness in the presence of people.

The fact that prepositions (or postpositions) are not a fully developed word class is also reflected in the fact that the few

African prepositions express a wide range of meanings. In order to avoid ambiguity, more explicit marking may be used after the English model. Swahili, for instance, expresses case relations mainly through verbal affixes (*analimia* as opposed to *analima*, see below) or the few prepositions like *kwa* (for) and *na* (with), new developments expanding these into longer prepositional constructions (Mkude 1986: 524):

Juma analimia trekta.
Juma anamlimia Asha.
Juma analimia Boko.
Juma analimia shida tu.

Juma analima kwa trekta.	instrumental: using a tractor
Juma analima kwa niaba ya Asha.	beneficiary: on behalf of
Juma analima huko Boko.	locative: in the direction of
Juma analima kwa sababu ya shida tu.	cause: because of

The case of prepositions illustrates again the contrastive hypothesis that the grammatical features of African English (in 3.4) have their counterparts in features of English-influenced African languages (prepositions are a problem for African speakers of English as they are not as prominent in African languages as in English). Thus participial, infinitive, passive and impersonal expressions, are strengthened, if they exist in an African language, or created, if they do not. Similarly, the fixed English word order can influence African word-order patterns: new patterns are introduced or the frequency distribution of existing ones alters in the direction of the English model. Swahili questions, for example, are usually marked by intonation and question words, but not by word order, but a number of modern texts in 'officialese' show a tendency to place the question word initially (ibid.: 523):

unatafuta nini?	nini unatafuta?	whom are you looking for?
unakwenda wapi?	wapi unakwenda?	where are you going?
unataka nani	nani unamtaka?	what do you want?

The verb phrase is usually most resistant to foreign influence, but Yoruba (cf. Banjo 1986: 543) has introduced a verb particle in equative constructions (*wà* for *be*), especially when they are in a context of language mixing (*wà* has to be used, when the intensifier is in English, but not when it is in Yoruba):

ó wà late = ó late	he/she is late
ó wà very late = ?ó very late	he/she is very late
ó late gangan	he/she is very late

Many African languages do not have a passive construction, but a sentence in Luo like

Simba ne olo go Gor. Or spoken: Simba nolo gi Gor.
Simba was beaten by Gor [two Kenyan football clubs].

may sound quite acceptable to a bilingual who is used to such constructions in English and Swahili, although it may be unknown to older monolingual speakers of Luo.

A more stylistic contrast is the prevalence of a verbal style in African languages compared to the nominal style in English. Such changes in style may cause chain reactions. Nominal style increases the importance of adjectives, but as many African languages have relatively few adjectives word-formation processes are set in motion. Influenced by English, derivational processes such as the formation of adjectives from nouns tend to be used more frequently than would otherwise be the case.

Frequency also governs the usage and collocational behaviour of African words. In Swahili *shamba* originally means *field*, occasionally it can also be translated as *farm* ('He has a *shamba* outside of town'). This extension of referential meaning is reflected in the new collocations of *shamba* in Swahili (Mkude 1986: 528):

shamba la kuku	poultry farm
shamba la nguruwe	pigsty

In general, the influence of English on differentiating syntactic or stylistic variation in African languages, e.g. the elaboration of the tense system or the development of more or less formal registers and the functionalization of previously free variation, can hardly be overestimated. This variation is certainly much more difficult to discover than straightforward lexical borrowings, and much less adequately researched so far. Newspaper style in African languages, for instance, is a very valuable field of research, not only because many journalists have had a thorough training in English, but also because their writings shape the stylistic experience of their readership.

Whiteley (1969a: 106) gives an interesting example of journalism, 'in which the material is either carelessly handled or translated literally from English':

> Mnasikiliza redio Tanzania kutoka Dar es Salaam. Na sasa mtasomewa hutuba ya Bwana Waziri alio wahutubia wafanya kazi wa pwani *akiwa yeye ni kama Waziri wa Leba.*

> You are listening to Radio Tanzania from Dar es Salaam. And now you will have read to you the speech of the Minister addressing workers on the coast, *in his capacity of Minister of Labour/as though he were the Minister of Labour.*

The parallel example from Akan is

> Radio Ghana na refɛ yi

which is the corresponding literal translation of

> This is London calling

and does not use the normal Akan word for speak, *kasen.*

The same criticism applies to the following Shona discourse formulae used by broadcasters (Ngara 1982: 91):

> Kupedzisa nhau, heyinoi misoro yadzo zvakare.
> To end the news here are the head(line)s again.

which should be more appropriately:

> Ngatichipedzisai nhau nokudzokorora ndima huru.
> Let us end the news by repeating the main points.

And

> Uku ndiko kupera kwenhau.
> (literally: 'This is the end of the news.')

would better be expressed by:

> Nhau dzinoperera pano.
> (literally: 'The news ends here.')

Other examples of the 'unfortunate' influence of English idioms come from literal translations from the Bible (ibid.):

Maria akawanikwa ava napamuviri.
Maria was found (to be) with child.

suggests that Mary had been missing, and when she was found it was discovered that she was with child. It is therefore better to say:

Maria akangoonekwa ava napumuviri.
(literally: 'Maria was unexpectedly seen to be with child.')

For similar reasons the formulae *Mambo uve netsitsi* (Lord have mercy) was replaced in Catholic prayer books by the more authentic Shona *Mambo tinzwireiwo tsitsi* (literally: 'Lord feel mercy for us').

As far as the phonological and morphological form is concerned, it is possible to distinguish three types (according to the depth of 'penetration'): material with no, with partial, or with complete substitution of form. If the loan form fits into the structural pattern of the borrowing language it is not changed, but simply imported; if it does not fit the African pattern it will be substituted to different degrees. At the level of vocabulary, these three types according to form are called loan-words (foreign forms), loan-blends (a mixture of foreign and indigenous forms) and loan-shifts, which include loan translations (indigenous forms according to the foreign model) and semantic loans (newly expanded indigenous forms). This distinction is important because loan-shifts usually meet with much less resistance, even among purists, than loan-words. In Tanzanian political terminology, for instance, a party leader could not really be called *cheyaman*, because this would contradict the national self-reliance philosophy, but a loan translation with Swahili word forms like *mwenyekiti* ('chair holder') fits very well.

Table 6.2 (with examples from Ojo 1977: 80) takes not only form but also meaning into consideration. It subdivides the concept of loan-word into loans with imported meanings and forms and loans that have indigenous (Yoruba) meanings but imported forms and it subdivides the concept of loan coinage into loan translations, which use indigenous translation equivalents

TABLE 6.2   Types of lexemic innovation from English into Yoruba

Type	Meaning	Form	Example	Standard English equivalent	Comments
Loan-word	E	E	títì	street	
			jíólójì	geology	probationary
	Y	E	mótò	'car', 'lorry'	from motor
			bíntò	been abroad'	'one who has
Loan translation	E	Y	onísègùn	'doctor'	
	E'	Y	ogba èwòn	'prison yard'	
Semantic extension	Y'	Y	ìjoba	'government	
New coinage	Y	E	ayókélé	'limousine'	spontaneous
			olùkó	teacher	induced

and more or less English meanings, semantic shifts, e.g.
extensions, which add the imported meaning to an existing
indigenous lexeme, and new coinages, which are newly created
indigenous forms for the imported meanings.

Ansre (1971: 145) quotes an example where it is not
immediately clear whether the speaker is using English or an
African language, in this case Ewe:

Mele *very sorry*, gake mena *every conceivable opportunity*-i
hafi wò *let*-m*down*.

He also gives an example of a type of influence that is more
difficult to identify since there are no morphological traces of
English, but changes in idiomatic preferences within the African
language. Even if semantically equivalent expressions have
existed in the language side by side for some time, foreign
influence may cause slight shifts in frequency (ibid.: 160 from
Twi):

Ne bo kɔ soro   (Its price has gone up.)

This expression seems, he tells us, to be a recent innovation due
to English influence, compared to the more traditional version:

Ne bo ayɛ den   (Its price has become hard.)

Direct translations from English may be acceptable although they
are often less idiomatic or they influence the frequency of words
and structures if there is a choice, for instance between two
different forms of a relative construction, (e.g. in Swahili, one
with the relative particle *ambao* and the other with a relative verb
infix, Eastman 1981: 3):

Kuna rafiki zangu wawili ambao wamevunja miguu yao . . .
There are two friends of mine who broke their legs. . . .

Other cases, however, clearly break the rules of African
languages, as for example when Swahili demonstratives precede
nouns, as with *hii* society instead of *society hii* for 'this society'
(ibid.).

Kirk-Greene (1963: 42f) quotes 'a passage of "modern" Hausa
that might have been better rendered in "orthodox" Hausa',
since the English influence is extremely pervasive:

Cikin wani *kilas* a *titisi* na Toro wani *tica* daga Ingila ya bai
sumorboyin shi *lifi*.
In a certain *class* at Toro T.T.C. a *teacher* from England gave his
small boy leave.

Sumorboyin ya hau *lori* tare da sauran *fasinjoji* ya sauka a *teshan
mota* na Jos.
The *small boy* travelled by *lorry* along with other *passengers* and got
down at Jos *motor station*.

Daga can ya shiga *teshan reliwe* ya sayi *tikitin taskilan*. Bai fito *kareji*
ba sai da ya kai garinsu.
Then he entered the *railway station* and bought a *third-class ticket*. He
did not leave the *carriage* until he reached home.

A can kam nan ya tafi *yadin fidabudi* inda wani danuwansa *makaniki*
ke aiki *gareji*, amma bai gan shi ba.
There he at once went to the P.W.D. *yard* where one of his brothers
was working as a *mechanic* in the *garage*, but he did not see him.

Ashe *leburori* duk da su sun yi *stiaraik* sun fita kan *basukurorinsu*
suna *masmitan* a wani *ofis* a bayan *aibiti*, inda ake masu *lacca* da
farfaganda.
You see, all the *labourers* had gone on *strike*. They had gone off on
their *bicycles* and were holding a *mass meeting* in an *office* behind the
hospital where they were listening to a *lecture* and *propaganda*.

Sometimes even greetings are taken over into African languages (although they are occasionally rejected by 'Greet me properly', i.e. traditionally). This can be found in Mina, where *mɔni* (<[good] morning) and *gudivi* (<good evening) are used (similarly *mɔni* and *gudimi* in several Nigerian languages). Another interesting example are swear words, which may however acquire a 'light' or innocuous meaning, as the following examples from Bemba: *saanamabiici(ki)* from *son of a bitch*, *mbulalishiiti* from *bloody shit*, *mbulalifuu(lu)* from *bloody fool*, *fwakiyo* from *fuck you*, *kontaelo* from *go to hell*, *konteemiti* from *God damn it* (Kashoki 1975: 723). These loans were of course brought into Bemba through the work of Bemba speakers in the copper mines, always an important area of language contact. The last examples also illustrate that changes in the pronunciation and corresponding spelling as well as morphological adaptations are necessary when loans are transferred from English into African languages.

6.5 Phonetic and grammatical integration of loan-words and their acceptability

The question of how foreign elements in the form ỏf loan-words can best be integrated into African languages[5] poses itself in pronunciation as well as in grammar. In pronunciation, the phonetic aspect is as interesting as the phonotactic. Whereas single English consonants rarely constitute a problem, English vowels often do. The vowels outside the normal African five to nine-vowel system (cf. 3.3) tend to converge with the nearest African vowel. Often this is even reflected in the spelling of the English loans, which has to be changed to a more phonemic form anyway. The phonemic spelling tends to conceal the English origin of the form.

The following examples (Table 6.3) from Zulu (Khumalo 1984: 210–12) exemplify the three tendencies (compare the tendencies in the pronunciation of African English in 3.3).

(A) the English vowels are adjusted to the nearest African equivalent;

(B) some English diphthongs are converted into single vowels, others to double monophthongs, usually with a connecting glide;

(C) a few particularly difficult consonants are substituted.

Most other English sounds can be integrated relatively easily, but this does not mean that there are not minor adaptations

TABLE 6.3 Phoneme adaptation of English loans into Zulu

English sound	Zulu sound	English source	Zulu loan-word
(A) /iː/	/i/	sweet	iswidi
/ɪ/	/i/	tin	ithini
/ɛ/	/e/	flag	ifulegi
/e/	/e/	bed	umbhede
/ɜː/	/e/	nurse	unesi
/a/	/a/	brush	ibhulashi
/ɜ/	/a/	dinner	idina
/ʌː/	/a/	farm	ifamu
/o/	/o/	pot	ibhodwe
/ɔː/	/o/	port	ebhodwe
/ʊ/	/u/	pulpit	ipulupiti
/uː/	/u/	shoemaker	ushumeka
(B1) /eɜ/	/e/	stairs	isitesi
/ɔʊ/	/o/	hotel	ihhotela
/ei/	/e/	game	igemu
(B2) /iɜ/	/iye/	beer	ubhiye
/ei/	/eyi/	tray	ithileyi
/ai/	/ayi/	bible	ibhayibheli
/ʌʊ/	/awu/	thousand	ithawuzeni
/ɔi/	/oyi/	boy	ibhoyi
(C) /θ/	/t/	theatre	itiyetha
/θ/	/f/	thimble	imfimbolo
/ð/	/ʃ/	(Anglican) Church	iSheshi
/r/	/l/	rubber	ilabha/irabha

noticeable, such as the aspiration in *ikhaphete* (< *carpet*).
Sometimes initial vowels are appended to the English root, as in
ithebula (< *table* [mathematical] and *uvulande* (< *veranda*),
sometimes final vowels are appended or they are clipped, as in
ijaji (< judge) or *ilokishi* (< *location*). Another problem may be
the combination of sounds, i.e. that even if the sound as such
occurs, it does not occur in combination with other sounds.

The phonotactic level also contributes to the alienation from
the English origin. As many African languages have a different
word structure, English loans have to be adapted. For instance,
restricted consonant–vowel sequences (e.g. CV–CV) have two
phonotactic consequences for loans: integrated loans should have
special final or initial vowels and should not have consonant
clusters. Not all consonant clusters have to be split, many African
languages can retain sonants like /l/, /r/ or /s/, irrespective of
whether they occur as the first or the second member of the set.
But many African languages only allow certain sequences of

(front or back) vowels in neighbouring syllables, a phenomenon called vowel harmony (e.g. *kɔto* [court] in Akan). Loan-words have to be adapted to this sequence, often more than traditional words (e.g. *ópùnà* 'opener' and *opúrétà* 'operator' in Yoruba; Salami 1972: 171). Table 6.4 gives abundant examples from Bemba, Swahili, Mina and Yoruba of these principles. Unfortunately, the patterns are not as neat as portrayed here. Final *-a*, for instance, occurs also regularly after voiceless palatal

TABLE 6.4 Phonotactic adaptations of English loans in Bemba, Swahili, Mina and Yoruba

---

P1: adapted *-a* from [-ə] as in

Bemba: talaiva (driver), meneja (manager), ticha (teacher), pikicha (picture)
Swahili: dikteta (dictator), golikipa (goalkeeper), dereva (driver), mposta ('postman' + human *m*-prefix) (this lexical group is reinforced by the similar form of deverbal nomina actoris in Swahili),
Mina: tchitcha (teacher), gɔta (gutter), taya (tyre), kakla (knife; < cutlery), wɔtchmeka (watchmaker), sɔdja (soldier) and
Yoruba: dérébà (driver), tírosa/torosa (trousers), fuláwà (flower);

P2: added *-u* after bilabial and labiodental consonants as in

Bemba: ibuku (book), isukulu (school)
Swahili: balbu (bulb), bafu (bath), stimu (steam), but also in buku (book; because of vowel harmony),
Mina: sukulu (school), bɔlu (ball) and
Yoruba: pompu (pump), máàpù (map), sikáàfu (scarf), but also kúkù (cook; again because of vowel harmony)

P3: added *-i* after alveolar, palatal or velar consonants[6] as in

Bemba: cikini (kitchen), lishiiti (receipt), foni (phone), treni (train)
Swahili: ofisi (office), deski (desk), stesheni (station), teksi (tax; taxi),
Mina: bɛdi (bed), briki (brick), brɛki (break), miniti (minute) and
Yoruba: ankasifi (handkerchief), gíláàssì (glass), sóòsì (church), tóòsì (torch);

P4: split consonant clusters as in

Bemba: supuni (spoon), ikolobo (globe), inkoloko (clock), pikicha (picture)
Swahili: baisikeli (bicycle), betri/beteri (battery), brashi/burashi (brush), spiringi (spring), musuli (muscle),
Mina: bɛlɛti (belt), dokita (doctor), and
Yoruba: ampilifáyà (amplifier), kiláàsì (class), bureeki (break), purasítà (plaster), tiṛéè (tray), siráìkì (strike), sitampu (stamp)

plosives and some other sounds in many languages, such as in Ganda (Uganda) *banka* (bank), *baala* (bar), *tanka* (tank), *makanika* (mechanic), but also *kada* (card), *payinta* (pint) and *loza* (rose; cf. Katamba/Rottland 1987 for a detailed discussion of the readjustmant of syllable structure in loan phonology). Other strategies include clippings of syllables, as in Mina *lɛtriki* (electricity). Even when these formal adaptations are not applied in standard orthography, since the orthography preserves the English form, intrusive vowels are very often heard in actual speech as in *hos(i)pitali* or *sok(i)si*.

Table 6.5 gives some alternatives to current English loan-words in Yoruba (Ojo 1977: 142–87; cf. Salami 1972: 169), either through better morphophonemic adaptation or by replacing the English word by parallel loan coinages from Yoruba material. The spelling again conceals some pronunciation problems, as the English [s] is partly substituted by [ʃ] (as in *senji*), partly retained (as in *unifásítì*).

Finally another example from Zulu (Khumalo 1984: 208) shows that the complete phonetic adaptation of a word may include many stages and rules:

breakfast > bre kfa st syllable structure adapted
   > bhu rea kfa st consonant substituted
   > bhu lea kfa st consonant substituted
   > bhu le kfa st vowel substituted
   > bhu le ku fa st vowel inserted in consonant cluster
   > bhu le ku fa si ti vowel inserted in consonant cluster
   > bhu le ku fa si final syllable deleted

Satisfactory phonological integration must be paralleled by

TABLE 6.5 Alternative forms to English loan-words in Yoruba

English original	Loan-word	Alternative adoption	Loan coinage
bible	báíbùlù	bíbéèlì	ìwé mímó
driver	déréba	díréfa	awako
injection	injékison	ínjékísonnì	abéré
licence	lánsénsì	láísénì	iwé awakò
leave	lîîfù	liifi	ìsimi
mechanic	mokáníkì	mónkáníkì	alágbède
change (coins)	sénjì	isénjì	eyo owó
chair	síà	síyà	àga
radio	wáyálèèsì	redió	èro gboùgboùn
university	yunifásítì	unifásítì	ilé èkó gíga

changes in the grammatical behaviour of loans. Good examples of this principle can be recognized in African languages which demand grammatical concord with prefixes (or suffixes) in noun classes.[7] Morphological marking, however, is an obstacle to integrating nouns, hence loan-words tend to be integrated into classes that require less salient marking or none at all. In Swahili, for instance, almost 90 per cent of the English loans are found in the classes 5 and 6 with singular prefixes *ji-* or, mostly, 0 (=no prefix) and plural *ma-*, as in *magazeti* (gazettes) or *mashati* (shirts), or in the classes 9 and 10 (cf. Eastman 1981: 3) with *n-* or no prefixes in singular and plural, as in *faili* (file), *sayansi* (science), *plasta* (plaster), *plagi* (plug). Often the classification of loans is inconsistent: the same lexemes can be found with concord prefixes for different classes (e.g. singular 9 + plural 6). Other class categorizations can be explained by morphological peculiarities (e.g. *kilabu* > club, which may be interpreted as a *n-* or a *ki*-class noun) or semantic peculiarities (e.g. *kisosa* > saucer, because the *ki*-class contains the diminutives). As most noun classifications are based on semantic criteria the integration of loans in the less openly marked classes undermines the logical basis of noun classification.[8]

English loan-words are, however, possible in all classes, e.g. in the Tswana class 1 *Mokeresete* (Christian; plural *Bakeresete*), in class 2 *motshine* (machine; plural *metshine*), in class 3 *lebotlele* (bottle; plural *mabotlele*), in class 4 *setempe* (stamp; plural

TABLE 6.6 Number marking in loan-words from English in Bemba and Shona

	Singular	Plural + prefix	Plural + pre-/+ suffix
Bemba			
book	ibuku	amabuku	amabuksi
pencil	pensulo	amapensulo	amapensulos
cup	kapu	amakapu	amakaps
paper	pepala	amapapa	(amapepala)
Shona			
minute	mineti		maminetsi
pill	piriti		mapiritsi
graduate	grajuweti		mapiritsi
African	muAfrikeni		maAfrikenzi
record	rekodhi	marekodhi	marekodzi
picture	pikicha	mapikicha	mapikichaz
paper	pepa	mapepa	mapepaz

ditempe), in class 5 *motokara* (motorcar; plural *dimotokara*), and so on. The examples in Table 6.6 illustrate the interesting cases where nouns show both the English and the African plural markers in Bemba (with the English forms used by urban and younger Bemba speakers) or in Shona (where sometimes the English marker is optional; from Ngara 1982: 86).

Integrative processes similar to those with nouns can be found with adjectives if they show concord prefixes. These prefixes can also indicate internal word formation processes, which can even be applied to integrated loanwords, such as *dòtí* (< dirt) in Yoruba forming the adjective *idòtí*, which cannot stem from *dirty* because of the tone pattern (Banjo 1986: 538). This may be the final stage of integration.

Whether a loan-word really becomes part of an African language (as in Swahili in the following examples), its acceptability or relative use, depend on several linguistic factors. There may be difficulties because of the linguistic form, as in *alawensi/ alowensi* with English diphthongs or in *eksidenti* (accident) or *hafutaimu* (half-time) with consonant clusters; such loans may be easily replaced by indigenous expressions, as for example *hedimasta* by *mwalimu mkuu* ('great teacher'). There may be difficulties because of the conceptual meaning, as with *boi* or *chifu*, which are associated with the older social systems of colonialism. Similar difficulties may arise with English forms in sensitive areas such as politics in general.

For the future it seems safe to say that English words which are formally well integrated into the structure of the African host language will survive easily; others may be replaced by corresponding expressions using African language material (e.g. calques or loan translations). The influence of English on African languages may become less evident. Nevertheless it will still be pervasive, especially the influence 'from below', i.e. in *ad hoc* usage. There will aways be a need for some adoption – when African resources have been exhausted, the multilingual African language user will try to incorporate both worlds by using forms of English origin and adapting them to the African environment. In fact, it is true to say that one of the most important functions of English in Africa is to contribute to the development of African languages at all linguistic levels, as world languages have done in other parts of the world and in other periods.

Notes

1. This became evident in some countries where language-planning directives demanded a rather abrupt change of language use. Then *ad hoc* translations are bound to reflect the English original and circulated word lists of alternatives often have little influence.

2. It goes without saying that this phenomenon cannot be interpreted as an inferiority of African languages compared to English, but rather as a temporal advantage of English, the international language of science and technology, which may be overcome in a relatively short time, as examples of parallel developments of expressions from various sources show. Although it is arguable whether all languages are equal, it is clear that all have at least the same potential to be adapted to fulfil the communicative needs of their speakers.

3. The writing systems of African languages often take the consonant spelling from English, but the vowels from languages with a more consistent system, e.g. Italian or French. This complicates the adoption of English vowels, because the spelling (and often also the pronunciation) could be taken from the spoken or the written form of the language. On this basis Salami (1972: 169) distinguishes between eye-loans and ear-loans and gives the following examples of double borrowings from Yoruba:

English origin	eye-loan	ear-loan
bible	bíbélì	báíbù
table	tábìlì	tébù/tébùrù
window	wíndò	fíndò
barracks	báráákì	bárékè
paradise	paradisè	párádáìsì

This, apart from slight differences in pronunciation, may also account for different forms of English loans in Kenyan and Tanzanian Swahili (e.g. *banki–benki* or *radio–redio*, respectively).

In Table 6.1 the examples from Mina in Togo follow the French spelling conventions, e.g. ch stands for [ʃ], and others reflect various attempts of rendering African pronunciations, e.g. Yoruba s is often pronounced [ʃ].

4. Another level that is usually neglected is the influence of English on African writing conventions, particularly punctuation. As punctuation is, apart from syntactic and semantic cohesion, closely tied to the rhythm of a language it is problematic if bilinguals apply their English punctuation rules to African languages.

5. Some writers even classify the transfer of loans on the basis of integration, distinguishing crude (i.e. not integrated) from refined (i.e. integrated) transfer, sometimes (e.g. Mkude 1986: 527) even adding underhand transfer (i.e. non-formal textual, syntactic or semantic influence). This section treats integration as a process different from transfer, as it may take some time until a foreign word is actually integrated. This is also reflected in the terminological

distinction between (simply transferred) foreign words and (integrated) loan-words in a language.

6. Final -*i* is an interesting example of the principle that some of these loan-word features even occur in languages that do not have them traditionally. In Luo, for instance, final -*i* occurs in loan-words that come into the language via the dominant regional lingua franca Swahili, such as *sati* (shirt), *koti* (coat), *ongeti* (blanket) and *tangi* (tank).

7. In African languages with a gender system (e.g. Iraqw in Tanzania) similar questions arise. In such systems the foreign nouns have to be assigned to a particular gender and that may imply that, for instance occupations that are typically related to males have to be treated as feminine in grammatical terms because they have a feminine suffix ending (but then a typically masculine suffix may be added to push them into the semantically more appropriate class).

8. English-influenced undermining of noun classifications may be an example for the acceleration of incipient indigenous changes in grammatical systems. Even if structures are not transferred completely the strengthening of parallel features and the neglect of contrastive features often considerably redress the proportional distribution of structures.

Chapter 7

Attitudes Towards English

In many African nations, language attitudes are seen as a central element in language policy, language use and language learning. As language attitudes are complex phenomena this chapter will describe fairly abstract stereotyped notions about the English language as a whole and more applied language beliefs about English in Africa. Besides this macro-level, the attitudes towards intralinguistic variation are revealed when African forms of English and their acceptability are discussed. At the heart of these psycholinguistic phenomena lies the relationship of English to the identity of African individuals and nations today.

7.1 Conceptual and methodological problems

In discussions of these questions many opinions about attitudes are expressed: however, few empirical studies have been made of attitudes towards English varieties in Africa. This can be attributed to two basic problems. *Methodologically*, it is very difficult to reach the high standards that have been set by recent sociolinguistic research in Britain or the USA. In countries with few reliable statistical data, poor postal services, and a population unused to questionnaires or foreign interviewers, test techniques need to be as direct, flexible and simple as possible. *Conceptually*, there is a very wide range of views about attitudes, from the extremely behaviourist to the extremely mentalist (cf. Agheyisi/Fishman 1970). A consequence of this conceptual difficulty is the surprising lack of congruence between language attitudes and overt language behaviour, i.e. language choice and usage. This divergence between the need for methodological simplicity and the obvious complexity of the phenomena to be observed makes the study of language attitudes a difficult undertaking.

For the purposes of this survey, it seems appropriate to distinguish between attitudes towards certain languages in general, or language stereotypes, attitudes towards specific sociolinguistic topics, or language beliefs, and attitudes towards particular language varieties. The conceptual difference between these types of attitudes is not easy to explain (and there are also other categorizations, e.g. in Cooper/Fishman 1974: 6); but for our purposes suffice it to say that language stereotypes are more subconscious and affective, and less based on rational explanation than language beliefs. The former represent idealized abstractions, the latter are revealed when it comes to practical issues. A third type, the study of attitudes towards variations within a language poses problems, since it touches on the question of norms. For a detailed analysis the general entity 'language' has to be broken up into smaller linguistic elements, such as features of pronunciation, vocabulary and grammar.

Before discussing the three types of attitude in detail, it is worth considering some research problems. As attitudes are sometimes felt to be a sensitive personal or, among people with a heightened national-language awareness, even a sensitive political matter, there is often a marked difference between attitudes uttered in public and those uttered privately – as well as those uttered in an interview situation. For this reason, the relationship between the interviewer and the informant is of crucial importance. Informants must be assured of the interviewer's good intentions and solidarity with the speech community if they are to express their opinions freely and openly.

Another important aspect insufficiently covered in the following sections, due to the general lack of empirical data, is the variation in attitudes. Although attitudes are not simply individual but also sociolinguistic phenomena which derive from the speech community, they vary with the community's sociolinguistic background. Attitudes are different in ESL and EIL environments, among English-speaking and non-English-speaking Africans, or at different socio-educational levels. But the following general tendencies may suffice to give an overall picture and to illustrate some of the research problems involved.

7.2 Stereotyped notions about English

Expressions of positive or negative feelings towards a language in general may reflect impressions of linguistic difficulty or simplicity, ease or difficulty of learning, the degree of importance or status it has in the community or even the importance of the people who use it as a first or second language. Sometimes one hears languages described as 'beautiful' or 'precise' by Europeans as well as Africans. These characterizations are to a large extent subconscious and it is not possible to explain them fully on a purely rational basis. They seem to be directly related neither to phonological, morphological or semantic features of the language so described, nor to the sociolinguistic background of the informants' speech community, although both must obviously contribute to the stereotype.

Interestingly enough, English is believed, in many countries in Africa, and indeed in many parts of the Third World generally, to possess certain qualities. These are often characterized by adjectives like 'beautiful', 'rich', 'logical', 'sophisticated' or even 'pleasing to the ear' (although these words may have slightly different meanings in an African context!). English seems to enjoy high international prestige as an idealized world language.[1] This can be measured and represented on attitude scales. The scale in Figure 7.1 resembles the Likert scale (ranging from 1 to 7), which is often used in psychological research, except that it has only six points from 1 (=disagree completely) to 6 (=agree completely), without a neutral mean (=don't know) as an easy way out. In order to find out whether there is some believed basis in linguistic features for this prestige it is necessary to ask informants what the labels attributed mean to them.

The label 'beautiful' seems to describe a very general aesthetic impression. 'Colourful' is less general and may apply to the lexical level. This level is certainly referred to quantitatively when a language is said to be 'rich', and qualitatively when it is said to be 'pure'. In these two cases it seems possible to argue that the stereotyped notions about English are in accordance with linguistic facts, because it cannot be denied that English has a very extensive vocabulary and may thus in this respect rightly be considered 'rich'; although since much of this vocabulary is noticeably borrowed from other languages it cannot come up to puristic standards. The stereotyped notion 'precise' is normally taken to refer to the exactness of lexical items, which is valued very highly by Africans in science and technology and in academic teaching (not because it is an intrinsic value of the language but rather because there is an intensive English-medium tradition in these fields). Similar to 'precise' is 'logical', because this is associated with exactness at the grammatical level. The stereotypes that seem to be based on acoustic and auditory–aesthetic evaluations, such as 'rhythmical' or 'pleasing to the ear',

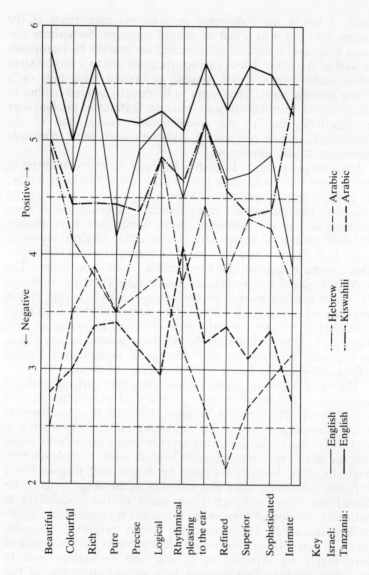

FIGURE 7.1 Stereotyped notions about English among students in Tanzania and Israel: a comparison

Note the largely parallel lines for English as opposed to the irregular lines for Arabic.

Source Figures for Israel from Cooper/Fishman 1977: 258, n=65; for Tanzania from Schmied 1985b: 246; n=55.

normally score less favourable results for English and are of course less easy to explain rationally. It is interesting here that French often seems to score better than English in these latter categories.

The notions 'refined', 'sophisticated' and 'superior' relate to the state of language development (if they are not wrongly associated with the language users anyway); this is why African languages are often ranked particularly low in this respect. Whereas the first two labels are taken to characterize a language that can be used in scientific discourse or for academic purposes, the third cannot be interpreted unambiguously: it can be seen as an intrinsic linguistic value ('a more differentiated language system') or as referring to a language's geographical range or international communicative power ('English is spoken all over the world'); it is, however, a dangerous term, as it may be given the undesirable interpretation of a colonial language attitude.

Other notions, such as 'intimate' or 'sacred', derive from particular purposes or preferences in language use. It goes without saying that as a 'sacred' language English cannot compete with Arabic (for Muslims) or Latin (for some Catholics) and that as an 'intimate' language, a language in which personal feelings, love, etc. are expressed and which is affectively very close to a speaker, English cannot compete with African languages; although there are instances, for example when a young man finds it easier to propose (a modern marriage!) in English.

Finally, it must be emphasized again that although it seems possible to support some stereotyped notions about English with some linguistic evidence, it is worth remembering that they are largely irrational manifestations of a more general feeling which associates English with the modern, successful, educated upwardly mobile, or with a member of a cosmopolitan élite, and this creates an uncritical idealizing image of the world language. This is supported by the fact that English is used not only by mother-tongue speakers but also by international organizations and other European experts in Africa. Thus English radio programmes in Botswana not only come from the BBC and Radio Botswana, but also from the United Nations and Deutsche Welle, for instance. Word association tests also show that English not only conjures responses like 'Britain/England' or 'colonialism', but also 'white people', 'educated' and even 'modern' and 'development'.

The idealized prestige thus accorded to English is only partly seen in relation to the other languages that may be used in the sociolinguistic environment, especially African languages, because a more critical and realistic attitude towards English often arises in discussions when more specific topics are dealt with.

7.3 Language beliefs and arguments for and against English in Africa

In many African newspapers letters to the editor are published which raise specific language issues and reveal the writers' attitudes. In public statements and discussions in which arguments for and against English are expressed attitudes towards English are revealed.

In general, several types of belief can be distinguished. In this section, a variety of arguments will be presented and discussed to illustrate these types. Whereas the stereotyped notions indicated in the previous section are normally based on language-inherent properties, or what are considered as such, most language beliefs can be said to be supported by communicative, national, personal, educational and cognitive arguments.

Communicative arguments are closely related to the sociolinguistic environment. This becomes obvious with statements such as 'An African language is more effective for communication than English' (A1), which may refer to a local environment (e.g. the ethnically homogeneous village) or to an African lingua franca (e.g. Swahili in East Africa). In many cases the statement would be reworded as follows: 'English is more effective than the African languages', because the greater spread and thus geographical range of English is taken into consideration. English may, however, be less effective, even inappropriate, for communication with the older generations, because it suggests that the young generation abandon old customs and values together with the language (e.g. food habits, festivities and greetings). Another communicative argument which is often heard from educated Africans is that 'Complex concepts can be expressed more easily in English than in an African language' (A2). This is not only a question of language or register development (for African languages see chapter 6), but is also determined by what is considered complex and by traditions of language use; since English has, through its position in the educational system, always been used to express (what are usually considered complex) technical, scientific or intellectual concepts, it is only to be expected that particularly the teachers, who have often had no formal training in African languages, are so used to it that only intensive efforts can change these habits.

National arguments are deployed within the context of the modern African nation-state in the attempt and need to maintain and strengthen it. Therefore, it is understandable that national arguments may at first sight work against English. Whereas the argument 'Favouring English means neglecting an important aspect of the national identity' (A3) refers to the cultural aspect of the nation-building process, the argument 'Favouring English may create class differences in the nation' (A4) refers to the democratic participation of all social groups in this process. Fortunately for the English language, many Africans believe that an African identity can also be expressed in English and that English may indicate class but does not necessarily create it – this depends on the educational opportunities (and financial background of the family). Although nationbuilding is very important for African nation-states, it is very complex, too. Thus many people in a nation-state with one African lingua franca (e.g. Kenya or Botswana) would not subscribe to a simplistic argument like 'A decline in the use of English would strengthen national unity' (A5), because they know that in reality it does not. But people in a nation-state with none or several lingue franche may still believe this (e.g. Zambia), although national unity could, of course, also be achieved by widespread overlapping multilingualism in African languages (if every African had to learn another national/African language at school).[2] There are also, however, national arguments put forward to support English in a nation-state. A strong ESL argument would be 'English-medium education means equal chances for all children in their future, because English is the basis for all further education' (A6), but this is often only moderately supported, since, as has been shown above (chapter 4), it is English language *teaching* and the achieved standard which are considered essential, and not English language use in other subjects. This interpretation is supported by the fact that an EIL argument like 'Only a sufficient knowledge of English can keep science and learning in the country in touch with world-wide developments' (A7) can meet with overwhelming consent in many anglophone African countries. The significance of English for international communication may be difficult to understand, because English is not only seen rightly as a medium for transmitting science and technology and information management (cf. Grabe 1988), but also as a means of communication with foreign development workers, guests and refugees. Generally EIL arguments are more convincing in most

African states than ESL arguments. Thus the statement 'The discouragement of English language teaching is harmful to our national interests' (A8a) would be much more fully supported than the stronger, ESL version 'The discouragement of English use is harmful to our national interests' (A8b).

Whereas these national arguments are related to the society as a whole, other instrumental and integrative arguments have a personal basis. This is most obvious when people claim 'English is useful for getting a better job' (A9), because English is seen as a personal asset, as an instrument to promote a personal career. Although this is believed by many Africans, because normally all Africans with steady positions in paid employment actually do know at least some English, English may again (cf. A4) be rather an indicator than an underlying reason for the good position, since it is also closely linked to educational background (cf. chapter 3). Nevertheless, even Africans who have little or no education themselves express the ambition that their children must learn English. The instrumental value of English (as to some extent any other additional language) is recognized by all, even those who have not benefited from it. In countries pursuing a rigorous national language policy, knowledge of the national language may be felt more important and 'For a career in the civil service it may be better not to use English but African languages' (A10), though this anti-English personal argument seems to apply to a few cases only. Personal integrative arguments are necessarily linked to national arguments, as when an individual wants to integrate into a larger community, a whole nation or a sub-group thereof. 'Speaking good English shows that someone belongs to the modern, educated society' (A11) would be a typical belief linking English with the modernizing, developing sector and the national élite. The opposite view would be that 'English is an élitist language thus separating educated Africans from the common people' (A12), which is closely linked to national arguments (especially A4).

The educational arguments are usually those most hotly debated. For a long time the belief was widespread that 'Switching to African languages as a medium of instruction would bring down the educational standards' (A13); but nowadays, with a decline in the standard of English (cf. 4.3), the validity of A13 cannot be taken for granted any longer. A closely related statement in situations where English is used as a medium of instruction would be 'If a student is good at English, he is good at other subjects, too' (A14). Although this belief is held by many people, it is difficult to prove. The educational counterpart to the national argument A3 is 'Favouring the students' use of English too much undermines principles of national education' (A15), but it is not heard very often. A very practical argument which is a great liability for English in schools is 'It is easier for students to understand concepts when they are explained in African languages' (A16). This argument sounds convincing, but in practice it poses problems (cf. A2: 'Complex concepts can be explained more easily in English').

The last, but possibly most important, arguments are cognitive. Some Africans think that 'Knowing African languages only means being less educated' (A17), believing that European languages are more 'demanding' for the brain. This belief may be a remnant of the old 'primitive languages' myth or it may be based on the observation that only those Africans who pass through further education have the chance to acquire 'good' English. An even more dangerous belief may be that 'People who do not know English, or European languages in general, lack certain basic cognitive concepts' (A18), which equates language choice with mental complexity. On the other hand, cognitive arguments against English are equally difficult to prove but are nevertheless often put forward. 'Being a foreign language English is not suitable for the African mind' (A19) is an argument that is only supported by the most ardent advocates of African languages. Similarly, 'English makes Africans too European-minded' (A20) may be used in discussions about linguistic and cultural imperialism (see chapter 4), but the relation between English and 'thinking European' is not considered as straightforward as this formulation suggests. We must also bear in mind that English is normally not replacing the African languages (and will probably never do so for the vast majority of Africans), but is rather an additional language for the wider domains beyond those for which the mother tongue is habitually used.

In this connection, one 'remedy' for improving attitudes towards English, especially among those who associate English with the colonial past or regard English as an evil influence which necessarily leads to Westernization, is the recognition of African varieties of English as pedagogical and sociolinguistic models.

7.4 Attitudes towards African varieties of English

As has been demonstrated above (see chapter 3) specifically African forms of English certainly exist, which can be heard and read as performance varieties in common usage at different levels of proficiency. But in contrast to ENL nations, England and the

United States in particular, it is not certain whether there are yet also institutionalized varieties of English in Africa, that is, national African standard Englishes which are generally accepted.

The acceptability of a national variety (if one exists) as a pedagogical and sociolinguistic norm for a speech community largely depends on the language's position in the nation. Whereas it seems clear, at least theoretically, that ENL nations establish their own national norms and codify them in dictionaries and grammars, these norms remain a subject of great controversy in ESL nations (cf. Prator 1968) and are hardly considered in EIL nations. The traditional position can be stated as follows: 'The fact is that what is correct in a language is just *what native speakers of the language say*. There is no other standard' (Hocking 1974: 58). The new liberal position is best exemplified in Halliday/McIntosh/Strevens (1964: 203f.):

> One of the most important changes that took place in the period between 1950 and 1960 was the acceptance that 'to speak like an Englishman' was not the obvious and only aim of teaching English to overseas learners. . . . Some American language teachers accept only American forms of English, but in the eyes of the British language-teaching profession one or other of the varieties of English that are growing up may in specific cases be of a kind more appropriate to the local educational systems than any form current in the British Isles. This acceptance is accorded to varieties of English such as those labelled 'Educated West African English' and so on; and obviously such acceptance makes a difference to the inventory of language teaching items.

This rather theoretical position has since been subscribed to not only by European and African linguists but also by prominent African writers and literary critics (cf. chapter 5.1). In addition to the rather defensive support of African English, there is occasionally also an aggressive one:

> If we can't decide on one Ghanaian language for the country after twenty-nine years of independence, then why shouldn't a borrowed language be 'butchered'. . . . In his heart of hearts, the youth, like many other silent Ghanaians, is protesting against an imposed language which prevents him from expressing himself in his own tongue.
>
> (Kwasi Duodu, 'The language problem', *People's Daily Graphic* 5 September 1986: 3)

Against such supporters of 'hybridization' the 'purist' side claims that 'Our people will not be fitted for citizenship of an intelligent democracy – the participatory democracy we are striving to build – until they can talk clearly, write and speak plainly, and read with understanding and enjoyment in English – the official language of the country!' (S.T. Asante, 'Falling Standard of English in Ghana', *People's Daily Graphic* 5 May 1985: 3). This opinion shows that English as an African language, in contrast to British Standard English as a European language, has to fight similar prejudices as other African languages, when cognitive arguments are put forward (cf. A18 above). Many of the arguments against African languages are also used against African varieties of English.

On the whole, the debate is far from coming to an end. 'There have been, perhaps, some rather premature christenings of "post-colonial Englishes" by liberal linguists anxious to grant linguistic independence to the new states of Asia and Africa' (Spencer's foreword in Sey 1973: ix). The general public, and especially many parents and teachers in Africa, would still prefer 'more or less' (British) Standard English as a model for African learners of English. This general ideal can be shown to be less stringently pursued at different linguistic sublevels. Whereas deviations in syntax are rarely tolerated, typically African features in pronunciation are now usually accepted. In fact, it would be considered ridiculous to mimic an Englishman's accent, a view that has also found its reflection in fiction: '. . . his attempts to adopt an air of importance were not just ridiculous but actually irritating in the special way in which the efforts of a Ghanaian struggling to talk like some special Englishman are irritating.' (Ayi Kwei Armah, *The Beautiful Ones Are Not Yet Born*. London: Heinemann 1968: 28).

This attitude has sometimes been called 'linguistic schizo-phrenia' (Kachru 1982: 44). Although Africans generally admire educated English (especially the learned style) and tend to cultivate it, 'hyper-correctness in pronunciation, especially the type that strives too obviously to approximate to RP, is frowned upon as distasteful and pedantic' (Sey 1973: 8). Thus the *chigololos* of Lusaka, students whose lives are full of pretence and illusions, often twist their tongues when talking to imitate whites, but they exaggerate and are ridiculed for speaking in a mannered foreign way. Even within African varieties it is interesting to see that features shared by many ethnic and social groups in a country are often accepted, although they may be conspicuous to outsiders and make intelligibility difficult, e.g. vowel mergers and a syllable-timed speech rhythm may be difficult for foreigners unaccustomed to these features. Other features, however, that are characteristic of some groups only are often ridiculed, stigmatized and not accepted. Such stigmatizations are, of course, culture-specific and reflect underlying sociopsychological relationships between groups. This means that features stigmatized by Africans are not necessarily the same as those stigmatized in Britain or those most saliently deviating from the British standard.

Most of the discussions about accepting a national African standard English have been concentrated in and on Nigeria. This can be attributed to two main causes: firstly, of all the ESL nations in Africa, Nigeria seems to have incorporated the English language most intensively into her national culture, and English enjoys a more stable sociolinguistic position than in most other African states. Secondly, the problem of identifying a national variety is more difficult than in other smaller and linguistically more homogeneous African states.

A closer look at the second problem reveals some of the difficulties involved in the development of a national variety. The first step is a detailed description of the performance varieties at all levels. The second is the identification of an acceptable level for a standard that would on the one hand be sufficiently close to other standards of English, especially the traditional British model, to ensure linguistic intelligibility, and on the other hand sufficiently distinct from them to convey African culture and identity. The third step is the codification of this national variety in dictionaries, grammars or teaching handbooks, the fourth the propagation of it in the national mass media. The final step would be the acceptance and widespread use of this national variety of English by an educated majority.

As has been demonstrated before, this development has not yet gained momentum in many African nations. An inter-African comparison leads to the conclusion that Ghana and particularly Nigeria have progressed most in the direction indicated above, if not in terms of public discussions about questions of acceptability and codification, then at least as far as description of a possible national variety is concerned. Jibril (1986: 59), for instance, argues that 'convergence between Northern and Southern varieties [Hausa, Yoruba and Igbo English in Nigeria] is taking place. If the sociolinguistic educational factors which favour this convergence continue to exist, a de-regionalized variety of Nigerian English may well emerge in the near future.' The state of the national discussion in Nigeria is summarized in Jibril (1987: 46f.):

> Perhaps the most controversial issue in English Language Studies in Nigeria is that of Nigerian English. Scholars such as Banjo, Adetugbo, Adesanoye and Odumuh affirm the existence of Nigerian English which they describe as the totality of the varieties of English used in Nigeria. It is distinct from Pidgin English though it may relate to it in a given continuum. Nigerian English has developed distinct phonetic, phonological, lexical and syntactic characteristics which are quite stable and which cannot be regarded as deviations from a native norm which Nigerians do not, in any case, aspire to approximate. This is also my position.
>
>   Within this school of thought, there are some scholars such as Odumuh (1984) who not only aggressively assert the existence of Nigerian English but also claim that there is already a standard version of it which we should codify and teach in our schools in place of a foreign grammatical model. This is an extreme position which few people share with Odumuh.
>
>   Most of those who accept Nigerian English as a reality neither propose it as a model nor seek to wipe it out of existence. They recognize, instead, that it is the natural result of attempting to learn a second language and of using that language in social and affective domains, among others. Nigerians will acquire Nigerian English whether or not they are taught in it, so attention is to be focussed on supplementing this variety of English with a native-like model in order to enhance the international intelligibility of Nigerians. In other words, English teaching, especially at the tertiary level, should be consciously bi-dialectal. . . .
>
>   However, other scholars, such as Oji . . . urge that 'The death-knell of Nigerian English should be sounded "loud and clear" as it has never existed, does not exist now, and will never see the sun of day' [sic]. Oji holds the position that well-educated Nigerians 'do not consciously speak or write the so-called Nigerian English' except in error, while the acceptance of error, he says, is illogical.

Other nations, such as Kenya and Zambia, may follow the Nigerian example in the future. But nowhere in Africa has a distinct national standard variety of English (apart from pidgins and creoles) developed as far as in India, or the Caribbean. This can be shown in very practical matters, such as the guidelines for language teaching or the reactions to radio broadcasts.

> The rules laid down by the book are 'Standart [sic] English'. But in many cases the authors were in a dilemma, whether to include as an error a certain form or expression on the simple grounds that it

deviates from Standart English; or whether to recognize that certain
deviations from Standart English have become so firmly established in
this or that part of Africa that to pillory them here would seem
fastidious and uncharitable. In the absence of any consensus about
the status of 'Nigerian English' or 'East African English' the dilemma
remains. However, the authors have partially overcome it by
disregarding a number of common lexical deviations from Standart
English, even though these cannot be said to have achieved formal
acceptance in the countries where they are used.

(Jowitt/Nnamonu 1985: vii)

When Radio Botswana ceased in January 1985 to rebroadcast
several BBC news magazine programmes local substitutes were
criticized for using inexperienced broadcasters with a poor
command of spoken English. Although this is a matter of
experience and of equipment it is also indicative of a variety
conflict. Le Page/Tabouret-Keller (1985) have shown that diffuse
speech communities, who do not feel that they control a unique
linguistic variety, often regard their speech forms negatively.

Again, differences between nations in Africa at various stages
of the ENL/ESL/EIL continuum can be identified. Where
English is used in sociocultural functions expressing an African
identity (i.e. in ESL nations), the acceptability threshold is lower;
where it is only used in international communicative sectors, it is
higher.

As in many other respects, South Africa is a special case here.
Although there have been codifications of South African English
pronunciation and vocabulary since the beginning of the century,
it is still a long way until 'something in the nature of a "General
Southern African English" (like "General American") might
ultimately emerge' (Branford, W. 1987: xi). For most of the
descriptions of South African English neglect the black majority
of the population, and future developments linguistically will
largely depend on also identifying a 'Black South African
English'. But this is not only a problem of linguistic description,
but also of the sociopolitical climate, which must allow a variety
to develop and stabilize so that it can become accepted as a
linguistic badge of black identity. This leads us to the fundamental issue of language attitudes.

7.5 English and African identity

The close relationship between language and identity has been
emphasized in recent sociolinguistic research, which includes
phenomena of forming, presenting and maintaining individual

and group identity. In this context 'identity' is closely related to 'identify', i.e. 'to recognize some entity as part of some larger entity', so that people can identify themselves with a group, a tradition, an attribute shared by others, etc.; speakers use language and associated phenomena and values to signal such an identity, whereas hearers take up these clues. The issue of identity shows itself on at least two levels, that of individual or personal and that of group or national identity.

On the personal level every utterance of the individual can be interpreted as an 'act of identity' (Le Page/Tabouret-Keller 1985), revealing the supposed properties of the various model groups with which the speaker wishes to be associated or distinguished from. The sociolinguist interested in English in Africa asks how Africanness is expressed through and in this language and in what way particular features of the varieties available in Africa are used by speakers to identify themselves with and dissociate themselves from language groups with whom these features are associated. Whereas in Britain 'dropping one's aitches' may not be fashionable, albeit an important feature of group solidarity, the same may apply to avoiding truly centrally pronounced central vowels, to neglecting vowel length distinctions, or even to 'confusing' 'r's and 'l's in Africa. Such speech markers are correlated with cognitive categories of group membership (cf. Williams 1989). Although indexical markers generally serve as perceptual clues on three levels, as group markers, individualizing markers and affective markers, only the first type concerns us here.

The interrelationship of language forms and personal identity is illustrated in the following general model:

There is a dyad consisting of speakers A and B. Assume that A wishes to gain B's approval. A then
(1) samples B's speech and
    (a) draws inferences as to the personality characteristics of B (or at least the characteristics which B wishes to project as being his);
    (b) assumes that B values and approves of such characteristics;
    (c) assumes that B will approve of him (A) to the extent that he (A) displays similar characteristics;
(2) chooses from his speech-repertoire patterns of speech which project characteristics of which B is assumed to approve.
(Giles/Powesland 1975: 158)

These principles of accommodation are largely unconscious or the effectiveness of the strategy depends largely on the fact that the receiver at least should not notice the strategy, although of course perhaps applying it, too, to convey a particular personal image. All this works within the general social network of power and solidarity relations in the community.

On the national level more or less conscious political decisions and development strategies are involved. Like many other things imported from Europe, such as religious denominations, money economies, legal systems, English is first of all a foreign object, although obviously a necessary one. A modern African society cannot reject a formerly European, but now international, language completely; but it cannot and will not, for reasons of practicality as well as of identity, follow the imported model very closely either.

This has hardly been stated explicitly by politicians or educationalists. The farthest they go is something like the following from a document issued by the Zimbabwean Ministry of Education and Culture (1982) shortly after independence:

> For Zimbabwe, L2 learning has to be associated more and more with features of the learners' culture and to reject what are considered alien and unacceptable features of the second-language culture – usually to *reinforce the individual's sense of his own culture*. Methods influenced by such considerations and certainly teaching materials will reflect attitudes towards *the desired cultural context* of L2 learning.

It is symptomatic that this refers explicitly to teaching methods and materials and not to language form. As the reality, of language-learning background as well as of language forms, clearly ridicules the maintenance of the imported model, an indigenous model will more implicitly than explicitly be accepted according to the motto: 'We cannot be like the others, but we do not even want to be like them anyway.'

The following model (Figure 7.2) illustrates some of the factors involved. Up to now, however, not enough empirical research data has been collected to show clearly how and to what extent these factors play a role. When, by whom and how consistently are features of African English consciously recognized, or are the processes only unconsciously effective?

The question of identity is sometimes not easy to deal with empirically. A change in behaviour, for instance, need not necessarily indicate a change in identity. It may merely signify a change in outward circumstances or possibilities. Can we talk of a factor of identity only when it implies difference from other group or personal identities and the conscious or unconscious opportunity of choice? Although language is more closely related

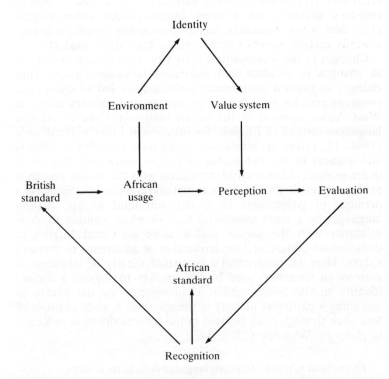

FIGURE 7.2   Factors in the process of perception, evaluation and recognition of African forms of English

to identity than many other factors it is difficult to prove an immediate link; yet a link does exist. As far as English in Africa is concerned the connection between this language and identity can be determined on three levels.[3]

I1: interlinguistic choice, i.e. the choice of using English and not other languages,

I2: intralinguistic choice, i.e. the choice of a particular variety of English, and finally

I3: conscious delimitation of certain varieties and features through overt or covert prestige.

These apply of course only if English is part of the speaker's repertoire (I1), when speakers have access to a wider range of registers, sociolects or, at least, interlanguages within English (I2), and when relatively stable community-specific attitudes towards certain varieties and features have developed (I3).

Changes in the sociopolitical matrix of a nation can also result in changes in national and individual language choice. Thus changes in general government policies have led to changes in language policies (cf. chapter 8) and several military coups in West Africa resulted in the (often temporary) use of African languages instead of English, for instance in Liberia. Breitborde (1988: 19) refers to 'interactions with new government officers and soldiers to use indigenous languages along with English in order to signify both their identification with the masses and their proficiency in English in order to obtain/retain a job'. Similarly a member of government or leader will tend to use African languages or a more mesolectal English when wanting to show solidarity with the masses and a more acrolectal English to demonstrate education,[4] modernization or adherence to Western values. Here language, and a particular variety of language, is seen as an identifier, used by the speaker to suggest a distinct identity to the hearer and/or is interpreted by the hearer as signalling a particular identity of the speaker. A vivid example of how such strategies can be used in the trifocal situation in Kenya is given by Whiteley (1973: 342):

> People tend to manipulate their language skills to their own advantage. Thus a man wishing to see a Government officer to renew a licence, for example, may state his request in Swahili to the girl typist as a suitable neutral language if he does not know her. To start out in English would be unfortunate if she did not know it, and on her goodwill depends his gaining access to authority reasonably quickly. She may reply in Swahili, if she knows it as well as he does and wishes to be cooperative; or in English if she is busy and not anxious to be disturbed; or in the local language if she recognizes him and wishes to reduce the level of formality. If he, in turn, knows little English, he may be put off at her use of it and decide to come back later; or, if he knows it well, he may demonstrate his importance by insisting on an early interview and gain his objective at the loss of goodwill from the typist. The interview with the officer may well follow a similar pattern, being shaped by the total repertoire available to each on the one hand, and on the other by their respective positions in relation to the issue involved.

Thus language choice can have its advantages and disadvantages. If somebody uses English in unacceptable contexts, sanctions

may even be imposed on the offender, as in the following story
told by Scotton (1978: 79):

> At a beer party near my home, two boys broke into talk in English.
> The reaction from the old men was bitter and they said, 'Who are
> those speaking English? Are they backbiting us? They are proud.
> Push them out!' Although the boys had not been addressing the beer
> party as such but had been talking only to each other, this use of
> English was regarded as an insult.

A similar story of intralinguistic variation, i.e. lect-variation
within one language, is given by Saah (1986: 374) from Ghana:

> My co-tenants and I had to use English because we were from areas
> where several different languages were spoken. We spoke different
> kinds of English due to our different educational backgrounds. My
> co-tenants, made up of illiterates and people with very little formal
> education, spoke 'broken English' or 'Pidgin' while I spoke the kind
> of English prescribed by grammar books. My co-tenants felt I was
> trying to distance myself from them because of the kind of English I
> spoke, while I found it difficult, as a graduate from a teachers'
> college, to speak their kind of English with its 'appalling grammar'.

Sometimes English is used deliberately to draw demarcation
lines. This also applies on the personal and on the political level.
Thus to avoid being associated with their own language group,
speakers may choose to use English to escape being asked too
many favours from their kinsmen. Similarly, Southern Sudanese
who don't want to be swallowed linguistically and culturally by
the North oppose Arabization by 'holding up the English flag', be
it in their schools or in their literary productivity. Gambians
might find it difficult to show they were different from the
surrounding Senegalese if they were not anglophone or even
anglophile. In South Africa the majority of Blacks prefer
English, as the language of liberation, to Afrikaans, the language
of oppression. Although usage in political slogans always
oversimplifies, this shows how English is used as a symbol. But
symbolic values beyond the purely functional perspective are
essential for creating or maintaining personal and national
identities.

If it is often 'said that the French of francophone Africans is
more like natively spoken French than the English of anglophone
Africans is like natively-spoken English' (Brann 1984: 314), this
may also reflect the growing distance and emancipation of many

anglophone African individuals and nations from their 'mother-land' and thus simply reflect the difference of importance attached to Africa by the European nations.

It may be necessary to express different identities through different languages or language varieties. Then code-switching takes place. In contrast to code-mixing,[5] which in principle does not indicate any change of social identity of the speaker (but possibly ambivalent feelings), code-switching usually does. A literary account of the necessity to express solidarity (through Igbo) and education (through English) at the same time is given by Achebe in his famous novel *Things Fall Apart* (London: Heinemann 1958: 74): 'The speech which had started off one hundred percent in Ibo was now fifty–fifty. But his audience still seemed highly impressed. They liked good Ibo, but they also admired English.' Often two (or even more) languages are so intricately mixed that it is difficult to say which language is spoken, as in the following examples of English and (Town) Bemba from the University of Zambia (Lusaka):

Balibomba [they worked] two days.
Tuma [only] half course *twa* [for] one day.
The other problem – *ama* [there are] parts *yengi sana* [very many].

The following example refers to a complex situation in Kenya (Scotton 1989: 338) where two Kikuyu speakers are inter-rupted by a Kisii and a Kalenjin speaker, who both switch from Swahili to English:

Kisii: Ubaya wenu ya Kikuyu ni ku-*assume* kila mtu anaelewa Kikuyu.
(=The bad thing about Kikuyus is assuming that everyone understands Kikuyu)
Kalenjin: Si mtumie lugha ambayo kila mtu hapa atasikia?
(=Shouldn't you use a language which every person here understands?)
WE ARE SUPPOSED TO SOLVE THIS ISSUE [with force].

The final definite switch to English indicating that the speaker wants to talk business at last, illustrates the markedness theory of code-switching, as it has been formulated by Scotton. She emphasizes the social parameters, as opposed to the formal ones: '. . . individual switches (i.e. points at which switches occur) do not carry any social message. Rather, it is the overall pattern of using two languages which conveys social meaning. And the message is that the participants have shared and simultaneous membership in two social identities, those symbolized by each of the languages used' (Scotton 1989: 334).

Code-switching is often signalled by some form of 'hesitation phenomenon', including such hesitation markers as *anyway, so* or *you know*, which provides time for the speaker to choose the correct way to express his thoughts. A speaker who wants to complain about a development tax assessment, for instance, can express his 'civilized' socioeducational status through English and his ethnic solidarity in an African language (Kru), because both elements are crucial elements in the Liberian social structure.

> Why should I have to pay this fee just because I have relatives in Sinoe? So . . . *i kpa* [=they took].

(Breitborde 1988: 17)

The following example shows that the switch (here from Swahili to English) may also be triggered by code-mixing or even the necessary use of single English words in a modern technical context, which finally results in a complete English structure:

> *Ile* (the) accident *ilitokea alipo*lose (occurred when he lost) control *na* (and) *aka*overturn and landed in a ditch.

(Abdulaziz 1972: 211)

Code-switching and particularly code-mixing are often criticized, not only by conservative school-masters, but despite these negative attitudes there is little evidence that it leads to 'semilingualism', with reduced competence in both languages. Furthermore the phenomena are governed by relatively consistent rules. Besides practical necessities, to include certain conversation participants in the conversation or to exclude them, code-switching is often related to the fact that certain domains are customarily associated with a certain language use and involves set phrases from these domains and attitudes associated with certain varieties and their users. Such associations and rules naturally apply to all languages in the multilingual matrix of an African community.

What is particular about English in comparison with other languages today is that English has a special range in terms of geographical, and perhaps parallel identificational, extension. It may signal international, national and subnational identities. It can be seen not only as the language spoken 'from Cairo to the Cape', but also as the language of the modern educated family, the language of the progressive, modernizing nation or the language of the international or pan-African technical communication network. An important change in language attitudes is evident in the fact that English today is no longer closely associated with the former Americo-Liberian settlers in Liberia, the colonial administration in Nigeria, the White Highland settlers in Kenya, white minority rule in the Republic of South Africa, and so on. African speakers can choose even within the English language between different varieties or variational features in order to signal (usually unconsciously) different associations of identity, if this type of variation lies within the speaker's repertoire. Few African speakers would wish to remind their listeners of the proverbial 'been-to', who imports Western life-style and 'Western English' wholesale into Africa, because their friends and colleagues would ridicule this non-African identity. In formal terms this means that English is intrinsically very flexible and has already developed a spectrum of variational forms. This sociolinguistically-based intralinguistic variation in English forms is most noticeable in pronunciation. The relationship of pronunciation and personal identity is emphasized in many discussions about obvious incongruencies between the prescriptive textbook ideal and the admitted everyday practice:

> What African students and, in fact, the socio-cultural setting mock at is an affected English accent, not a natural, polished modified Received Pronunciation. Only very few Nigerians or Ghanaians would like to surrender their African personality and speak the prestigious English R.P., that is, if R.P. can be taught by non-R.P. speaking African language teachers, who form the bulk of the teaching staff.
>
> (Yankson 1989a: 149)

As languages are generally multidimensional and multifunctional entities, different functions (i.e. in the broadest sense, communicating information or signalling identity) can be 'attached' to different formal dimensions of language. To what extent is it correct, for instance, that syntactic unity is 'the common bond' of a language, since grammar carries the communicative information, whereas pronunciation expresses the speaker's individuality or personality (cf. Hudson 1980: 48)? If this holds true the simplest way of explaining accepted varieties of African English is the concept of 'nuclear fission' on different levels of the acceptability hierarchy. Part of English (syntax and morphology) is taken over as a recognized culture-free international means of communicating information, part of it (pronunciation and discourse) is seen as European-based and must be modified on the basis of common usage and acceptability as a culture-specific means of signalling sociolinguistic identity. What has been suggested on an empirical basis for Indian English (by Sahgal/Agnihotri 1985) can be confirmed for African English: syntactic deviation is tolerated to a lesser degree than phonetic deviation and it is not so often associated with a particular social or ethnic group. This does not mean that everything is allowed in pronunciation because some deviations are clearly stigmatized, whereas others are rarely noticed.

Thus sociolinguistic research on English in Africa attempts to define specific African national identities as resting on various distinct concepts of cultural identity as well as on various overlapping regional identities; in this overall framework language is seen as a means of expressing, together with a message, a personal and/or a group identity, which is chosen by the speaker and interpreted by the hearer.[6] Thus if a market woman responds in English to a white man's question in an African lingua franca, she expresses one part of her identity, just as when she talks in her mother tongue to her market neighbours to express another. Similarly, a hotel manager may talk in basilectal English to his African cleaners and in acrolectal English to his foreign guests. These examples support the idea of modern ethno-psychological research that personal identity is often to be seen as the sum of heterogeneous overlapping identities. Fundamental categories of human social identity, such as age, sex, ethnicity, social class and situation, are reflected in language and its variation, and thus attitudes towards language phenomena can give us important clues to the dimensions of human nature.

Notes

1. The high prestige of English can also be seen in the EIL country Egypt, where research by El-Dash/Tucker (1975) shows that Egyptian English always occupies a safe middle position between Classical and Colloquial Arabic (except in 'religiousness'). This study is also interesting because it uses the matched guise technique, recordings of the same speaker in different dialects, to avoid the influence of differences in voice quality, etc. Because it is extremely difficult to find really ambilingual speakers and listeners and adequate places for recording and testing, this technique has hardly been used in Africa.

2. This is an important educational aim where English is used as a link language. In Nigeria, for instance, plans exist to introduce a major Nigerian language as a subject in addition to the mother tongue and English; in Zambia it has been suggested that French should be abolished as a secondary school subject and replaced by African languages.

3. Milroy (1987: 171), who calls inter- and intralinguistic choice code-switching and style-shifting respectively, argues rightly that the distinction has no theoretical justification, because speakers in multilingual communities may express similar culture- or network-specific social meanings or identities by either means.

4. Although English usually signals 'plus education', 'socially meaningful features seem to vary both in their saliency and their connotations from situation to situation (Scotton 1976a: 928). Thus when a newsreader uses English this does not emphasize his education, but the status of English as an official language, and the signal 'plus education' may be interpreted as positive by superiors at work, but as negative by friends from early schooldays.

5. The distinction between code-switching and code-mixing is unclear on the formal as well as on the interpretative/indexical level. A standard definition from the formal perspective is that code-switching is intersentential and code-mixing is intrasentential, thus the former 'does not necessitate the interaction of the grammatical rules of the language-pair involved in the speech event, whereas CM [code-mixing] does' (Bokamba 1989: 279). Often however code-switching is used as a cover term for both phenomena.

6. The choices and interpretations occur, of course, largely subconsciously, although most of the underlying stereotyped notions can be elicited, and only when external practical necessities, such as knowledge of languages and varieties, do not prevent a choice. Similar problems are related to other identifiers, such as reading habits or clothes, which also depend on availability but indicate identity if there is a choice.

Chapter 8

Language Policy and the Future of English in Africa

This survey of English in Africa has so far shown that while English is already deeply rooted in the multilingual life of some African countries, in other countries it is seen as a rival to national languages and as only a temporary necessity. The future of English in African countries will largely depend on the language policies of their respective national governments. This is why it is necessary to analyse the processes and alternatives in language policies more closely. From a more general perspective the past and the future development of English in Africa can be summarized in a model of life-cycles of African varieties.

8.1 Alternatives in language policies

The following flow diagram (Figure 8.1) combines the most important general processes involved in language planning in an idealized model, and can serve as the basis for a discussion of the role of English. It emphasizes that there are two sides to language planning, a linguistic and a political one, usually of a top-down nature, i.e. the decisions are taken at the top level and several filters may be responsible for quite different results at the bottom. The processes are modelled on the developments and discussions in the Sudan, Nigeria, Kenya, Tanzania, Zambia and Zimbabwe, where such processes are richly documented.

The sociolinguistic situation, including the knowledge and use of a language, and the attitudes towards it among certain groups of the population, is the basis for all political measures. These measures may be taken because of sociopolitical evaluations of the functions of languages,[1] such as the desire to ensure efficient communication between the administration in all parts of the

LINGUISTIC SIDE   POLITICAL SIDE

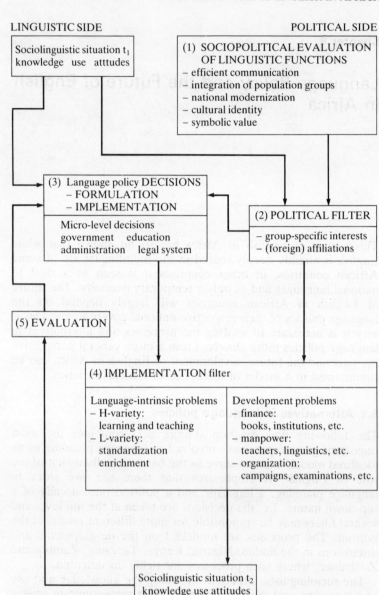

Sociolinguistic situation t_1
knowledge use atttudes

(1) SOCIOPOLITICAL EVALUATION
    OF LINGUISTIC FUNCTIONS
    – efficient communication
    – integration of population groups
    – national modernization
    – cultural identity
    – symbolic value

(3) Language policy DECISIONS
    – FORMULATION
    – IMPLEMENTATION

Micro-level decisions
government   education
administration   legal system

(2) POLITICAL FILTER
    – group-specific interests
    – (foreign) affiliations

(5) EVALUATION

(4) IMPLEMENTATION filter

Language-intrinsic problems
– H-variety:
   learning and teaching
– L-variety:
   standardization
   enrichment

Development problems
– finance:
   books, institutions, etc.
– manpower:
   teachers, linguistics, etc.
– organization:
   campaigns, examinations, etc.

Sociolinguistic situation t_2
knowledge use attitudes

FIGURE 8.1   Flow diagram of phases and factors in language policy

country, to integrate certain population groups into the wider national unity, to foster national industrialization and moderniza- tion, to create or stabilize the cultural identity of the nation as a whole, or simply to promote a certain language or language variety because of its symbolic value. How these factors are weighed obviously depends on the government's more general philosophy concerning nation-building and development (cf. Table 8.1). The outcome of these language policy processes will basically be either exoglossic, i.e. neglecting African languages in favour of the European language(s), or endoglossic, i.e. favour- ing African languages at the expense of the European lan- guage(s). (For a comprehensive description along these lines see Reh/Heine 1982.)

It is worth noting here that whereas language policy decisions are sometimes announced very loudly the filters work more quietly. The reason why policy and practice are so incongruent in many African nations is that before, during and even after the many stages of the decision-making process, especially at the micro-level, filtering occurs during the implementation phase in schools and offices. The second filtering process takes place in practical implementation, because not only language-intrinsic problems but also general development problems need to be overcome; and again political influences may be a help or a hindrance. The final phase in our flow diagram, often neglected, is the evaluation phase. After a certain period the sociolinguistic situation needs to be re-examined and compared with the envisaged results of the language policy formulation phase. If it is considered necessary, a reformulation or reimplementation of the language policy may take place.

What is the role of English in the whole process and in each phase? The linguistic functions are generally in favour of English when sociopolitical priority is given either to efficient com- munication on higher levels, i.e. of a nation-wide and interna- tional scope, or to national modernization, because this normally involves strong foreign affiliations. Here the interdependence of the priority allocation and the political filter can be seen. International affiliations normally work in favour of a more international variety of English; but when the cultural identity 'card' is played, it is in favour of an African variety of English. The integration of different population groups can only be seriously attempted by means of a very extensive English language teaching programme, when no African lingua franca is available as a link language.

The political filter very often works in favour of English,

because politicians in power tend to wish to maintain the status quo (including their own position). This is, however, only one group with specific interests, and not only the national but also the regional and international groups may want to have a say in the matter. Although English-speakers are not really a pressure group as such, they are, through their generally higher level of education, certainly well represented in many influential and privileged groups. Even after an overall formulation of language policy against English these groups may water down all micro-level decisions within their scope of influence or refuse to help with the implementation. They may, however, reinforce decisions in favour of English.

The implementation filter acts partly against, and partly in favour of, English. As a socially 'high' variety (Ferguson 1959) English normally poses enormous intrinsic problems for wide-spread language learning and teaching because its structures are less familiar to the learners than those of the African languages around them. On the other hand, African languages may still be going through a phase of language standardization and enrichment; furthermore they will certainly lack the grammars, dictionaries and textbooks for all educational and age levels, such as are already available for English. This now touches on general questions of development, which often support English indirectly as they support the status quo, i.e. what is practicable or already available within the constraints of finance, manpower and organization. This is the reason why old books are still in use and old teaching methods still in practice in many African schools (see Blakemore/Cooksey 1981 in general).

The final question about our flow diagram, of particular interest to the linguistic scholar, must be: where does linguistic research come into the picture? On the linguistic side there are the necessary descriptions of the sociolinguistic situation, which should be the basis of language policy decisions and evaluations. As has been shown above, research into knowledge of, use of and attitudes towards languages in Africa is rare and, what is more, research methods in this field are still being developed. Therefore, the linguistic and sociolinguistic bases for decision-making are often insufficient, since not enough fieldwork data are available. In the other areas of the language policy process linguists could be valuable partners for politicians, administrators and educationalists, complementing their views in the identification, preparation, implementation and evaluation of language policy projects.

After all these considerations of language policy in principle, a closer look at some practical examples of how English has been treated in language policy projects or campaigns seems valuable. This, however, is more difficult than it appears, for three reasons.

First, as most language policy campaigns in Africa were launched to promote African languages, project descriptions normally do not deal with English explicitly unless simply to mention it as a remnant of colonialism that has to be replaced. Secondly, as evaluations of language policies are very rare, repercussions on English, the reverse side of language policy, can only be indirectly estimated. Thirdly, as English has quite a positive image among Africans, campaigns to promote English have seldom been necessary; it has been sufficient to adopt a *laissez-faire* policy, or to provide the means to allow more English classes to take place, books to be published, etc.

Although most of the decisive governmental and institutional efforts in language policy have been undertaken in the last thirty years, language policy in Africa has, of course, a much longer tradition. From the times of the first missionaries and the first soldiers and administrators onwards political micro-decisions on language had to be made: in which language was the church service to be conducted, in which language was the teaching to be carried out, in which language were military commands to be given, in which language were official decrees to be proclaimed, etc.? The following example (Table 8.1) from what is today Tanzania illustrates a particularly complicated historical development of language policies resulting from the changing underlying dominant political objectives of two different colonial powers, as language policies have, of course, always been subordinate to more general political objectives.

Language planning should, however, not only be able to explain developments in the past but also provide guidelines for the future. It is thus possible to use our flow diagram (Figure 8.1) to analyse various policy alternatives for a particular country. This is particularly challenging for politically and linguistically complex cases such as South Africa.[2] Any future government on the basis of majority rule will have to deal with the sociolinguistic and educational heritage of the apartheid system. Although there are the two sides of language planning, status planning, i.e. language use down to the micro-level, and corpus planning, i.e. vocabulary expansion, grammar codification and various methods of standardization (cf. chapter 6), this model will concentrate on the former, which includes the role of English, Afrikaans and the various black African languages. As the implementation filter is less of a problem in South Africa than in other African states the

TABLE 8.1 The historical development of language policies in East Africa/Tanzania: a typological approach

Phase	Beginning	Name and status	Sociolinguistic concept	Languages promoted	Superordinate political objectives
I	1885	German East Africa; colony	exoglossic bilingual	G + Sw	modernization
II	1907	German East Africa; colony	endoglossic bilingual	Sw + G	efficiency, penetration
III	1919	Tanganyika British mandate	endoglossic bilingual	Sw + E	East African integration, neglect
IV	1945	Tanganyika British trust territory	exoglossic bilingual	E + V	modernization, nation-building
V	1961	Tanganyika/ Tanzania (United) Republic	exoglossic bilingual	E + Sw	modernization, nation-building
VI	1967	Tanzania United Republic	endoglossic monolingual	Sw	self-reliance, nationalization
VII	1981	Tanzania United Republic	endoglossic bilingual	Sw + E	efficiency, modernization

Key: (G = German, Sw = Swahili, E = English, V = vernaculars

sociopolitical evaluations and the political filter are decisive. Reagan (1987) has broadly identified five options:

(1) English as the sole medium of instruction;
(2) initial instruction in the mother tongue and switch to English in the fourth year;
(3) national languages at least throughout primary education;
(4) Afrikaans–English dual medium education;
(5) (regional) national language – English dual medium education.

The first option certainly has the support of the English mother-tongue speakers (of British and Indian origin), is gaining ground among the coloured groups, which were historically strongly oriented towards Afrikaans, and has symbolic value as the language of liberation among Blacks. It is associated with the liberal opposition and has pragmatic international value. It would, however, contribute to maintaining a social stratification in the country. The second option is attractive because it helps the children to adjust to the school environment and would give them time to acquire some mastery of English – and is thus favoured by many other African nations. Yet, in the South African situation it may be felt to be too close to the structure of 'Bantu education'. This also discredits the third alternative, which smacks too much of the old *divide-and-rule* policy. The fourth alternative, which is in principle a continuation of the present bilingual policy, would be pressed for by the Afrikaner community, still the majority of the white population, but is unlikely to be accepted by the black majority. The fifth alternative could be followed on a decentralized or a regional basis with the dominant language (e.g. Zulu in Natal, Southern Sotho in the Orange Free State and Afrikaans in the Western Cape) in addition to English. This would be a compromise combining mother-tongue education with English and ensure that white children acquire competence in one black language (except perhaps in the Western Cape).

Whatever the political and educational future may look like in detail the place of English is hardly threatened in South Africa, because it combines more positive evaluations and more reinforcements and fewer restrictions through the various filters than anywhere else on the continent.

Language policy is particularly demanding because languages are a very sensitive political topic since they affect the personal identity of every speaker (cf. chapter 9.3). In the name of linguistic democracy all African languages may expect some form of official recognition and promotion. In a highly complex multilingual society it is of course neither feasible nor desirable to allocate official functions to every minority language, because that would enclose their speakers in little self-contained ghettos. As African societies are developing into pluralistic, closely knit, political, economic and communicative networks, languages of wider communication are also important for nations and individuals. This means that only some kind of functionally adjusted multilingualism can achieve a satisfactory equilibrium between the legitimate pride in the mother tongue and the wider communicative range of additional languages. Thus African

citizens expect from their politicians as decision-makers satisfactory functional roles for the African mother tongues or languages
of ethnic affiliation combined with adequate access through
education to languages of wider communication. This means that
the functional distribution of English and African languages in a
modern nation-state is not an either/or, but a more/less option.

On the whole it is quite remarkable how stable the position of
English has been. Since independence, more than three decades
ago, the position of English in most African states has not
changed drastically. This explains why it is still possible to talk of
'English-speaking' states as opposed to 'French-speaking' or
'Portuguese-speaking' states (although they have always been
'African-speaking'). This post-independence development (see
chapter 1.3) makes it very likely that despite some ups (as in
Zambia) and downs (as in Tanzania) English will remain one of
the most important languages in Africa.

8.2 Life-cycles of African Englishes

In concluding our discussion of English in Africa I shall try to
analyse a more general pattern in the development of the
language since it first came to Africa. For this we can adopt
Moag's (1982) tentative model of the life-cycles of non-native
varieties, which was developed in the South Pacific. When it is
applied to Africa five phases can be distinguished, they form two
circles, however, instead of one[3] (cf. Figure 8.2):

(1) The phase of *contact* begins with the appearance of the first
English traders in the early days of colonialism in the seventeenth
century. English is used, together with other languages, European and African, for basic communicative needs in travel and
trade. From this marginal encounter marginal languages emerge,
which come to be known as pidgins and these are partly
developed later into creole languages (thus entering their own
life-cycles). Only few African interpreters are needed and those
are trained in Europe. English thus remains a typical foreign
language variety (EFL), being learnt from native speakers by
Africans who have to deal with British sailors and merchants. As
only West Africa is of importance to the British at this time (from
the sixteenth to the eighteenth century) this phase is hardly felt in
other parts of Africa.

(2) The phase of *institutionalization* begins with the rise of
imperialism in the nineteenth century, when growing religious
and scientific, but also economic and political interest in Africa

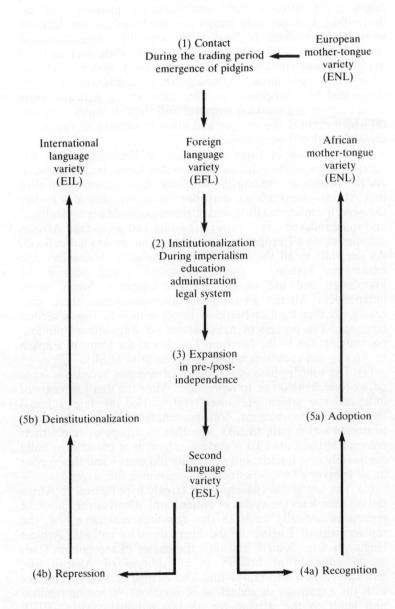

FIGURE 8.2 The life-cycles of African Englishes

arises in Europe. The missionaries and explorers are thus followed by soldiers and administrators, planters and industrialists. This not only means increased contacts for Africans with native speakers of English but also the establishment of institutions that work only through and in English, such as (part of) the administrative hierarchy, the legal system and the educational institutions. Although these institutions are still dominated by Europeans, an élite minority of Africans starts using English as a working language and English comes to be the oil which ensures the smooth and efficient running of the newly created 'anglophone' colonies.

(3) The phase of *expansion* begins in the 1940s when the independence of the African nation-states looms on the horizon. As the British are among the first colonizing nations to realize that African independence must one day come, they also realize the need for modernization and Africanization. Many agricultural and some industrial enterprises are embarked on to take African colonies along a European path of development into nationhood. As the staff in all the institutions is gradually Africanized the educational system is greatly expanded – and with it the knowledge and use of the English language. Some newly independent African governments even accelerate these processes, so that English becomes firmly established as a second language. The process of nativization, i.e. linguistic adaptation, not only applies to the functions but also to the forms of English in Africa, and second language varieties arise (ESL).

(4) The fourth phase is the phase of *decision* because it leads either to *recognition* or to *repression*. After the first few years of independence which are often still carried by late colonial impulses, African nations, both governments and peoples, have to decide which path to take, whether to accept or reject their colonial foundations. To a certain extent, it is possible to build completely new foundations or modify old ones – and this applies to all spheres of socio-political life, including languages.

(5) The last phase (which is still largely hypothetical in Africa today) completes the cycles of either path. Whereas the choice of repression logically leads to the *deinstitutionalization*, i.e. the replacement of English in the institutions by national African languages (e.g. Somali, Swahili), the choice of recognition leads to an *adoption* of English in all spheres of African life, ultimately, even into family life. The change of norms coincides with the expansion or reduction of functions; deinstitutionalization leads to the striving for an international variety (EIL), adoption may gradually lead to the recognition of a new, African

mother-tongue variety (ENL), independent of but still related (see Gimson 1982) to the parent mother-tongue variety, (British) Standard English.
A few special aspects may help to clarify the model presented above. First, in African countries which were not incorporated into the British Empire (e.g. what is Togo today) institutionalization does not take place; these nations take a short-cut from the foreign to the international language variety. Secondly, African nations have followed this cycle at different speeds and have reached different stages, or even stopped at different stages of the cycle. Thirdly, nations may be indecisive as to which cycle to follow in phase four (Kenya, for instance, is not certain whether to pursue a path of recognition or whether to follow the other path of repression, as Tanzania did for some time). Finally, as African nations have only embarked on the last phases fairly recently (later than Asian nations) it is not yet possible to say whether the two paths will really develop full circle.
This leads us to a concluding clarification of the terminology used. Moag (1982) referred to his model as life-cycles because he believes that the 'New Englishes' may emerge, develop, mature and die, just like human beings. I tend to believe that African Englishes accompany the life-cycles of the new modern African nation-states: after the birth of the new nations in the contact phase, their (forced) dependent infancy in the institutionalization phase, their growing independence in the childhood of the expansion phase, they are at last allowed to decide for themselves (in the adolescence of the new nation-state) whether to recognize or repress the inherited values and adopt or replace them in mature adulthood. For the language that means that either a new mother-tongue variety evolves or it 'falls back' to its international functions, in both ways the development comes full circle typologically, from a European to an African ENL variety or from an EFL to an EIL variety, both serving international functions.
Today the real situation is diverse and dynamic in many African states. As with other elements of the new African nation-state (e. g. the political system), Africans will decide to what extent they take over the European elements they inherited and to what extent they incorporate and develop older traditional African features to form new syncretistic elements. But whether they develop English into their essential means of expression or only use it when necessary in the international context, they will have to live with it, since the importance of English today is not based on ideological, political or cultural dominance, but on the

possibilities it offers in world-wide communication, in information retrieval, in technology and in economic exchange and cooperation. This means that English has come to Africa to stay – in some form or other.

Notes

1. Different functions of an official language are, for instance, distinguished by Okonkwo (1975), who sees the 'expressive' and 'communicative' functions as essential for first languages, the 'unifying', 'separatist' or 'participatory' functions as basic parameters in language planning in multilingual nations.
2. A similar case is obviously independent Namibia, which is often seen as a South Africa in miniature, except that the majority of the population belong to one ethnic group, the Ovambo. With its international and regional affiliations (OAU, SADCC) Namibia is certainly moving closer towards ESL status, as most African nations did immediately after independence. The envisaged move towards English as the only official language (United Nations 1981) may however be delayed by the dominance of Afrikaans in administration and commerce, as well as by the demand for a liberationist language policy with adequate emphasis on the African languages (Phillipson/ Skutnabb-Kangas/Africa 1986).
3. The main differences between the Pacific-based and the African-based model are:
    (a) Moag's model has only one life cycle, mine has two; the possibility of choosing between recognition and repression emphasizes the linguistic self-determination of the people.
    (b) Moag's variety returns to EFL status, mine returns to EIL status; this reflects the importance of English as an inter-African and international means of communication (=EIL) beyond British, American, etc. mother-tongue speakers (=EFL).
    (c) Moag's terminology differs slightly, because I avoid the term 'transportation', as it may place too much emphasis on the settler (as in Australia or South Africa) and prefer the term 'contact', which can be seen as the starting-point of an independent creole life-cycle; I add the term 'deinstitutionalization' as a counterpart of 'institutionalization' and I replace 'restriction' by 'repression' to emphasize the psychological decision-taking.
    (d) Moag merges the functional and the formal levels and sees 'indigenization' at work from the beginning of the EFL phase to the end of the ESL phase (his Figure 1 on p. 271), I restrict my terminology to the functional side and have, of course, a parallel cycle of formal development, which is constantly increasing towards the new ENL variety or increasing up to ESL status, then decreasing to EIL status.
    (e) Moag quotes Fishman's view that 'a society cannot tolerate the

luxury of two languages occupying the same functional territory'
(Moag 1982: 282) to indicate that second-language status must be
temporary, whereas I have stressed the multilingual nature of
Africa throughout this book. That implies that English may retain
a relatively stable position with ups and downs around ESL
status, from ENL/ESL to ESL/EIL, for a very long time.

Chapter 9

Problems and Perspectives of Empirical Research

Research problems have been mentioned in practically every section of this study, but a summary may serve here as an indication of more general related issues. These emphasize the comparative systematic and the applied perspective as predominant research priorities, without neglecting the fascinating possibilities of research on English in Africa for linguistic theory. In the context of the continent's vast development problems, however, ethical considerations as to the usefulness and methodological adaptability of sociolinguistic research must be taken seriously.

9.1 Research perspectives and priorities

Despite the great number of examples of linguistic and sociolinguistic phenomena presented in this survey, research on English in Africa is still far from covering the field comprehensively in any sense. As was stated at the beginning of this survey these examples from various parts of a large continent can help to initiate comparative research in other parts, where they will be confirmed or challenged. Although there are many promising individual research approaches they are not always compatible, which makes it very difficult to generalize about parallels and differences between various regions or social groups of English users; and they are not always systematic in covering several linguistic or sociolinguistic aspects in the networks of form and use, function and attitude relating to English in Africa. Obviously compatibility and systematicity suggest a more co-ordinated type of research than is often possible; this applies to both sociolinguistic and linguistic research.

A UNESCO advisory group of linguists (UNESCO 1972: 7) suggested the use of national censuses and language surveys to collect language data systematically. Although asking language questions in national censuses would be the best way to gather information from practically everybody, it also has its disadvantages. The lack of time and facilities prevents one from asking more than the most important questions in a census, and the fact that a census is always conducted by the ruling authorities may have a negative effect on the informants. Where people have enough problems with their daily survival they are less inclined to make an attempt to answer 'strange questions' asked by representatives of a state that has always had more demands on them than help for them. Language surveys (cf. the *Survey of Language Use and Language Teaching in Eastern Africa* in 2.2) have the advantage that language specialists interact directly with language users, which makes more precise and often more reliable questions and answers possible. It has always been doubtful whether self-reports are reliable and consistent, but the interpretation of statistical results is only possible for linguists who have participated in the field research. On the basis of such surveys more abstract sociolinguistic profiles may be drawn up for larger areas or whole nations.

Research at the macrolevel must be complemented by detailed study at the microlevel. Whereas large-scale quantitative studies identify general factors and problems of the sociolinguistic setting, fine-grained qualitative studies add the individual level, both techniques feed into and reinforce one another. The microlevel is also affected by numerous problems related to normal linguistic fieldwork, aggravated by the development situation (cf. Pausewang 1973). The general problems of observing and analysing language use and usage have been described in detail in many sociolinguistic handbooks (e.g. Milroy 1987). The specific ones are often neglected because they are not part of the 'scientific' approach. Tape recordings in Africa, for instance, are not only difficult because of the well-known observer's paradox but also because of the lack of equipment, energy and experience, or simply because it is not easy to avoid noisy environments. Standardized questionnaires for individual informants may prove impossible when friends and neighbours keep joining in during the interviews, which are therefore often better replaced by group discussions. In such situations culture-specific research methods may be forced on the researcher. Like non-standard speakers of native English, non-native speakers often feel too inhibited to speak English once they become aware that language is the major concern, although they enjoy talking about, again culture-specific, matters they can identify with, such as traditional stories and current economic topics. This may open up interesting sociocultural comparisons beyond 'narrow-minded' linguistic matters.

With regard to the theoretical perspectives which underlie fieldwork, many sociolinguists (e.g. Jibril 1982a) have asked themselves whether the Labovian paradigm is invalid for empirical fieldwork in Africa, or whether it merely has to be adapted. Others have favoured a more comprehensive approach, such as the ethnography of speaking suggested by Dell Hymes, or the network compromise suggested by the Milroys. Up to now the data are far too limited to give any general answer to such questions. It goes without saying, however, that the local situation must be taken into account as far as possible, not only because of the ethical implications discussed below, but also because any sociolinguistic research must reassess its own parameters critically within any specific situation.

Many sociolinguistic concepts have to be tested on much more empirical data to verify or refine them. The ENL–ESL–EIL model of macrolinguistic classification used in this book is a hypothesis assumed to have formal repercussions at all levels of linguistic analysis: phonetics, grammar, discourse. Görlach (1989) has even tried to apply it to the investigation of differences in word-formation processes and norms.

In general, linguistic research on the formal side of English in Africa can be either item-based or text-based.[1] Item-based research records features of African English at the level of pronunciation, grammar, vocabulary, discourse, etc., from the daily language experience of participants or from recorded performance. The advantage of this procedure allows the researcher to go through a large amount of spoken and/or written language material and to 'make a note' of anything that appears marked. Using this method makes it difficult, however, to judge the African features compiled according to their frequency and co-occurrence.

Text-based research collects written and/or spoken texts from various fields, domains or situations and analyses features in these texts. The advantage of this procedure is that it provides not only the raw data but also some guidelines as far as the frequency and combinations of features are concerned. All these quantitative measures are only valid, however, when the compilation of texts is done on a systematic basis so that the resulting corpus is roughly representative of actual language use and usage.[2] The text- and the item-based approaches characterized here overlap to some extent with the qualitative–quantitative paradigm. Whereas a qualitative study on language use would follow only a few multilingual speakers closely and examine diaries of language use, for instance, a quantitative study would administer questionnaires to various sections of the population. Parallel investigations could be carried out on language attitudes. What applies to descriptive analyses of English varieties is also true of African languages, with the additional problem that a model of reference must be found that can be accepted as some kind of standard. But this only illustrates again that constantly new challenges arise. From these examples it should become clear that thorough linguistic research can never restrict itself to one method alone and that different approaches must complement one another.

All approaches of formal analyses must, however, be conducted with an eye open for the variational parameters of language use: the medium, the situation, place, time and aim of communication, the number and type of interlocutors present, and their age, relationship, social status as well as ethnic, linguistic, (religious?), educational and regional characteristics, and so on. These parameters are particularly important for the socio- and psycholinguistic interpretation of the data. They are of course vital for theoretical conclusions, but also for applications in textbook writing and dictionary compilation, where stylistic and other restrictions of usage must be considered and indicated.

Such applications of empirical linguistic work have been described above in the fields of education, literary study and language policy in particular. It is important to remember that although linguistic work cannot help to solve the pressing basic needs of the developing world in any short-term way, linguists should be asked and allowed to make a supportive and long-term contribution towards the future of Africa. This can be in an indirect, descriptive way, as they compile and analyse data for dictionaries or grammars of African usage; or in a more direct, advisory way, when they recommend tolerating or 'unteaching' certain African forms of English in schools. Scholarly dictionaries and local usage can complement each other. The fruits of linguistic work can then be made available to African and European literary critics or even businessmen, who can be made aware of the connotations of African–English expressions, particularly if they differ from international English, to educational planners and politicians, who can apply language data for the benefit of the general public affected by their decisions, to teachers and school-children, who can be provided with more satisfactory applied textbooks, and to many others. All sociolinguistic work that studies the linguistic clues of speaker/writer identity can help to ensure that this identity be realized and appreciated and that prejudices and disadvantages are avoided. As linguistic research can ultimately contribute towards better communication it also contributes to better understanding and social harmony – and this is certainly an important value in many African societies.

9.2 Sociolinguistic research in Africa and the theoretical challenge

Whereas we have already seen that English in Africa can and must attract the assistance of such diverse branches of linguistics as sociolinguistics, corpus linguistics and language acquisition studies, it is also evident that it can from its particular perspective throw new light on them all. Theoretical and empirical approaches in science form a reciprocal relationship and must cross-fertilize each other.

Being a relatively new research area English in Africa can be used as a testing ground for concepts, methods and theories that have been developed in other areas and historical periods. As is the case with creole languages, it allows us to observe language processes of which in Europe and North America we can only see the effects. We can, for instance, compare the domains of loan-words from English and their phonetic and grammatical adaptation into African languages with those of Latin loan-words into Old and French loan-words into Middle English. The 'creolization' (in the sense of extreme morphosyntactic simplification) of English in the Middle Ages is being repeated in Africa today, and the acceptance of an 'indigenized' variety runs parallel to the development of a national identity. What happened then in Europe repeats itself in Africa only with a reversed diglossia: English being the low variety in medieval but the high variety in modern times, if we see English as a whole. If we distinguish different varieties of English within Africa, we witness the emancipation of a local variety in opposition to a superimposed foreign norm. Such processes have been studied in some detail by sociolinguists in Africa; transferring expressions and theories developed from present-day research in Africa to historical phenomena in Europe allows a fresh view, as well, possibly, as a new interpretation of old data. For the sociolinguist the great number of African countries provides so many examples that

Africa is almost a living laboratory of languages, with varying influences in the form of missionaries, settlers or educational policies in pre- and post-independence periods. Thus we can relate processes not only to the variety divergence between Kenya and Tanzania or the convergence between Northern and Southern Nigeria, but also to the expansion of Standard English from the fifteenth century. Why can Africa (or Tanzania to mention the most famous attempt) not abolish the diglossic situation and do away with English as late medieval England did with French? One major argument in favour of English in Africa is obviously that English is not merely the language of the former imperialists, it is also the language of science and technology and of international communication – and after all, even after the triumph of 'vernacular' English over the colonial language, Norman French, in the fourteenth century, the English had to a certain extent to accept another form of diglossia, with Latin in the Renaissance. It is worth looking at the way in which the English managed to solve their scientific terminology problems in the sixteenth century. To what extent were they able to use direct loans, with or without explanations or loan translations from Latin and Greek? Language planners in Africa can still learn from the discussions and processes in Early Modern English – and English specialists can observe similar historical discussions again today, in a very different context.

Another challenge to sociolinguists in Africa are the problems of categorization, which occur in descriptive linguistics, as in sociolinguistics. It has been observed by Africanists that African languages cannot be adequately described through European but only through African eyes. English in Africa very often falls between all categories (e.g. when article usage is described). Those developed for European languages do not apply, but neither do those for African languages. This usually favours an eclectic approach, using whatever categories seem to explain the processes best, but this may lead to a lack of descriptive coherence.

However, Africa is not only a challenge, it can also be a confirmation. In some ways research on African English can provide support for new concepts developed in the European or American context. The concept of vernacular culture, developed by Milroy (cf. 1987), is certainly evident in conscious African non-standard usages of English. Do we, therefore, have to work out how tightly Africans are knit into their social network or construct an index of 'Africanness' and relate it to language structure? Do Africans who emphasize that they are not like

Europeans also use more Africanized forms of English? Can we, for instance, distinguish political leaders on the basis of their 'Africanness' in English? Giles/Hewstone/Ball (1983) describe accent divergence as involving the exaggeration of pronunciation differences between oneself and one's addressee with the intention of dissociating oneself from the latter. This may also be the case with speakers of African English. These tendencies confirm the view that language is not only a communicative and social system, but also contributes to the construction of society and even of reality.

African English can be as inspiring to language theory as pidgins and creoles have been, in two important respects: the origin and development of certain African forms of English on the one hand and the recognition of these forms as an acceptable standard on the other. In order to discuss parallels and differences in the origin of African English and African pidgins, it may be useful to construct another typology of input-specific types of language acquisition.[3] The main distinction is usually seen as that between formal, guided and structured language learning and informal and natural language acquisition, as has been stressed by Krashen (e.g. 1981). When we look at English in Africa today we can, to a varying degree, depending on the status of English in the country, say that English is normally learnt in the educational system. This gives us the opportunity to compare varieties of school English in Africa with other school interlanguages in different parts of the continent, as well as with other more informally acquired interlanguages, i.e. in the few families that use English as a first language at home, and so on.

Whereas the context in which English learning takes place in Africa is in principle similar to that of general guided language teaching and learning elsewhere, the first languages that form the substrate in African English may be partly similar to African pidgins and creoles. The similarities with these languages are striking in many formal as well as sociolinguistic respects. As Thomason/Kaufman (1988) have shown 'creolization' and 'nativization' are two aspects of more general language contact phenomena and differ from each other more in degree than in kind. They are both types of group second-language acquisition, which is different from individual second-language acquisition (Mufwene 1990). Both substrate-specific types are characterized by a limited target language input during the learning process, because they were cut off from native speakers for social and/or political reasons. Whereas pidgin speakers were, when they developed their new language, separated from their 'masters',

TABLE 9.1   Parallels and contrasts between English-related Pidgins and
African Englishes

	African English	African Pidgins
Substrate	African	African
Target-language input	restricted	very restricted
Functional range	restricted	very restricted
Prestige	low	very low
Learning	formal	informal
Vocabulary	expansion?	reduction
Target variety	Standard English	English?
Intelligibility	high	low

who spoke English as a mother tongue, either socially, on
plantations exploiting slave labour, or even geographically, when
these masters left the trading stations or colonies, African
English began to develop to a noticeable extent only after the
massive expansion of education and after the political independence of the former African colonies. Independence had
repercussions not only in terms of physical distance – that is, after
the native-speaker teachers, administrators and some of the
settlers had left the country – but also in terms of psychological
distance; that is, it became more and more obvious that Africans
were no longer keen to be assimilated in any way into an Empire,
but were markedly different – and consciously so. The question
of African English in relation to pidgin and creole languages is
interesting also because African English is clearly taught with the
standard language as a target norm in the background, and is
thus more independent of English mother-tongue dialectal inputs
than the pidgins and creoles, with whom African English shares
the substratum of African languages.

From a comparative point of view African English can be seen
at the extreme end of a long chain of varieties stretching from
American varieties of English to Caribbean creoles, to West
African Pidgin, to varieties of West and of Eastern and Southern
African English, each with distinct subvarieties and several
connected intermediate stages: Gullah, Barbados creole, Liberian
English, Krio and Sheng, to name only the most prominent
examples. The important point in this chain is that there is no
pidgin–creole connection between West and East African
English. This means that if features of Black American English
also occur in East African English they are either substrate
features (of West and East African languages, which, however,

show quite distinct differences even within the predominant Niger–Kongo language family) or they are universal features of normal second-language acquisition (under whatever difficult sociolinguistic circumstances) and not just of pidginization/ creolization in the strict sense. We thus have a 'substrate versus universals' discussion over African English, as within pidgin and creole studies. This may help to decide a number of critical issues between substratum-minimalists and substratum-maximalists concerning the origin of specific forms.

9.3 Ethical considerations of research on English in the Third World

Ethical issues are important wherever the personal identity of people is involved. It may therefore be surprising that linguists do not in general have recourse to a widely accepted ethical code in the same way that medical researchers do. Whereas neurolinguists and psycholinguists may take ethical guidelines from neighbouring fields, sociolinguists rarely refer to anthropological ethical codes (e.g. Rynkiewich/Spradley 1971). Whereas sociolinguists in developed countries usually have to consider problems of candid recordings, of preserving the anonymity of their informants, or of restricting access to data to *bona fide* researchers (cf. Milroy 1987: 87–93), different issues arise in developing countries.

As this book aims at stimulating empirical research by both European and African scholars, it seems appropriate to look more closely at the sociopolitical and sociocultural implications of sociolinguistic research on English in Africa and the role of European scholars in it. Although Africa, as part of the Third World, with many of its nations counted among the *least* developed in this world, is known to have many more basic needs and problems, research into English may be justified in three different ways. In the first place English is seen by many Africans as a means of escaping from 'underdevelopment' on the road to modernization, which often means Westernization. Thus the language itself is seen as having a contribution to make to development and to liberation from economic and political restrictions. Secondly, English is an integral part of the life of many African nations today; not being socially neutral but rather characterizing the leading educated socioeconomic groups. Thus *intra*nationally it is an indicator of, and a factor in, the sociopolitical hierarchies of African nations. Thirdly, English plays a very important role in *inter*national communication today, and African nations must be able to use it. Thus it is internationally a means African nations can use to raise their voices and put forward their claims and demands in the world forum.

Because languages are an important part of national culture, English in Africa may as a result be a sensitive psychological and political issue. This makes the role of the European researcher, and particularly perhaps the British mother-tongue speaker difficult: Africans may feel patronized by the First World or by the former colonialists, or they may feel that an English culture is being forced upon them together with the language, preventing them from demonstrating their African identity.

These reservations, raised by language-conscious Africans in many discussions, may make empirical fieldwork by Europeans awkward. In such a case it may be an advantage if a researcher can argue that English is no longer the language of the English (or of mother-tongue speakers in general) but that it is used even by many Europeans as a second language, for instance to discuss problems of English in Africa.

In more general terms, it is worth bearing in mind the following three principles of 'objectivity and commitment in linguistic science' (cf. Labov 1982). According to the principle of linguistic autonomy, members of a speech community may choose for themselves which language (or language variety) they want to use. The principle of linguistic democracy leads linguists to support languages and language use when this fosters communication and understanding between different groups, but not when this creates social barriers. The principle of the debt incurred entails that researchers who have gained linguistic data from a speech community must make these data accessible to that speech community.

For English in Africa this means that people should not be at a disadvantage because they do not know enough English, nor should they be denied access to English if they wish to learn or use it. English should, in our opinion, be used as a means of liberation, participation and development, as a means of expressing identity and not oppressing it. And linguistic research should attempt to contribute towards this aim and hopefully present research results to the community concerned, which can be used accordingly. Even if European researchers do their best to follow these principles, they may still feel awkward doing research in a speech community without that speech community's participation. Therefore collaboration[4] between European and African linguists is in any case desirable and fruitful for both

sides: the Africans' experience in the sociolinguistic environment
helps Europeans to collect and interpret the data; the Europeans'
experience in different environments may permit interesting
comparisons. Research in Africa should be specific in so far as
this is practicable and relevant to Africa. It can, however, be
fascinating to see how new research techniques and themes
emerge from the challenges of Africa. This may also later shed
light on phenomena in other parts of the world.

Notes

1. This distinction obviously has a sociolinguistic foundation, when we
   think of Hudson's (1980) suggestion to take the linguistic item as the
   basic unit or when we consider the more traditional alternative of the
   individual speech act. Both must be seen as a multidimensional unit
   which must be characterized by as many descriptive parameters as
   possible.
2. The corpus linguistic approach offers additional possibilities for
   automatic data analysis of non-native English (cf. Schmied 1990c).
   Although some of the analyses can be done with well-known
   statistical or word-processing programmes, which are easily available
   world-wide today, the equipment and co-ordination necessary may be
   beyond the reach of many African linguists and university departments at present. This only makes co-operation in research
   methodology between North and South more imperative. The new
   International Corpus of English, its principles, guidelines and
   methods may provide a model for future research (Greenbaum 1990).
3. The fascination that theoretical linguists find in language acquisition
   and sociolinguistics is of course that they allow them to observe
   linguistic change in real time. Such developing systems 'are probably
   the only languages where notions like "free variation" apply'
   (Romaine 1988: 60). What Romaine says about pidgins holds to some
   extent for African varieties of English as well, which oscillate
   between an indigenous performance norm and an international
   institutionalized norm.
4. Collaboration between African and European researchers is a diverse
   cultural and political matter and not without its pitfalls. In some
   universities in economically most affected countries the saying goes
   that you can recognize those colleagues that have 'a link' already
   from the stationery on their desks. In others computer equipment is
   the symbol of progressive co-operation. Unfortunately, some African
   governments rely so much on these links that they allow national
   resources to dry up and leave the support of their researchers to
   foreign sponsoring agents. This has two serious consequences: first,
   direct national influence on research priorities is limited and can only
   be compensated by the establishment of a national scientific research

council and secondly, many African researchers spend more time writing new research applications and proposals than carrying out actual empirical research.

Further Reading

As this introductory work was arranged by topic the following suggestions will be listed according to region or country to enable the reader to find basic information on a particular area. They will comment briefly on some of the most important writings, which are relatively easily accessible and contribute significantly to our knowledge about English in that particular area. The suggested thirty titles are intended also as a bridge between the previous chapters and the about 800 titles in the following bibliography.

The best introduction to the historical development of the English language on the West African coast is still Spencer (1971A), although a lot more has since been published from the creolist perspective (e.g. Hancock 1986).

West Africa is covered by several important books. Sey's *Ghanaian English* (1973) is one of the best country surveys and lists grammatical, semantic and phonetic features plus some sample texts. Ubahakwe (ed. 1979) is a conference report that gives a comprehensive view of the discussion in Nigeria.

The continuum of Liberian English from the creole to the standard variety is described with examples in Singler (1981). Cameroon is the only African country covered by a volume in the text series *Varieties of English Around the World* (Todd 1982a). It offers a short introduction together with a selection of forty-one annotated texts, printed, written and oral, partly in phonetic transcription and partly on an accompanying tape. They range from Cameroon Pidgin to Standard English, with or without the influence of French.

For the sociolinguistic situations in Eastern Africa the

SLULTEA volumes are invaluable sources, although the emphasis is usually not on English but on African languages: Bender/Bowen/Cooper/Ferguson (eds 1976) for Ethiopia, Ladefoged/Glick/Criper (eds 1971) for Uganda, Whiteley (ed. 1974) for Kenya, Polomée/Hill (eds 1980) for Tanzania, Ohannessian/ Kashoki (eds 1978) for Zambia and the general books by Whiteley (ed. 1971) and Gorman (ed. 1970).

The Sudan offers an interesting case study of different language policies in the north and the south of the country. Sandell (1982) describes these and places particular emphasis on language teaching and its problems: syllabus design, examination papers and development support. Schmied (1985a) gives a broad survey of sociolinguistic and interlinguistic problems of English in Tanzania as the country moves from ESL towards EIL status. Ngara (1982) is interesting on Zimbabwe, because he describes language contact and influence of English and Shona in both directions.

South Africa provides a wealth of publications. The broad frame is set by Lanham/Prinsloo (1978) and Hauptfleisch (1978a and b, 1979, 1983), the historical development of (White) South African English by Lanham/Macdonald (1979) and a black sociopolitical perspective is added by Dunjwa-Blajberg (1980). The more practical reference works comprise J. Branford (third edition 1987), which covers exclusively words and meanings peculiar to (mainly White) South African English, Mesthrie (1989), which adds the Indian component and W. Branford (1988), which includes South Africanisms in a general *Oxford English Dictionary*.

Africa is also covered by readers in English in different parts of the world, as Bailey/Görlach (eds 1982) and Cheshire (ed. 1991), which both include condensed overviews on English in West, East and South Africa. The nativization perspective is emphasized in the collection by Kachru (ed. 1982). Todd/Hancock's *International English* (1986) combines brief entries on West, North, East and South African English and on some individual countries (Cameroon, Kenya, etc.) with explanations of the most interesting variational categories and concepts of English around the world. Invaluable information on the status and the teaching of English in individual countries can also be obtained from the British Council, which published some conference proceedings on English in Nigeria (Freeman/Jibril eds 1984) and in East Africa (British Council 1986 and 1988). For the SADCC states the conference proceedings in Ngara/Morrison (eds 1989) are very useful.

The most easily accessible scholarly journals which contain
many articles on English in Africa despite their world-wide
perspective are *World Englishes* and *English World-Wide*. They
usually give either broad overviews of the current sociolinguistic
situation, such as Breitborde (1988) on Liberia, or detailed case
studies or research reports, such as Mesthrie (1987) on word
order in South African Indian English. The scholarly and the
popular perspective are combined in *English Today* (e.g. Tripathi
1990 on Zambia). The number of journals published in Africa is
still relatively small, which is not surprising in view of the
enormous difficulties involved. Thus an undertaking such as the
Journal of English as a Second Language (published characteristically in the largest African ESL state, Nigeria) particularly
deserves to find the support of many readers. It could also
encourage the exchange of information and ideas, to which this
book and this bibliography also wish to contribute.

Bibliography

The following bibliography offers a wide selection of titles that may serve as a work of reference or guide for special research. It does not include African language works that contrast African languages with Standard English, unless at least some aspects of interference, teaching problems or language use are discussed. Newspaper articles and primary literature quoted with full references in the text of this book are also omitted. With few exceptions, the list contains only titles that are relatively easily publicly available. Thus unpublished papers, MA theses and other grey literature are not included, except where no other comparable information is available. From the remaining titles about 800 were selected subjectively from a larger data base as to their relative value for the treatment of English in Africa. For this reason only part of the educational, political, literary or pidgin and creole literature is mentioned. A wider perspective of English as a world language is offered in Viereck, Wolfgang/Edgar W. Schneider/Manfred Görlach (1984) *A Bibliography of Writings on Varieties of English, 1965–1983*. Amsterdam: John Benjamins.

ABDELMAGID, MUSTAFA MUHAMMAD (1972) 'The role of English in education in the Sudan'. PhD thesis (Edinburgh).

ABDULAZIZ, MOHAMED H. (1971) 'Tanzania's national language policy and the rise of Swahili political culture'. Whiteley, Wilfried H. (ed.), 160–78.

ABDULAZIZ, MOHAMED H. (Mkilifi-) (1972) 'Triglossia and Swahili–English bilingualism in Tanzania'. *Language in Society* 1, 197–213. Repr. Fishman, Joshua A. (ed.) (1978) *Advances in the Study of Societal Multilingualism*. The Hague: Mouton, 129–49.

ABDULAZIZ, MOHAMED H. (1982) 'Patterns of language acquisition and use in Kenya: rural–urban differences'. *International Journal of the Sociology of Language* **34**, 95–102.

ABDULAZIZ, MOHAMMED H. (1991) 'East Africa (Tanzania and Kenya)', (overview article). Cheshire, Jenny (ed.), 391–401.

ACHEBE, CHINUA (1965) 'English and the African writer'. *Transition* 4 (No. 18), 27–30.

ACHEBE, CHINUA (Second Edition 1973) 'The role of the writer in a new nation'. Killam, G.D. (ed.) *African Writers on African Writing*. London: Heinemann, 7–13.

ACHEBE, CHINUA (1975) 'The African writer and the English language'. Achebe, Chinua. *Morning Yet on Creation Day*. London: Heinemann, 55–62.

ADASKOU, K./D. BRITTEN/B. FAHSI (1990) 'Design decisions on the cultural content of a secondary English course for Morocco'. *ELT Journal* 44, 3–10.

ADEGBIJA, EFUROSIBINA (1989a) 'Lexico-semantic variation in Nigerian English'. *World Englishes* 8, 165–77.

ADEGBIJA, EFUROSIBINA (1989b) 'The implications of the language of instruction for nationhood: an illustration with Nigeria'. *ITL. Review of Applied Linguistics* 85/86, 25–50.

ADEKUNLE, MOBOLAJI A. (1970) 'Toward a realistic approach to problems of English instruction in West Africa'. *English Language Teaching Journal* 24, 269–78.

ADEKUNLE, MOBOLAJI A. (1972) 'Multilingualism and language function in Nigeria'. *African Studies Review* 15, 185–207.

ADEKUNLE, MOBOLAJI A. (1974) 'The standard Nigerian English in sociolinguistic perspective'. *Journal of the Nigerian English Studies Association* 6 (1), 24–37.

ADEKUNLE, MOBOLAJI A. (1978a) 'Language choice and the Nigerian linguistic repertoire'. *West African Journal of Modern Languages* 3, 114–26.

ADEKUNLE, MOBOLAJI A. (1978b) 'Oral English in Nigeria: the sociolinguistic realities'. *Lagos Review of English Studies* 1 (1), 11–21.

ADEKUNLE, MOBOLAJI A. (1979) 'Non-random variation in the Nigerian English'. Ubahakwe, Ebo (ed.), 27–42.

ADENIRAN, ADEKUNLE (1974) 'A functionalistic view of stylistic restriction in Nigerian English'. *Journal of the Nigerian English Studies Association* 6 (1), 20–1.

ADENIRAN, ADEKUNLE (1979a) 'Nigerian élite English as a model of Nigerian English'. Ubahakwe, Ebo (ed.), 227–41.

ADENIRAN, ADEKUNLE (1979a) 'Personalities and policies in the establishment of English in Northern Nigeria (1900–1943)', *International Journal of the Sociology of Language* 22, 57–77.

ADESANOYE, F.A. (1973) 'A Study of Varieties of Written English in Nigeria'. PhD thesis (Ibadan).

ADESANOYE, F.A. (1979) 'Formality as an aspect of unreadability in Nigerian English'. Ubahakwe, Ebo (ed.), 184–99.

ADESINA, SEGUN (1977) *Planning and Educational Development in Nigeria*. Lagos: Educational Industries Nigeria Ltd.

ADETUGBO, ABIODUN (1977) 'Nigerian English: fact or fiction'. *Lagos Notes and Records* **6**, 128–41.

ADETUGBO, A. (1979a) 'Appropriateness and Nigerian English'. Ubahakwe, Ebo (ed.), 137–66.

ADETUGBO, A. (1979b) 'Nigerian English and communicative competence'. Ubahakwe, Ebo (ed.), 167–83.

ADEY, A.D. (1977) 'South African "Black" English: some indications'. *English Usage in South Africa* **8**, 35–9.

ADEYANJU, THOMAS K. (1979) 'English grammatical structure and the Hausa student: problem areas'. *IRAL (International Review of Applied Linguistics in Language Teaching)* **17**, 349–57.

ADEYINKA, A.A. (1973) 'The impact of secondary school education in the Western State of Nigeria'. *Comparative Education* **9** (3), 151–5.

AFOLAYAN, ADEBISI (1968) 'The Linguistic Problem of Yoruba Learners and Users of English'. PhD thesis (London).

AFOLAYAN, ADEBISI (1974) 'Politeness in English'. *Journal of the Nigerian English Studies Association* **6** (1), 57–64.

AFOLAYAN, ADEBISI (1977) 'Acceptability of English as a second language in Nigeria'. Greenbaum, Sidney (ed.) *Acceptability in Language.* Paris: Mouton, 13–25.

AFOLAYAN, ADEBISI (1978) 'Towards an adequate theory of bilingual education for Africa'. Alatis, James E. (ed.), 330–90.

AFOLAYAN, ADEBISI (1984) 'The English language in Nigerian education as an agent of proper multilingual and multicultural development'. *Journal of Multilingual and Multicultural Development* **5**, 1–22.

AFOLAYAN, ADEBISI/OBAFEMI AWOLOWO (1987) 'English as a second language: a variety or a myth?' *Journal of English as a Second Language* **1**, 4–16.

AFRICA, H.P. (1977) 'The use of English in Zambia'. *Bulletin of the Zambia Language Group* **3**, 21–5.

AFRICA, H.P. (1980) 'Language in education in a multilingual state: A case study of the role of English in the educational system of Zambia'. PhD thesis (Toronto).

AFRICA, H.P. (1983) 'Zambian English: myth or reality'. Lusaka: University of Zambia, Dept of Literature and Languages.

AGHEYISI, REBECCA M. (1971) 'West African Pidgin English: Simplification and Simplicity'. PhD thesis (Stanford).

AGHEYISI, REBECCA N. (1977) 'Language interlarding in the speech of Nigerians'. Kotey, Paul F.A./Haig Der–Houssikian (eds), 97–110.

AGHEYISI, REBECCA N. (1984) 'Linguistic implications of the changing role of Nigerian Pidgin English'. *English World-Wide* **5**, 211–33.

AGHEYISI, REBECCA N. (1988) 'The standardization of Nigerian Pidgin English'. *English World-Wide* **9**, 227–41.

AGHEYISI, REBECCA/JOSHUA A. FISHMAN (1970) 'Language attitude studies: a brief survey of methodological approaches'. Anthropological Linguistics **12**, 137–57.

AKERE, FUNSO (1978a) 'Grammatical competence and communicative competence in relation to the users of English as a second language'. *Lagos Review of English Studies* **1**, 22–32.

AKERE, FUNSO (1978b) 'Socio-cultural constraints and the emergence of Standard Nigerian English'. *Anthropological Linguistics* **20**, 407–21. Repr. Pride, John (ed.) (1982), 85–99.

AKERE, FUNSO (1979) 'Evaluation criteria for a local model of English pronunciation: an experimental study of attitudes to the accents of English used by Africans'. *Indian Journal of Applied Linguistics* **5**, 80–100.

AKERE, FUNSO (1980a) 'Verbal strategies in communal meetings. Code-switching and status manipulation in a bi-dialectal Yoruba speech community'. *Language Sciences* **2** (1), 102–26.

AKERE, FUNSO (1980b) 'Evaluation criteria for a local model of English Pronunciation'. *Lagos Review of English Studies* II, 19–39.

AKERE, FUNSO (1981) 'Sociolinguistic consequences of language contact: English versus Nigerian languages'. *Language Sciences* **3** (2), 283–304.

AKERE, FUNSO (1982) 'Language use and language attitudes in a Yoruba suburban town: a sociolinguistic response to the factors of traditionalism and modernity'. *Anthropological Linguistics* **24**, 344–62.

AKINNASO, F. NIYI (1980) 'The sociolinguistic basis of Yoruba personal names'. *Anthropological Linguistics* **22**, 275–304.

ALATIS, JAMES E. (ed.) (1978) *International Dimensions of Bilingual Education*. Georgetown: Georgetown University Press.

ALEXANDRE, PIERRE (1968) 'Some linguistic problems of nation–building in Negro Africa'. Fishman, Joshua A./Charles A. Ferguson/Jotirindra Das Gupta (eds), 119–27.

ALLAN, EDWARD JAY/HAZEL MAE RELTON (1977) 'Language use and attitudes among employers of HSIU graduates in Addis Ababa'. Kotey, Paul F.A./Haig Der-Houssakian (eds), 111–19.

ALLAN, KEITH (1978) 'Nation, tribalism and national language: Nigeria's case'. *Cahiers d'Etudes Africaines* **18** (3), 397–415.

ALLAN, KEITH (1979) 'Nation, tribalism and national language. The problem of choosing a national language in a multilingual nation like Nigeria'. *Journal of the Language Association of East Africa* **4** (1), 77–84.

ALLSOPP, RICHARD (1977) 'Africanisms in the idiom of Caribbean English'. Kotey, Paul F.A./ Haig Der-Houssikian (eds), 429–41.

ALO, MOSES (1984) 'A lexical study of educated Yoruba English'. PhD thesis (Reading).

ALO, MOSES (1989) 'A prototype approach to the analysis of meanings of kinship terms in non-native English'. *Language Sciences* **11**, 159–76.

AMAYO, AIREN (1980) 'Tone in Nigerian English'. *Papers from the Regional Meeting Chicago Linguistic Society (CLS)* **16**, 1–19.

AMUDA, ATOYE A. (1986) 'Yoruba/English code-switching in Nigeria: aspects of its functions and form'. PhD thesis (Reading).

ANASIUDU, B.N. (1987) 'Nigerian English slang: coinage processes'. *Nsukka Journal of Linguistics and African Languages* **1**, 30–42.

ANGOGO, RACHEL M. (1978) 'Language and politics in South Africa'. *Studies in African Linguistics* **9**, 211–21.

ANGOGO, RACHEL M./I.F. HANCOCK (1980) 'English in Africa: emerging standards or diverging regionalisms?' *English World-Wide* 1, 67–96.

ANICHE, GODFREY C. (1982) 'Standard Nigerian English and the educated user'. *Indian Journal of Applied Linguistics* 8, 71–81.

ANSRE, GILBERT (1964) 'A study of the official language in Ghana'. *CSA*, 211–18.

ANSRE, GILBERT (1970) *Language Policy and the Promotion of National Unity and Understanding in West Africa.* Legon: University of Ghana, Institute of African Studies.

ANSRE, GILBERT (1971) 'The influence of English on West African languages'. Spencer, John (ed.), 145–64.

ANSRE, GILBERT (1977) 'Four rationalisations for maintaining the European language in education in Africa'. *Kiswahili* (Dar-es-Salaam) 47 (2), 55–61. Repr. (1979) *African Languages* 5 (2), 10–17.

APRONTI, E.O. (1972) 'Language and national integration in Ghana'. *Présence Africaine* 81, 162–9. Repr. *Legon Journal of the Humanities* 1, 54–61.

APRONTI, E.O. (1974) 'Sociolinguistics and the question of national language: the case of Ghana'. *Studies in African Linguistics* Supplement 5, 1–20.

ARMSTRONG, R. (1968) 'Language policies and language practices in West Africa'. Fishman, Joshua A./Charles F. Ferguson/Jyotirindra Das Gupta (eds), 227–36.

ASMOA, E.A. (1955) 'The problem of language in education in Ghana'. *Africa* 25, 60–78.

ATOYE, RAPHAEL O. (1980) 'Sociolinguistics of phonological interference in Yoruba-English'. PhD thesis (Sheffield).

AWONIYI, T.A. (1975) 'The Yoruba language and the formal school system: a study of colonial language policy in Nigeria 1882–1952'. *The International Journal of African Historical Studies* 8 (1), 63–80.

AWONUSI, VICTOR O. (1985) 'Sociolinguistic variation in Nigerian (Lagos) English'. PhD thesis (London).

AWONUSI, VICTOR O. (1990) 'Coming of age: English in Nigeria'. *English Today* 22, 31–5.

AYODELE, SAMUEL O. (1982) 'Nigerian primary school teachers' mastery of English language pronunciation'. *ITL, Review of Applied Linguistics* 57, 41–52.

AYODELE, SAMUEL O. (1983) 'A description of the varieties of Nigerian English for pedagogic purposes'. *British Journal of Language Teaching* 21 (2), 101–8.

AZUIKE, MACPHERSON N. (1984) 'Style, context and the written text: a linguistic examination of written English in Nigeria today'. PhD thesis (Exeter).

BABALOLA, SOLOMON ADEBAYE Q. (1975) 'The role of Nigerian languages and literatures in fostering national cultural identity'. *Presence Africaine* 94, 53–83. Repr. Riemenschneider, Dieter (ed.) (1983), 148–51.

BAILEY, GUY/GARRY ROSS (1988) 'The shape of the superstrate: morphosyn-tactic features of ship English'. *English World-Wide* 9, 193–212.

BAILEY, RICHARD (1984) 'Notes on South African English'. *South African Journal of Linguistics* 2 (3), 1–35.

BAILEY, RICHARD (1985) 'South African English Slang: form, function and origins'. *South African Journal of Linguistics* 3 (1), 1–42.

BAILEY, RICHARD/MANFRED GÖRLACH (eds) (1982) *English as a World Language.* Ann Arbor: University of Michigan Press.

BAKER, PHILIP (1969) 'The language situation in Mauritius with special reference to Mauritian Creole'. *African Language Review* 8, 73–97.

BAKER, STEPHEN B. (1983) 'Some thoughts on English language teaching in Zambia'. *World Language English* 2, 225–8.

BAMGBOSE, AYO (1969) 'The relationship of the vernacular and English throughout the primary and secondary school'. *Journal of the Nigerian English Studies Association* 3 (1), 79–88.

BAMGBOSE, AYO (1971) 'The English language in Nigeria'. Spencer, John (ed.), 35–48.

BAMGBOSE, AYO (1973) *Language and Society in Nigeria.* Stanford: Stanford University Press.

BAMGBOSE, AYO (1978) 'Models of communication in multilingual states'. *West African Journal of Modern Languages* 3, 60–4.

BAMGBOSE, AYO (1982) 'Standard Nigerian English: issues of identifica-tion.' Kachru, Braj B. (ed.), 99–111.

BANJO, AYO (1969) 'A contrastive study of aspects of the syntactic and lexical rules of English and Yoruba'. PhD thesis (Ibadan).

BANJO, AYO (1970a) 'A historical view of the English language in Nigeria'. *Ibadan* 28, 63–8.

BANJO, AYO (1970b) 'The English language and the Nigerian environ-ment'. *Journal of the Nigerian English Studies Association* 4 (1), 45–51.

BANJO, AYO (1971a) 'Standards of correctness in Nigerian English'. *West African Journal of Education* 15 (2), 123–7.

BANJO, AYO (1971b) 'Towards a definition of standard Nigerian spoken English'. *Annales de l'Université d'Abidjan Serie* 5 (1), 165–75.

BANJO, AYO (1975) 'Language policy in Nigeria'. Smock, David R./ Kwamena Bents-Enchill (eds), 206–19.

BANJO, AYO (1976) 'The university and standardization of the English language'. *West African Journal of Modern Languages* 1, 93–8.

BANJO, AYO (1986) 'The influence of English on the Yoruba language'. Viereck, Wolfgang/W.D. Bald (eds), 533–45.

BANJO, AYO/PETER YOUNG (1982) 'On editing a second-language dictionary: the proposed Dictionary of West African English (DWAE)'. *English World-Wide* 3, 87–91.

BARBAG-STOLL, ANNA (1975) 'Some aspects of semantic shifts in English loanwords in West African Pidgin English!' *Africana Bulletin* 22, 131–8.

BARBAG-STOLL, ANNA (1976) 'The role of the English language in the development of African nationalism'. *Africana Bulletin* 24, 35–42.

BARBAG-STOLL, ANNA (1978) 'Nigerian Pidgin English as a medium of literary expression'. *Africana Bulletin* **27**, 55–63.

BARBAG-STOLL, ANNA (1983) *Social and Linguistic History of Nigerian Pidgin English as Spoken by the Yoruba with Special Reference to the English Derived Lexicon.* Tübingen: Stauffenberg.

BARBEAU, D. (1972) 'Le pidgin English comme moyen d'expression littéraire chez les romanciers du Nigeria'. *Annales de l'Université d'Abidjan*, ser. D **5**, 5–30.

BARNARD, G.L. et al. (1956) *Report on the Use of English in Gold Coast.* Accra: Government Printer.

BARNOUW, ADRIAN J. (1934) *Language and Race Relations in South Africa.* The Hague: Martinus Nijhoff.

BARTON, H.D. (1980) 'Language use among Ilala residents'. Polomé, Edgar C./C.P. Hill (eds), 176–205.

BEARDSLEY, R. BROCK;XS/CAROL M. EASTMAN, (1971) 'Markers, pauses and code switching in bilingual Tanzanian speech'. *General Linguistics* **11**, 17–27.

BEETON, D.R. (1968) 'Some aspects of English usage in South Africa'. *Taalfasette* (Pretoria) **6**, 7–16.

BEETON, D.R./HELEN DORNER (1975) *A Dictionary of English Usage in Southern Africa.* Cape Town: Oxford University Press.

BENDER, M. LIONEL/J. DONALD BOWEN/ROBERT L. COOPER/CHARLES FERGUSON (eds) (1976) *Language in Ethiopia.* London: Oxford University Press.

BERRY, JACK (1961) 'English loanwords and adaptations in Sierra Leone Krio'. Le Page, Robert B. *Creole Language Studies II. Proceedings of the Conference on Creole Language Studies held at the University College of the West Indies, March 28–April 4, 1959.* London: Macmillan, 1–16.

BERRY, JACK/JOSEPH H. GREENBERG (1966) 'Sociolinguistic research in Africa'. *African Studies Bulletin* IX (2), 1–9.

BERRY, JACK/J.H. GREENBERG (eds) (1971) *Current Trends in Linguistics 7: Linguistics in Sub-Saharan Africa.* The Hague: Mouton.

BHAIJI, A.F. (1976) 'The medium of instruction in our secondary schools: a study report'. *Papers in Education and Development* (Department of Education, University of Dar es Salaam) **3**, 111–24.

BIBER, DOUGLAS (1988) *Variation across Speech and Writing.* Cambridge: Cambridge University Press.

BIBER, DOUGLAS (1989) 'A typology of English texts'. *Linguistics* **27**, 3–43.

BICKLEY, WERNER (1982) 'The international uses of English: research in progress'. Brumfit, Christopher J. (ed.), 81–94.

BIRNIE, J.R. (1981) 'Ghanian English: the shape of things to come'. Banjo, Ayo et al. (eds) *West African Studies in Modern Language Teaching and Research.* Lagos: Federal Ministry of Education, The National Language Centre, 128–36.

BISHOP, VAUGHN FREDERICK (1974) 'Multilingualism and national orientations in Kano, Nigeria'. PhD thesis (Evanston, Illinois).

BLAKE, JOHN W. (1977) *West Africa – Quest for Good and Gold: 1454–1578*. London: Curzon Press.

BLAKEMORE, KENNETH/BRIAN COOKSEY (1981) *A Sociology of Education for Africa*. London: George Allen & Unwin.

BOADI, L.A. (1971) 'Education and the role of English in Ghana'. Spencer, John (ed.), 49–65.

BOAHENE-AGBO, KWAKU (1985) 'The Republic of Ghana: an example of African multilingualism'. *Annual Review of Applied Linguistics* 6, 66–77.

BOKAMBA, EYAMA G./JOSIAH S. TLOU (1977) 'The consequences of the language policies of African states *vis-à-vis* education'. Kotey, Paul F.A./Haig Der-Houssikian (eds), 39–53.

BOKAMBA, EYAMBA G. (1981) 'Language policies and national development in Sub-Saharan Africa: Issues for the 1980s'. *Studies in the Linguistic Sciences* 11 (1), 1–25.

BOKAMBA, EYAMBA G. (1982) 'The Africanization of English'. Kachru, Braj B. (eds), 77–98.

BOKAMBA, EYAMBA G. (1989) 'Are there syntactic constraints on code-mixing?' *World Englishes* 8, 277–92.

BOKAMBA, EYAMBA G. (1991) 'West Africa' (overview article). Cheshire, Jenny (ed.), 493–508.

BOKAMBA, EYAMBA G. (ed.) (1979) *Language Policies in African Education*. Washington, DC: University Press of America.

BOTHA, J.J. (1982) 'Computer-based education and the teaching of English for specific purposes: report on a project in progress'. *System* 10, 277–84.

BOURENANE, KARIMA RADJA ROUDESLI (1984) 'English learning in Algeria: an analysis of errors and attitudes'. PhD thesis (Austin, Texas).

BRANFORD, JEAN (3rd Edition 1987) *A Dictionary of South African English*. Cape Town: Oxford University Press.

BRANFORD, WILLIAM (1976) 'A dictionary of South African English as a reflex of the English-speaking cultures of South Africa'. Villiers, André de (ed.), 297–316.

BRANFORD, WILLIAM (1976) 'English in the South African Republic – an interim report'. *English Around The World* 14, 1–2+6.

BRANFORD, WILLIAM (1987) *The South African Pocket Oxford Dictionary*. Cape Town: Oxford University Press.

BRANFORD, WILLIAM (1990) *A Dictionary of South African English on Historical Principles*. Cape Town/Oxford: Oxford University Press.

BRANN, CONRAD MAX BENEDICT (1978) 'Functions of world languages in West Africa'. *West African Journal of Modern Languages* 3, 6–28.

BRANN, CONRAD MAX BENEDICT (1979) 'A typology of language education in Nigeria'. McCormack, William C./Stephen A. Wurm (eds), 463–507.

BRANN, CONRAD MAX BENEDICT (1980) *Mother Tongue, Other Tongue, and Further Tongue*. Maiduguri: Maiduguri University Press.

BRANN, CONRAD MAX BENEDICT (1981) 'The future of European languages in Africa'. *Liber amicorum Henri Brugmans: au service de L'Europe*. Amsterdam: European Cultural Foundation, 46–54.

BRANN, CONRAD MAX BENEDICT (1984) 'Afro-Saxons and Afro-Romans: Language Policies in Sub-Saharan Africa'. *History of European Ideas* 5, 307–21.

BRANN, CONRAD MAX BENEDICT (1985a) *Official and National Languages in Africa: Complementarity or Conflict.* Québec: Centre International de Recherche sur le Bilinguism.

BRANN, CONRAD MAX BENEDICT (1985b) 'A sociolinguistic typology of language contact in Nigeria: the role of translation'. Ugboajah, Frank Okwa (ed.) *Mass Communication, Culture and Society in West Africa.* München: Hans Zell Publishers (K.G. Saur), 122–32.

BRANN, CONRAD MAX BENEDICT (1985c) 'Language policy, planning and management in Nigeria: a bird's eye view'. *Sociolinguistics* 15 (1), 30–1.

BREITBORDE, LAWRENCE B. (1977) 'The social structural basis of linguistic variation in an urban African neighborhood'. PhD thesis (Rochester).

BREITBORDE, LAWRENCE B. (1983) 'Levels of analysis in sociolinguistic explanation: bilingual codeswitching, social relations, and domain theory'. *International Journal of the Sociology of Language* 39, 5–43.

BREITBORDE, LAWRENCE B. (1988) 'The persistence of English in Liberia: sociolinguistic factors', *World Englishes* 7, 15–23.

BRIGHT, J.A. (1962) 'The teaching of English in Uganda'. *English Language Teaching* 16 (2), 89–95.

BRINK, A.P. (1976) 'English and the Afrikaans writer'. *English in Africa* 3, 35–46.

BRITISH COUNCIL (1986) *Proceedings of the Conference on English in East Africa. 24–7 March 1986.* Nairobi.

BRITISH COUNCIL (1988) *The Place of Grammar in the Teaching of English.* An International Conference held at the British Council, Nairobi.

BROSNAHAN, L.F. (1958) 'English in Southern Nigeria'. *English Studies* 39 (3), 97–110.

BROSNAHAN, L.F. (1961) 'Problems of linguistics inequivalence in communication (English – Nigerian)'. *Ibadan* 13, 26–30.

BROSNAHAN, L.F. (1963) 'Some aspects of the linguistics situation in tropical Africa'. *Lingua* 12, 54–65.

BROWN, LALAGE (ed.) (1973) *Two Centuries of African English.* London: Heinemann.

BROWN, P.P. (1949) 'West Africa; learning a European language'. *Yearbook of Education* 1949, 338–41.

BRUMfiT, ANNE (1971) 'The development of a language policy in German East Africa'. *Journal of the Language Association of Eastern Africa* 2 (1), 1–9.

BRUMfiT, ANNE (1980) 'The rise and development of a language policy in German East Africa'. *Sprache und Gesellschaft in Afrika* 2, 219–331.

BRUMfiT, CHRISTOPHER J. (ed.) (1982) *English for International Communication.* Oxford: Pergamon.

BUGHWAN, D. (1970) 'An investigation into the use of English by the Indians in South Africa, with special reference to Natal'. PhD thesis (University of South Africa).

BUGHWAN, D. (1972) 'Indian South Africans – their language dilemma'. *Humanitas* (Pretoria) **2** (1), 61–5.

BUTLER, G. (1964) 'The future of English in Africa'. *Optima* **14** (2), 88–97.

CANDLER, W.J. (1977) 'Teaching English as a second dialect in Liberia'. *English Language Teaching Journal* **31**, 321–5.

CARROL, B.J. (1961) 'English as a medium of instruction'. *Educational Review* **14**, 54–63.

CARROL, BRENDON J. (1962) 'An English language survey in West Africa'. *English Language Teaching* **16** (4), 205–10.

CHAMPION, ERNEST A. (1974) 'The contribution of English language and West African literature to the rise of national consciousness in West Africa'. PhD thesis (Bowling Green State University).

CHANDLER, L. (1975) 'Language contact and interference in South Africa'. *English Usage in South Africa* **6** (2), 13–19.

CHESHIRE, JENNY (ed.) (1991) *English Around the World: The Social Contexts*. Cambridge: Cambridge University Press.

CHIA, EMMANUEL (1979) 'A sociolinguistic survey of Cameroon urban centres'. *The Linguistic Reporter* **22** (3), 6–7.

CHICK, J. KEITH (1985) 'The interactional accomplishment of discrimination in South Africa'. *Language in Society*, 299–326.

CHICK, J. KEITH (1989) 'Intercultural miscommunication as a source of friction in the workplace and in educational settings in South Africa'. García, Ofelia/Ricardo Otheguy (eds), 139–60.

CHICK, J. KEITH (1991) 'Sources and consequences of miscommunication in Afrikaans English – South African English encounters'. Cheshire, Jenny (ed.), 446–51.

CHILIVUMBO, ALIFEYO B. (1976) 'Malawi's culture in the national integration'. *Présence Africaine* **98**, 234–41.

CHIKALANGA, I.W. (1983) 'Teaching primary English in Zambia'. *Zambia Education Review* **4** (1), 1–18.

CHIMUKA, S.S./KASHOKI, MUBANGA E./H.P. AFRICA ROBERT SERPELL (eds) (1978) *Language and Education in Zambia*. Communication **14**. Lusaka: Institute for African Studies, University of Zambia.

CHINEBUAH, ISAAK K. (1976) 'Grammatical deviance and first language interference'. *West African Journal of Modern Languages* **1**, 67–78.

CHISANGA, TERESA (1987) 'An investigation into the form and function of educated English in Zambia as a possible indigenized non-native variety'. PhD thesis (York).

CHISHIMBA, MAURICE M. (1982) 'Language teaching and literacy: East Africa'. *Annual Review of Applied Linguistics* **3**, 168–88.

CHISHIMBA, MAURICE M. (1984) 'Language policy and education in Zambia'. *International Education Journal* **1**, 151–80.

CHISHIMBA, MAURICE M. (1984) 'African varieties of English: text in context'. PhD dissertation (Illinois at Urbana-Champaign).

CHISHIMBA, MAURICE M. (1991) 'Southern Africa' (overview article). Cheshire, Jenny (ed.), 435–45.

CHOMBA, SIMON R. (1975) 'English as a medium of instruction: the problem of culture'. *Bulletin of the Zambia Language Group* **2** (1), 42–55.

CHRISTOPHERSEN, P. (1953) 'Some special West African English words'. *English Studies* **34**, 282–91.

CHRISTOPHERSEN, P. (1973) 'English in West Africa: a review article'. *English Studies* **54**, 51–8.

CHUMBOW, SAMMY BEBAN (1980) 'Language and language policy in Cameroon'. Kofele-Kale, Ndiva (ed.) *An African Experiment in Nation-Building: The Bilingual Cameroon Republic since Reunification*, Boulder, Colorado: Westview Press, 281–311.

CHUMBOW, SAMMY BEBAN (1984) 'Foreign language in a multilingual setting: the predictability of the "mother tongue effect"'. *IRAL (International Review of Applied Linguistics in Language Teaching)* **22**, 287–97.

CLARK, JOHN PEPPER (1968) 'The legacy of Caliban. An introduction to the language spoken by Africans and other 'natives' in English literature from Shakespeare to Achebe'. *Black Orpheus* **2** (1), 16–39.

CLARKE, J.D. (1930) 'The language question in West Africa'. *Oversea Education* **1** (2), 44–52.

COANGAE, SIMON/KEBASENYA LETSIDIDI/LYDIA NYATI (1987) 'English for Special Purposes: the case of Botswana'. Osbiston, Rachel (ed.), 91–109.

COLLINS, H.R. (1968) *The New English of Onitsha Chapbooks*. Ohio. Ohio University, International Studies.

COLLISON, G.O. (1972) 'Language and concept development in Ghanaian elementary school children'. PhD dissertation (Harvard).

CONRAD, ANDREW W./FISHMAN, J.A. (1977) 'English as a world language: the evidence'. Fishman, Joshua A. et al. (eds), 3–76.

CONSTABLE, D. (1974) 'Bilingualism in the United Republic of Cameroon: proficiency and distribution'. *Comparative Education* **10**, 233–46.

CONSTABLE, D. (1976) 'Investigating language attitudes: Cameroon'. *West African Journal of Modern Languages* **1**, 31–40.

CONSTABLE, D. (1977) 'Bilingualism in the United Republic of Cameroon'. *English Language Teaching Journal* **31**, 249–53.

COOK, P.A.W. (1953) 'The Place of African languages and English both in School Education and in Education out of School'. *UNESCO*, 22–40.

COOPER, ROBERT L./JOSHUA A. FISHMAN (1974) 'The study of language attitudes'. *Linguistics* **136**, 5–19.

COOPER, ROBERT L./JOSHUA A. FISHMAN (1977) 'A study of language attitudes'. Fishman, Joshua A./Robert L. Cooper/Andrew W. Conrad, 239–76.

CRAMPTON, DIANA (1986) 'Language policy in Kenya'. *Rassegna italiana di linguistica applicata* **18** (3), 109–22.

CREIDER, CHET A. (1984) 'Language differences in strategies for the interactional management of conversation'. *Studies in the Linguistic Sciences* **14** (2), 57–65.

CRIPER, C./W. DODD (1984) 'Report on the teaching of the English language and its use as a medium of education in Tanzania'. Dar es Salaam: Ministry of National Education.

CRIPER, L. (1971) 'A classification of types of English in Ghana'. *Journal of African Languages* 10 (3), 6–17.

CRIPWELL, KENNETH R. (1974) *L'anglais en Afrique. Guide pour l'enseignement de l'anglais comme langue étrangère*. Paris: Les Presses de l'UNESCO.

CRIPWELL, KENNETH R. (1975) 'Governmental writers and African readers in Rhodesia'. *Language in Society* 4, 147–54.

CROW, HUGH (1970 repr.) *Memoirs of the late Captain Hugh Crow of Liverpool*. London: Frank Cass & Co.

CRYSTAL, DAVID (1985) 'How many millions? The statistics of English today'. *English Today* 1, 7–9.

CSA (CONSEIL SCIENTIFIQUE POUR L'AFRIQUE) (1964) *Colloque sur le Multilingualisme/ Symposium on Mutlilingualism*. London: Bureau des Publications CCTA/CSA Publications Bureau.

CYFFER, NORBERT (1977) 'Sprachplanung in Nigeria'. *Afrika Spektrum* 12, 239–62.

DADA, AYORINDE (1985) 'The new language policy in Nigeria: its problems and its chances of success'. Wolfson, Nessa/Joan Manes (eds), 285–93.

DAKIN, J./BRIAN TIFFEN/H.G. WIDDOWSON (1968) *Language in Education. The Problem of Commonwealth Africa and the Indo-Pakistan Sub-Continent*. London: Oxford University Press.

DALBY, DAVID (1970) 'The place of Africa and Afro-America in the history of the English language'. *African Language Review* 9, 280–98.

DALGISH, GERARD M. (1982) *A Dictionary of Africanisms. Contributions of Sub-Saharan Africa to the English Language*. Westport, Connecticut/London: Greenwood Press.

DATTA, ANSU K. (1978) 'Languages used by Zambian Asians'. Ohannessian, S./M.E. Kashoki (eds), 244–68.

DE FÉRAL, CAROLE (1977a) 'Le cas du pidgin Camérounais'. *West African Journal of Modern Languages* 3, 144–53.

DE FÉRAL, CAROLE (1977b) 'Le pidgin English au Cameroun: présentation sociolinguistique'. *Bulletin ALCAM* (Yaoundé: ONAREST) 2, 107–28.

DE FÉRAL, CAROLE (1980) *Le Pidgin-English Camerounais: essai de définition linguistique et sociolinguistique*. Publ. de l'Institut d'Etudes et de Recherches Interethniques et Interculturelles, University of Nice.

DECKER, DONALD M. (1978) 'The importance of the English language in today's world'. *English Around the World* 19, 1, 7.

DELANY, M. (1967) 'A phonological contrastive analysis North American English – Standard Swahili'. *Swahili* 37, 27–46.

DEMOZ, ABRAHAM (1963) 'European loanwords in an Amharic daily newspaper', Spencer, John (ed.), 116–22.

DEMOZ, ABRAHAM (1977) 'Language and law in Africa'. Kotey, Paul F.A./ Haig Der-Houssikian (eds), 135–40.

DENTON, JOHNNIE MAE (1976) 'Towards a model of ESL for Krio Speakers in Sierra Leone'. PhD thesis (Austin, Texas).

DILLARD, J.L. (1979) 'Creole English and Creole Portuguese: the early records'. Hancock, Ian F. et al. (eds), 261–68.

DOKE, CLEMENT (1939) 'European and Bantu languages in South Africa'. *Africa* 12, 308–19.

DORCAS, WALE O. (1979) 'Register in oral discourse'. Ubahakwe, Ebo (ed.), 107–26.

'DOSSIER: NATIONAL LANGUAGES'. *The Courier* No. 119 (Jan/Feb 1990). Paris: UNESCO.

DOWNES, WILLIAM (1984) *Language and Society*. London: Fontana.

DUMINY, P.A. (1972) 'Language as medium of instruction, with reference to the situation in a number of Ciskeian secondary schools'. *Comparative Education* 8, 119–32.

DUMINY, P.A./A.H. MACHARTY/E.D. GASA (1980) 'The introduction of Africaans and English to Zulu pupils in the primary school'. *Tydskrift wir Rasse-Aangeleenthede (Pretoria)* 31 (3), 93–104.

DUNJWA-BLAJBERG, JENNIFER (1980) *Sprache und Politik in Südafrika. Stellung und Funktion der Sprachen unter dem Apartheidssystem*. Bonn: Informationsstelle Südliches Afrika e.V.

DUNSTAN, E. (1969) *Twelve Nigerian Languages. A handbook on their sound systems for teachers of English*. London: Longman.

DUPONCHEL, LAURENT (1976) 'L'enseignement des langues étrangères en Cote-d'Ivoire'. *West African Journal of Modern Languages* 1, 89–92.

DUROJAIYE, SUSAN M. (1978) 'The English language in Nigeria'. *English Around the World* 19, 2, 8.

DWAMINA, WINGROVE CHARLES (1972) 'English Literature and Language Planning in West Africa'. PhD thesis (State University of New York, Buffalo).

DWYER, DAVID SMITH, DAVID (1966) *An Introduction to West African Pidgin-English*. East Lansing: African Studies Centre.

DYAMINI, PETRONELLA (1975) 'English as a medium of instruction in Zambian primary schools: theory and practice (Implications for urban schools)'. *Bulletin of the Zambia Language Group* 2 (1), 30–5.

EASTMAN, CAROL M. (1981) 'Language planning, identity planning and world view'. *International Journal of the Sociology of Language* 32, 45–53.

EASTMAN, CAROL M. (1983) *Language Planning: An Introduction*. Novata, CA: Chandler & Sharp.

EASTMAN, CAROL M. (1985) 'Establishing social identity through language use'. *Journal of Language and Social Psychology* 4, 1–20.

EASTMAN, CAROL M. (1986) 'Cultural synthesis: a language plan for the 1980s'. *ACLALS Bulletin* 7 (6), 1–13.

EDWARDS, PAUL (ed.) (1967) *Equiano's Travels*. London: Heinemann (originally (1789) *The Interesting Narrative of the Life of Olaudah Equiano or Gustavus Vassa the African*. London).

EGBE, DANIEL I. (1979) 'Spoken and written English in Nigeria'. Ubahakwe, Ebo (ed.), 86–106.

EGBE, DANIEL I. (1981) 'Aspects of English grammar and usage'. *Papers in Linguistics* 14 (2), 271–96.

EKONG, PAMELA (1982) 'On the use of an indigenous model for teaching English in Nigeria'. *World Language English* 1, 87–92.

EKONG, PAMELA A. (1978) 'On describing the vowel system of a standard variety of Nigerian spoken English'. PhD thesis (Ibadan).

EKPENYONG, J.O. (1965) 'The use of English in Nigeria'. Press, John (ed.) *Commonwealth Literature: Unity and Diversity in a Common Culture*. London: 144–50. Repr. Riemenschneider, Dieter (ed.) (1983), 142–45.

EKWENSI, CYPRIAN (1956) 'The dilemma of the African writer'. West African Review **27**, 701–4, 708.

EL-DASH, LINDA/G. RICHARD TUCKER (1975) 'Subjective reactions to various speech styles in Egypt'. *Linguistics* **166**, 33–54.

EL-HIBIR, BABIKER IDRISS (1976) 'Sources of common errors in written English of Sudanese secondary school students'. PhD thesis (Wales).

ELUGBE, BEN O./AUGUSTA O. OMAMOR (forthcoming) *Nigerian Pidgin: Background and Prospects*. Ibadan: Heinemann.

ENGHOLM, EVA (1965) *Education Through English. The Use of English in African Schools*. Cambridge: Cambridge University Press.

EPSTEIN, A.L. (1959) 'Linguistic innovation and culture on the Copperbelt, Northern Rhodesia'. J.A. Fishman (ed.), 320–39.

ESHETE, ALEME (1974) 'The pre-war attempts to promote the use of the English language in the educational system of Ethiopia in place of French'. *Ethiopian Journal of Education* **6** (2) 15–29.

ESSILFIE, THOMAS (1983) 'English in multilingual countries: Problems of pedagogy and acquisition – the case of Botswana'. *Paper presented at conference on 'English in Southern Africa'*. Lusaka.

ESSILFIE, THOMAS (1989) 'The African linguist and his chores: language teaching programmes in SADCC universities and the philosophy behind them'. Ngara, Emanuel/Andrew Morrison (eds), 211–18.

EZE, SMART N. (1980) *Nigerian pidgin English sentence complexity*. Wien: AFRO-PUB.

FABIAN, JOHANNES (1986) *Language and Colonial Power*. Cambridge: Cambridge University Press.

FAKUNDE, GLENGA (1989) 'The three-language formula for Nigeria: problems of implementation'. *Language Problems and Language Planning* **13**, 54–9.

FANAROFF, D. (1972) *South African English Dialect: A Literature Survey*. Pretoria: HSRC.

FARACLAS, NICHOLAS (1991) 'The pronoun system in Nigerian Pidgin: a preliminary study'. Cheshire, Jenny (ed.), 509–18.

FARINE, A. (1968) 'Le bilinguisme au Cameroun'. *Canadian Journal of African Studies* **2** (1), 7–12.

FARSI, A.A. (1966) 'Some pronunciation problems of Swahili speaking students'. *English language Teaching* **20**, 136–40.

FASHOLA, J.B. (1976) 'Oral competence at the university: a critical appraisal of the Nigerian situation'. *West African Journal of Modern Languages* **1**, 107–17.

FASOLD, RALPH W. (1984) *The Sociolinguistics of Society*. Oxford: Basil Blackwell.

FASOLD, RALPH W. (1990) *The Sociolinguistics of Language*. Oxford: Basil Blackwell.

FAWCETT, R.P. (1970) 'The medium of education in the lower primary school in Africa with special reference to Kenya'. Gorman, Thomas (ed.), 51–69.

FAYER, JOAN H. (1982) 'Written Pidgin English in Old Calabar in the 18th and 19th centuries'. PhD thesis (Pennsylvania, Philadelphia).

FAYER, JOAN H. (1986) 'Pidgins as written languages: evidence from 18th century Old Calabar'. *Anthropological Linguistics* **28**, 313–19.

FERGUSON, CHARLES A. (1959) 'Diglossia'. *Word* **15**, 325–40.

FISHMAN, JOSHUA A. (1965) 'Who speaks what language to whom and when?' *La Linguistique* **2**, 67–88.

FISHMAN, JOSHUA A. (1967) 'Bilingualism with and without diglossia, diglossia with and without bilingualism'. *Journal of Social Issues* **23** (2), 29–38.

FISHMAN, JOSHUA A. (1971) 'National languages and languages of wider communications in the developing nations'. Whiteley, Wilfried H. (ed.), 27–49.

FISHMAN, JOSHUA A. (ed.) (1968) *Readings in the Sociology of Language.* The Hague: Mouton.

FISHMAN, JOSHUA A. (ed.) (1986) *The Firgusonian Impact.* Vol. 2. Illinois: Mouton.

FISHMAN, JOSHUA A./CHARLES F. FERGUSON/JYOTIRINDRA DAS GUPTA (eds) (1968) *Language Problems of Developing Nations.* New York: John Wiley & Sons.

FISHMAN, JOSHUA A./ROBERT L. COOPER/ANDREW W. CONRAD (1977) *The Spread of English: The Sociology of English as an Additional Language.* Rowley, Mass: Newbury House.

FLETCHER, R.W.Y. (1975) 'The new junior secondary school curriculum in Lesotho'. *Education in Botswana, Lesotho and Swaziland* **10**, 9–12.

FODOR, ISTVÁN (1966) 'Linguistic problems and "language planning" in Africa'. *Linguistics* **25**, 18–33.

FOLARIN, B. (1979) 'Context, register and language varieties: a proposed model for the discussion of varieties of English in Nigeria'. Ubahakwe, Ebo (ed.), 77–85.

FONLON, BERNARD (1976) 'The language problem in Cameroon: a historical perspective'. *Abbia* **22**, 5–40. Repr. *Comparative Education* (Oxford) **5**, 25–49 and Smock, David R./Kwamena Bentsi-Enchill (eds), 189–205.

FORDE, DARYLL (ed.) (1956) *Efik Traders of the Old Calabar. The Diary of Antera Duke.* London: for I.A.I. by Oxford University Press.

FORSON, BARNABAS (1979) 'Code-switching in Akan–English bilingualism'. PhD thesis (University of California, Los Angeles).

FREEMAN, RICHARD/MUNZALI JIBRIL (eds) (1984) *English Language Studies in Nigerian Higher Education.* London: British Council.

FYLE, CLIFFORD N./ELDRED D. JONES (1980) *A Krio-English Dictionary.* Oxford: Oxford University Press.

GARCÍA, OFELIA/RICARDO OTHEGUY (eds) (1989) *English across Cultures, Cultures across English. A Reader in Cross-cultural Communication.* Berlin: Mouton de Gruyter.

GIBBS, JAMES (comp. & ed.) (1986) *A Handbook for African Writers.* Oxford: Saur.

GILBERT, GLENN G. (1985) 'Hugo Schuchardt and the Atlantic Creoles: a newly discovered manuscript "On the Negro English of West Africa"'. *American Speech* 60, 31–63.

GILES, H./P.F. Powesland (1975) *Speech Style and Social Evaluation*. London: Academic Press.

GILES, HOWARD/MILES HEWSTONE/PETER BALL (1983) 'Language attitudes in multilingual settings: prologue with priorities'. *Journal of Multilingual and Multicultural Development* 4, 81–100.

GILMAN, CHARLES (1979) 'Cameroonian Pidgin English, a neo-African language'. Hancock, Ian F. et al. (ed.), 269–80.

GILMAN, CHARLES (1980) 'The origin of Cameroonian pidgin dialects'. *Anthropological Linguistics* 22, 9 363–72.

GIMSON, A.C. (1982) 'The Twentyman lecture 1981: The pronunciation of English: Its intelligibility and acceptability in the world'. *The Incorporated Linguist* 21, 25–8.

GIMSON, A.C. (Fourth Edition 1989) *An Introduction to the Pronunciation of English*. London: Edward Arnold.

GLICK, R. (1969) 'The relationship between selected sociolinguistic variables and the ability to read English among Ugandan children'. PhD thesis (University of California, Los Angeles).

GOKE-PARIOLA, ABIODUN (1978) 'Language transfer and the Nigerian writer of English'. *World Englishes* 6, 127–37.

GOKE-PARIOLA, ABIODUN (1982) 'A socio-political perspective of English language pedagogy in Nigerian High Schools'. PhD thesis (Michigan).

GÖRLACH, MANFRED (1984) 'English in Africa – African English'. *Revista Canaria de Estudios Ingleses (La Laguna, Tenerife)* 8, 33–56.

GÖRLACH, MANFRED (1987) 'Colonial lag? The alleged conversative character of American English and other "colonial" varieties'. *English World-Wide* 8, 41–60.

GÖRLACH, MANFRED (1988) 'English as a world-language – the state of the art'. *English World-Wide* 9, 1–32.

GÖRLACH, MANFRED (1989) 'Word-formation and the ENL/ESL/EFL categorization'. *English World-Wide* 10, 279–314.

GÖRLACH, MANFRED (1990) 'Lexical problems of English in Africa'. Schmied, Josef (ed.), 27–46.

GORMAN, THOMAS P. (1968) 'Bilingualism in the educational system of Kenya'. *Comparative Education* 4, 213–21.

GORMAN, THOMAS P. (1971) 'A survey of educational language policies; and an enquiry into patterns of language use and levels of language attainment among secondary school entrants in Kenya'. PhD thesis (Nairobi).

GORMAN, THOMAS P. (1971) 'Sociolinguistic implications of a choice of media of instruction'. Whiteley, Wilfried H. (ed.), 198–220.

GORMAN, THOMAS P. (1973) 'Language allocation and language planning in a developing nation'. Rubin, Joan/Roger Shuy (eds) *Language Planning: Current Issues and Research*. Washington DC: Georgetown University Press, 72–82.

GORMAN, THOMAS P. (1974) 'The development of language policy in Kenya with particular reference to the educational system'. Whiteley, Wilfried H. (ed.), 397–453.

GORMAN, THOMAS P. (1974) 'The teaching of languages at secondary level: some significant problems'. Whiteley, Wilfried H. (ed.), 481–545.

GORMAN, THOMAS P. (ed.) (1970) *Language in Education in Eastern Africa*. Nairobi: Oxford University Press.

GOUALA, PIERRE MACAIRE (1981) 'Problems of learning English in the Congo due to mother-tongue interference'. Nairobi: ACO Project (mimeo).

GOWER, R.H. (1952) 'Swahili borrowings in English'. *Africa* 22, 154–6.

GRABE, WILLIAM (1988) 'English, information access, and technology transfer: a rationale for English as an international language'. *World Englishes* 7, 63–72.

GRANT, NEVILLE (1987) 'Swahili speakers'. Swan, Michael/Bernard Smith (eds), 194–211.

GRAVES, G.F. (1978) 'Social control and the use of English in developing countries'. *Compare* 8, 119–22.

GREAT BRITAIN (1953) 'African education, a study of educational policy and practice in British Tropical Africa'. London: HMSO.

GREENBAUM, SIDNEY (1988) *Good English and the Grammarian*. Harlow: Longman.

GREENBAUM, SIDNEY (1990) 'Standard English and the International Corpus of English'. *World Englishes* 9, 79–83.

GREENBAUM, SIDNEY (ed.) (1985) *The English Language Today*. Oxford: Pergamon.

GREENBERG, JOSEPH H. (1966) 'Interdisciplinary perspectives in African linguistic research'. *African Studies Bulletin* Vol. IX, 8–23.

GREENFIELD, P.M. (1972) 'Oral or written language: the consequences for cognitive development in Africa, the United States and England'. *Language and Speech* 15, 169–78.

GREGORY, MICHAEL/SUSANNE CARROLL (1978) *Language and Situation. Language Variants and their Social Contexts*. London: Routledge & Kegan Paul.

GREIS, NAGUIB AMIN FAHMY (1963) 'The pedagogical implications of a contrastive analysis of cultivated Cairene Arabic and the English language'. PhD thesis (Minnesota).

GRIEVE, D.W./A. TAYLOR (1952) 'Media of instruction: a preliminary study of relative merits of English and an African vernacular as teaching media'. *Gold Coast Education* 1, 36–52.

GUY, B. (1964) 'The future of English in Africa'. *Optima* 14 (2), 88–97.

GYASI, IBRAHIM K. (1991) 'Aspects of English in Ghana'. *English Today*, 23.

HALL, G.R. (1928) 'Talking by ear: Kru-boy English'. *West Africa* 12, 988–9.

HALLIDAY, M.A.K./ANGUS MCINTOSH/PETER STREVENS (1964) *The Linguistic Sciences and Language Teaching*. London: Longman.

HANCOCK, IAN F. (1969) 'A provisional comparison of the English-based Atlantic creoles'. *African Language Review* 8, 7–72. Repr. Hymes,

Dell (ed.) (1971) *Pidginization and Creolization of Languages*. Cambridge: Cambridge University Press, 287–90.

HANCOCK, IAN F. (1970) 'Some aspects of English in Liberia'. *Liberian Studies Journal* **3,2**. Repr. Dillard, Joe Lee (ed.) (1971) *Perspectives on Black English*. The Hague: Mouton, 248–55.

HANCOCK, IAN F. (1971a) 'Some aspects of English in Liberia', *Liberian Studies Journal* **3**, 207–13.

HANCOCK, IAN F. (1971b) 'West Africa and the Atlantic creoles'. Spencer, John (ed.), 113–22.

HANCOCK, IAN F. (1971c) 'Repertory of pidgin and creole languages'. Dell Hymes (ed.) *Pidginization and Creolization of Languages*. Cambridge: Cambridge University Press. Repr. Rev. Valdman, Albert (ed.) (1977) *Pidgin and Creole Linguistics*. Bloomington: Indiana University Press, 362–91.

HANCOCK, IAN F. (1971d) 'A study of the sources and development of the lexicon of Sierra Leone Krio'. PhD thesis (London).

HANCOCK, IAN F. (1974) 'English in Liberia'. *American Speech* **49**, 224–9.

HANCOCK, IAN F. (1976) 'Nautical sources of Krio vocabulary'. *International Journal of the Sociology of Language* **7**, 23–36.

HANCOCK, IAN F. (1979) 'Creole English and Creole Portuguese: the early record'. Hancock, Ian F. et al. (eds), 261–8.

HANCOCK, IAN F. (1986) 'The domestic hypothesis, diffusion and componentiality. An account of Atlantic Anglophone creole origins'. Muysken, Pieter/Noval Smith (eds), 71–102.

HANCOCK, IAN F. et al. (eds) (1979) *Readings in Creole Studies*. Ghent: Story-Scientia.

HANCOCK, IAN F./P. KOBBAH (1975) 'Liberian English of Cape Palmas'. Dillard, Joan (ed.) *Perspectives on Black English*. The Hague: Mouton, 248–71.

HANCOCK, IAN F./RACHEL ANGOGO (1982) 'English in East Africa'. Bailey, Richard/Manfred Görlach (eds), 306–23.

HARLECH-JONES, BRIAN (1979) 'Is there an African English?' *ELTIC Reporter* **4**, 25–30.

HARRIES, LYNDON (1966) 'Language and law in Tanzania'. *Journal of African Law* (London) **10**, 164–7.

HARRIES, LYNDON (1976) 'The nationalization of Swahili in Kenya'. *Language in Society* **5**, 153–64.

HATFIELD, V. (1950) 'New emphasis on English in the Kenya African primary school'. *Overseas Education* **21**, 161–3.

HAUPTFLEISCH, TEMPLE (1975) *Research into the Position of the Official language in the Educational System of Whites in South Africa: A Literature Survey*. Pretoria: Human Sciences Research Council.

HAUPTFLEISCH, TEMPLE (1978a) *Language Loyalty in South Africa. Vol. I. Bilingual Policy in S.A. Opinions of White Adults in Urban Areas*. Pretoria: Human Sciences Research Council.

HAUPTFLEISCH, TEMPLE (1978b) *Language Loyalty in South Africa. Vol. 2. Using and Improving Usage in the Second Language*. Pretoria: Human Sciences Research Council.

HAUPTFLEISCH, TEMPLE (1979) *Language Loyalty in South Africa. Vol. 3: Motivation to Language Use: Opinions and Attitudes of White Adults in Urban Areas.* Pretoria: Human Sciences Research Council.

HAUPTFLEISCH, TEMPLE (1983) *Language Loyalty in South Africa, Vol. 4. Language Purity and Language Shift.* Pretoria: Human Sciences Research Council.

HAUPTFLEISCH, TEMPLE (1989) 'Citytalk, theatretalk: dialect, dialogue and multilingual theatre in South Africa'. *English in Africa* 16, 71–91.

HAWKES, C.N. (1973) 'The written English of Ghanaian Primary Six pupils in relation to their exposure to English as the medium of spoken intruction'. PhD thesis (York).

HAWKES, NICOLAS (1976) 'The medium of instruction in primary schools in Ghana'. *West African Journal of Modern Languages* 1, 57–66.

HAYNES, R. (1982) 'The emergence of an English based creole in Zambia: possibilities and implications'. *The English Teachers' Journal* 6 (2), 2–13.

HAYWOOD, DAVID (1970) *South African English Pronunciation.* College Park Maryland: McGrath.

HEINE, BERND (1976) 'Knowledge and use of second languages in Musoma Region – a quantitative study'. *Kiswahili* 46 (1), 49–59.

HEINE, BERND (1977) 'Vertical and horizontal communication in Africa'. *Africa Spectrum* 12, 230–8.

HEINE, BERND (1979) *Sprache, Gesellschaft und Kommunikation in Afrika: zum Problem der Verständigung und sozio-ökonomischen Entwicklung im sub-saharischen Afrika.* München: Weltforum-Verlag.

HEINE, BERND/OSWIN KÖHLER (1981) *Linguistik – Ostafrika (Kenya, Uganda, Tanzania). Gliederung der Sprachen und Dialekte.* Berlin & Stuttgart: Gebr. Borntraeger.

HELLINGER, MARLIS (1990) 'Creolistics and sociolinguistics' *English World-Wide* 11, 59–77.

HILL, C.P. (1980a) 'Library users and their reading preferences'. Polomé, Edgar/C.P. Hill (eds), 206–28.

HILL, C.P. (1980b) 'Some developments in language and education in Tanzania since 1969'. Polomé, Edgar/C.P. Hill (eds), 362–404.

HILL, CLIFFORD (1982) 'Up/down, front/back, left/right: a contrastive study of Hausa and English'. *Pragmatics and Beyond* 3, 13–42.

HILL, PETER (1965a) 'Some notes on structural differences between English and Swahili'. *Swahili* 35 (1), 24–7.

HILL, PETER (1965b) 'Some problems in the change-over from Swahili to English as the medium of instruction'. *English Language Teaching* 20, 49–54.

HILL, TREVOR (1973) 'The pronunciation of English stressed vowels in Tanzania'. *Bulletin of the Language Association of Tanzania* 4 (2), 3–9.

HIRSON, BARUCH (1981) 'Language in control and resistance in South Africa'. *African Affairs* (London) 319, 219–37.

HOCKING, B.D.W. (1970) 'Types of interference'. Gorman, Thomas P. (ed.), 129–38.

HOCKING, B.D.W. (1974) *All What I Was Taught and Other Mistakes.* A handbook of common errors in English. Nairobi: Oxford University Press.

HOFMANN, JOHN E. (1977) 'Language attitudes in Rhodesia'. Fishman, Joshua A./Robert L. Cooper/Andrew W. Conrad (eds), 277–301.

HÖFTMANN, H. (1963) 'Untersuchung zur Eingliederung moderner Begriffe in Bantusprachen, dargestellt am Swahili, Zulu und Herero'. *Ethno-graphisch-Archäologische Zeitschrift* **4**, 60–5.

HOLM, JOHN (1988/89) *Pidgins and Creoles*. 2 vols. Cambridge: Cambridge University Press.

HOPKINS, TOMETRO (1977) 'The development and implementation of the national language policy in Kenya'. Kotey, Paul F.A./Haig Der-Houssikian (eds), 84–96.

HUDSON, RICHARD (1980) *Sociolinguistics*. Cambridge: Cambridge University Press.

HYDER, M./ABDULAZIZ, MKILIFI M.H. (1977) 'Kenya'. Sow, Alfa Ibrahim (ed.) *Langues et politiques de langues en Afrique noire*. Paris: Nubia.

IGZAW, MESFIN (1978) 'Teaching English in Ethiopia'. *English around the World* **18**, 1–2, 7.

IKARA, BASHIR (1976) 'English as a factor in the process of Hausa language modernization'. PhD thesis (Leeds).

IKEKEONWU, CLARA J. (1982) 'Borrowings and neologisms in Igbo'. *Anthropological Linguistics* **24**, 480–6.

IKWUE, IKWUYATUM O. (1984) 'Effective educational language planning in Nigeria'. *International Education Journal* **1**, 39–60.

ILOKA, GODWIN (1979) 'The role of teaching English as a national language: the case of Nigeria'. *The English Journal* **68**, 9, 19–21.

INYAMA, N.F. (1990) 'Language and characterization in Cyprian Ekwenzi's "People of the City" and Jagua "Nana"'. Jones, Eldred/Eustace Palmer/Marjorie Jones (eds) *The Question of Language in African Literature Today*. London: James Currey.

ISAACS, R.H. (1970) ' "Learning through language" – an intensive preparation course for pupils entering English medium secondary schools from Swahili medium primary schools in Tanzania'. Gorman, Thomas P. (ed.), 70–83.

IWARA, A.V. (1981) 'Mother-tongue education: problems and perspectives in a post-colonial African state: Nigeria'. *Presence Africaine* **119**, 90–103.

JACOBS, ROBERT (1966) *English Language Teaching in Nigeria. An assessment of the situation with recommendations for action*. Lagos: The Ford Foundation.

JAMA, VIRGINIA (1982) 'The English language in Somalia'. *English Around the World* **26**, 1, 4–5. Repr. (1983) *Le lingue del mondo* **48**, 49–53.

JAMES, S.L. (1979) 'Three basic functions of the English language in Nigeria'. Ubahakwe, Ebo (ed.), 257–67.

JIBRIL, MUNZALI (1979) 'Regional variation in Nigerian spoken English'. Ubahakwe, Ebo (ed.), 43–53.

JIBRIL, MUNZALI (1982a) 'Phonological variation in Nigerian English'. PhD thesis (Lancaster).

JIBRIL, MUNZALI (1982b) 'Nigerian English: An Introduction'. Pride, John B. (ed.), 73–84.

JIBRIL, MUNZALI (1986) 'Sociolinguistic variation in Nigerian English'. *English World-Wide* 7, 47–75.

JIBRIL, MUNZALI (1987) 'Language in Nigerian education'. *Indian Journal of Applied Linguistics* 13 (1), 38–51.

JIBRIL, MUNZALI (1991) 'The sociolinguistics of prepositional usage in Nigerian English'. Cheshire, Jenny (ed.), 519–44.

JOHNSON, ALEX C. (1981) 'Language and society in West African literature: a stylistic investigation into the linguistic resources of West African drama in English'. PhD thesis (Ibadan).

JOHNSON, ALEX C. (1985) 'Multilingualism and language policy in Sierra Leone'. *Bayreuth African Studies Series* 5, 115–44.

JOHNSON, BRUCE C. (1975) 'Stable triglossia at Larteh, Ghana'. Herbert, Robert H. (ed.) *Patterns in Language, Culture, and Society: Sub-Saharan Africa. Working Papers in Linguistics* 19, Columbus: Ohio State University 93–102. Repr. 1978 *West African Journal of Modern Languages* 3, 128–36.

JOHNSON, BRUCE C. (1977) 'Language functions in Africa: a typological view'. Kotey, Paul/Haig Der- Houssikian (eds), 54–67.

JONES, ELDRED (1960) 'Sierra Leone and the English language'. *West African Journal of English* 4, 10–18.

JONES, ELDRED (1971) 'Krio: an English-based language of Sierra Leone'. Spencer, John (ed.), 66–94.

JONES, FREDERICK C.V. (1983) 'English-derived words in Sierra Leone Krio'. PhD thesis (Leeds).

JONES, THOMAS JESSE (1922) *Education in Africa. A Study of West, South, and Equatorial Africa*. London: Edinburgh House Press.

JONES, THOMAS JESSE (n.d. (1925)) *Education in East Africa. A Study of East, South, and Equatorial Africa by the African Education Commission, under the Auspices of the Phelps-Stokes Fund and Foreign Mission Societies of North America and Europe*. New York: Phelps-Stokes Fund.

JOWITT, DAVID/SILAS NNAMONU (1985) *Common Errors in English*. Harlow: Longman.

KACHRU, BRAJ B. (1985) 'Standards, codification, and sociolinguistic realism: the English language in the outer circle'. Quirk, Randolph/ Henry Widdowson (eds) *English in the World: Teaching and Learning of Languages and Literature*. Cambridge: Cambridge University Press, 11–30.

KACHRU, BRAJ B. (1986a) *The Alchemy of English. The Spread, Functions and Models of Non-native Englishes*. Oxford: Pergamon.

KACHRU, BRAJ B. (1986b) 'The power and politics of English'. *World Englishes* 5, 121–40.

KACHRU, BRAJ B. (ed.) (1982) *The Other Tongue: English Across Cultures*. Urbana: University of Illinois Press.

KANYORO, MUSIMBI R.A. (1991) 'The politics of the English language in Kenya and Tanzania'. Cheshire, Jenny (ed.), 402–19.

KAPLAN, R.B. (1966) 'Cultural thought patterns in inter-cultural education'. *Language Learning* 16, 1–20.

KAPLAN, R.B. (1987) 'Cultural thought patterns revisited'. Conner U./R.B. Kaplan (eds) *Writing Across Languages: Analysis of L2 Text*. Reading, MA: Addison-Wesley.

KASHOKI, MUBANGA E. (1971) 'Language and nation in Zambia: the problem of integration'. *Journal of the Language Association of Eastern Africa* 2, 91–104.

KASHOKI, MUBANGA E. (1974) 'Language: a blueprint for national integration'. *Bulletin of the Zambia Language Group* 1 (2), 21–49.

KASHOKI, MUBANGA E. (1975) 'Migration and language change: the interaction of town and country'. *African Social Research* 19, 707–29.

KASHOKI, MUBANGA E. (1978) 'The language situation in Zambia'. Ohannessian, Sirarpi/Mubanga E. Kashoki (eds), 9–46.

KASHOKI, MUBANGA E. (1982) 'Rural and Urban multilingualism in Zambia: some trends'. *International Journal of the Sociology of Language* 34, 137–66.

KASSULAMEMBA, FREDERICK T. (1984) 'The learning of postmodification structure by adult second language learners of English: a case for Tanzania'. PhD thesis (Reading).

KATAMBA, FRANCIS/FRANZ ROTTLAND (1987) 'Syllable structure and English loan-words in Luganda'. *Afrikanistische Arbeitspapiere* (Köln) 9, 77–101.

KELLEGHAN, T. (1961) 'Some implications of bilingualism for education in Nigeria'. *Ibadan* 11, 31–3.

KHALID, ABDALLAH (1977) *The Liberation of Swahili*. Nairobi: The Kenya Literature Bureau.

KHUMALO, J.S.M. (1984) 'A preliminary survey of Zulu adoptives'. *African Studies* (Witwatersrand University) 43, 205–16.

KILLAM, DOUGLAS (1976) 'Notes on adaptation and variation in the use of English in writing by Haliburton Furphy, Achebe, Narayan and Naipaul'. Niven, Alistair (ed.), 121–35.

KIRK-GREENE, A.H.M. (1963) 'Neologisms in Hausa: a sociological approach.' *Africa* 33 (1), 25–44.

KIRK-GREENE, ANTHONY (1971) 'The influence of West African languages on English'. Spencer, John (ed.), 123–44.

KLOSS, HEINZ (1978) *Problems of Language Policy in South Africa*. Wien: Wilhelm Braunmüller.

KNAPPERT, J. (1968) 'The function of language in a political situation', *Linguistics* 39, 59–67.

KNAPPERT, J. (1970) 'The problem of national languages and education in Africa'. *La Mondo Lingvo-Problemo* 2 (4), 21–37.

KOFELE-KALE, NDIVA (1980) *An African Experiment in Nation-Building: The Bilingual Cameroon Republic Since Reunification*. Boulder, Colorado: Westview Press.

KOTEY, PAUL F.A./HAIG DER-HOUSSIKIAN (eds) (1977) *Language and Linguistic Problems in Africa*. Columbia, SC: Hornbeam Press.

KRASHEN, S.D. (1981) *Second Language Acquisition and Second Language Learning*. Oxford: Pergamon Press.

KUJORE, OBAFEMI (1985) *English Usage. Some Notable Nigerian Variations*. Ibadan: Evans Brothers (Nigeria Publishers) Ltd.

KUMENE, D.P. (1963) 'Southern Sotho words of English and Afrikaans origin'. *Word* 19, 347–75.

KWOFIE, E.P. (1972) 'The language question and language consciousness in West Africa'. *Bulletin of the African Studies Association of the West Indies* (Mona) 5, 5–20.

LABOV, WILLIAM (1982) 'Objectivity and commitment in linguistic science: the case of the Black English trial in Ann Arbor'. *Language and Society* 11, 165–201.

LADEFOGED, PETER/RUTH GLICK/CLIVE CRIPER (1971) *Language in Uganda*. Nairobi: Oxford University Press.

LAITIN, DAVID D. (1979) 'Language choice and national development: a typology for Africa'. *International Interactions* 6, 291–321.

LAITIN, DAVID D./CAROL M. EASTMAN (1989) 'Language conflict: transactions and games in Kenya', *Cultural Anthropology* 4, 51–72.

LANHAM, L.W. (1963) 'Teaching English pronunciation in Southern Africa'. *Language Learning* 13, 153–70.

LANHAM, L.W. (1965) 'Teaching English to Africans: a crisis in education'. *Optima* (Johannesburg) 15, 197–204.

LANHAM, L.W. (1967) *The Pronunciation of South African English. A Phonetic-Phonemic Introduction*. Cape Town/Amsterdam: A.A. Balkema.

LANHAM, L.W. (1976) 'English as a second language in South Africa since 1820'. Villiers, André de (ed.), 279–96.

LANHAM, L.W. (1978) 'An outline history of the languages of Southern Africa'. Lanham, L.W./K. Prinsloo (eds), 13–28.

LANHAM, L.W. (1978) 'South African English'. Lanham, L.W./K. Prinsloo (eds), 138–65.

LANHAM, L.W. (1982) 'English in South Africa'. Bailey, Richard/Manfred Görlach (eds), 353–83.

LANHAM, L.W. (1984) 'Stress and intonation and the intelligibility of South African Black English'. *African Studies* 43 (2), 217–30.

LANHAM, L.W. (1985) 'The perception and evaluation of varieties of English in South African Society', Greenbaum, Sidney (ed.), 242–51.

LANHAM, L.W./C.A. MACDONALD (1979) *The Standard in South African English and Its Social History*. Heidelberg: Groos.

LANHAM, L.W./K. PRINSLOO (eds) (1978) *Language and Communication Studies in South Africa*. Cape Town: Oxford University Press.

LASS, ROGER (1987) 'How reliable is Goldswain? On the credibility of an early South African English source'. *African Studies* 46 (2), 156–62.

LASS, ROGER/SUSAN WRIGHT (1986) 'Endogeny vs. contact: 'Afrikaans influence' on South African English'. *English World-Wide* 7, 201–25.

LAVER, J. (1968) 'Assimilation in educated Nigerian English'. *English Language Teaching Journal* 22, 156–60.

LAWRENCE, LORRAINE/CHARLES SARVAN (1983) 'Zambian English: an enquiry'
Zambia Educational Review **4** (1), 27–39.

LAWRENCE, LORRAINE (1989) 'Language in education: an evaluation of the
teaching of structure in Zambian grade 8 classes '. PhD thesis
(University of Zambia, Lusaka).

LEECH, GEOFFREY N./MICHAEL H. SHORT (1981) *Style in Fiction*. London:
Longman.

LE PAGE, ROBERT B./ANDRÉE TABOURET-KELLER (1985) *Acts of Identity*.
Cambridge: Cambridge University Press.

LÈGERE, KARSTEN (1984) 'Fragen der Diskussion um die Sprachpolitik eines
künftig unabhängigen Namibia'. *Zeitschrift für Phonetik, Sprachwis-
senschaft und Kommunikationsforschung* **37**, 595–605.

LEWIS, M./W. MASTERS (1987) *Better English: A Handbook of Common
Errors*. Harare: Longman Zimbabwe.

LEITH, DICK (1983) *A Social History of English*. London: Routledge &
Kegan Paul.

LIEBERSON, STANLEY J./EDWARD J. MCCABE (1982) 'Domains of language
usage and mother-tongue shift in Nairobi'. *International Journal of the
Sociology of Language* **34**, 83–94.

LINDFORS, BERNTH (1966) 'African vernacular styles in Nigerian fiction'.
College Language Association Journal **9**, 265–73.

LINDFORS, BERNTH (1969) 'Nigerian fiction in English, 1952–1967'. PhD
thesis (UCLA).

LISIMBA, M. (1975) 'A note on the feelings and attitudes to the
introduction of a national language'. *Bulletin of the Zambia Language
Group* **2** (1), 1–6.

LLOYD, TREVOR O. (1984) *The British Empire 1558–1983*. Oxford: Oxford
University Press.

LOWENBERG, PETER H. (1986) 'Non-native varieties of English: nativization,
norms, and implications'. *Studies in Second language Acquisition* **8**, 1–
18.

LUBEGA, STEPHEN (1987) 'English as an international language: the concept
and misconceptions'. *Journal of English as a Second Language* **1**, 62–
73.

MACADAM, BRYSON (1970) 'The English medium scheme in Zambia'.
Gorman, Thomas P. (ed.), 37–50.

MACADAM, BRYSON (1970/71) 'English medium in the Zambian primary
system'. *Teacher Education in New Countries* **11**, 221–28.

MACADAM, BRYSON (1973) 'The development of the Zambian primary
course'. *Educational Development International* **1** (2), 58–60.

MACADAM, BRYSON (1978) 'The new Zambia primary course'. Ohannessian, Sirarpi/Mubanga E. Kashoki (eds) *Language in Zambia*.
London: International African Institute, 329–54.

MACMILLAN, D. (1980) *Language Policies for African Primary Education*.
Washington, DC: World Bank.

MACMILLAN, M. (1970) 'Aspects of bilingualism in university education in
Sudan'. Gorman, Thomas P. (ed.), 144–68.

MCCORMACK, WILLIAM C./STEPHEN A. WURM (1979) *Language and Society. Anthropological Issues*. The Hague: Mouton.
MCGINLEY, KEVIN (1978) 'The future of English in Zimbabwe'. *World Englishes* 6, 159–65.
MCGREGOR, G.P. (ed.) (1968) *English for Education? Papers on the Teaching of English as a Second Language*. Lusaka: Government Printer.
MCGREGOR, G.P. (1971) *English in Africa*. London: Heinemann.
MACHUNGO, INES/GILBERTO MATUSSE (1989) 'Language and literature in education in Mosambique'. Ngara, Emanuel/Andrew Morrison (eds), 133–9.
MACKENZIE, NORMAN H. (1959) 'The place of English in African education'. *International Review of Education* 5, 216–23.
MAFENI, BERNARD (1971) 'Nigerian Pidgin'. Spencer, John (ed.), 95–112.
MAGURA, BENJAMIN J. (1984) 'Style and Meaning in African English'. PhD thesis (Illinois).
MAGURA, BENJAMIN J. (1985) 'Southern African Black English'. *World Englishes* 4, 251–6.
MALAN, KAREN C. (1981) 'An investigation of non-standard English syntax in 12-year old coloured children'. *The South African Journal of Communication Disorders* 28, 68–80.
MALHERBE, E.G. (1946) *The Bilingual School: A Study of Bilingualism in South Africa*. London: Longmans, Green & Co.
MALHERBE, E.G. (1966) *Demographic and Socio-Political Forces Determining the Position of English in the South African Republic: English as Mother-Tongue*. Johannesburg: The English Academy.
MALHERBE, E.G. (1978) 'Bilingual education in the Republic of South Africa'. Spolsky, B./Robert Cooper (eds) *Case Studies in Bilingual Education*. Rowley, MA: Newbury House, 167–202.
MALONG, ROWBONE (Second Edition 1978) *Ah Big Yaws? A Guard to Sow Theffricun Innglissh*. Cape Town: David Philip.
MATEENE, KAHOMBO (1985) 'Failure in the obligatory use of European languages in Africa and the advantages of a policy of linguistic independence'. *Osnabrücker Beiträge zur Sprachtheorie (OBST)* 31, 41–73.
MATTAR, O.M.S. (1978) 'A study of the written English of some Egyptian students in the University of Alexandria with suggestions for improvement in the teaching of English'. PhD thesis (London).
MAZRUI, ALI (1966) 'The English language and political consciousness in British Colonial Africa'. JMAS 4, 295–311. Repr. as 'English and the emergence of modern African politicians'. Mazrui, Ali (1975), 86–102.
MAZRUI, ALI (1966) 'The English language and political consciousness in British colonial Africa'. *Journal of Modern African Studies* 4, 295–311.
MAZRUI, ALI (1967) 'The English language and the origins of African nationalism. *Mawazo* 1, 1. Repr. Mazrui, Ali, (1975) 39–53.
MAZRUI, ALI (1968) 'Some sociopolitical functions of English literature in Africa'. Fishman, Joshua A./Charles A. Ferguson/Jyotirinda Das Gupta (eds), 183–97.

MAZRUI, ALI (1971) 'Islam and the English language in East and West Africa'. Whiteley, Wilfried H. (ed.), 179–97.

MAZRUI, ALI (1973) 'The English language and the origins of African nationalism'. Bailey, R.W./J.L. Robinson (eds) *Varieties of Present-Day English*. New York: Macmillan, 56–76.

MAZRUI, ALI (1974) 'Language and Black destiny'. Mazrui, Ali *World Culture and Black Experience*. Washington, DC: University Press, 82–110.

MAZRUI, ALI (1975) 'The racial boundaries of the English language: an African perspective'. Savard, J.-G./R. Vigneault (eds) *Les états multilingues: problèmes et solutions*. Québec: Université Laval, 61–86.

MAZRUI, ALI (1975) *The Political Sociology of the English Language. An African Perspective*. The Hague: Mouton.

MAZRUI, ALI/MOLLY MAZRUI (1967) 'The impact of the English language on African international relations. *Political Quarterly* 38 (2). Repr. Mazrui, Ali (1975), 185–99.

MBANGWANA, PAUL (1987) 'Some characteristics of sound patterns of Cameroon Standard English'. *Multilingua* 6, 411–24.

MBANGWANA, PAUL (1989) 'Flexibility in lexical usage in Cameroon English'. García, Ofelia/Ricardo Otheguy (eds), 319–33.

MBASSI-MANGA, FRANCIS (1973) 'English in Cameroon: a study of historical contact patterns of usage and current trends'. PhD thesis (Leeds).

MBASSI-MANGI, FRANCIS (1976) 'The state of contemporary English in Cameroon'. *Cameroon Studies in English and French* 1, 49–63.

MBUNDA, FULGENS/C.J. BRUMFIT/D. CONSTABLE/C.P. HILL (1980) 'Language teaching in secondary schools'. Polomé, Edgar E./C.P. Hill (eds), 306–40.

MELBER, HENNING (1985) 'Ein sprachloses Volk stirbt einen lautlosen Tod: Fremdherrschaft, Befreiungskampf und Dekolonisation: Probleme der Sprachpolitik für ein befreites Namibia'. *Osnabrücker Beiträge zur Sprachtheorie (OBST)* 31, 13–39.

MESTHRIE, RAJEND (1987) 'From OV to VO in language shift: South African Indian English and its OV substrates'. *English World-Wide* 8, 263–76.

MESTHRIE, RAJEND (1988) 'Toward a lexicon of South African Indian English', *World Englishes* 7, 5–14.

MESTHRIE, RAJEND (1989) *A Lexicon of South African Indian English*. Leeds: Peepal Tree Press.

MESTHRIE, RAJEND (1991) 'Syntactic variation in South African Indian English: the relative clause'. Cheshire, Jenny (ed.), 462–73.

MEZIANI, AHMED (1983) 'Modality in English and Maroccan Arabic'. *IRAL (International Review of Applied Linguistics in Language Teaching)* 21, 267–82.

MILROY, LESLEY (1987) *Observing and Analysing Natural Language*. Oxford: Basil Blackwell.

MKUDE, DANIEL J. (1986) 'English in contact with Swahili'. Viereck, Wolfgang/Wolf-Dietrich Bald (eds), 513–32.

MOAG, RODNEY (1982) 'The life cycle of non-native Englishes: A case study'. Kachru, Braj B. (ed.), 270–88.

MOGOTSI, MAMOEKETSI MARIA (1987) 'A semantic analysis of borrowed words in Southern Sotho'. BA thesis (University of South Africa, Pretoria).

MOLNOS, ANGELA (1969) *Language Problems in Africa. A bibiliography (1946–1967) and a summary of the present situation, with special reference to Kenya, Tanzania and Uganda.* Nairobi: Information Circular 2 East African Research Information Centre (EARIC).

MOODY, JAMES (1973) 'Possible sources of errors in the English of first year students at the University of Zambia: some implications for the teaching of English in Zambia'. *The Bulletin of the Zambia Language Group* 1 (2), 67–82.

MOODY, JAMES (1982) 'The concept of register and its application to colloquial English conversation in Zambia'. Unpublished paper (University of Zambia, Lusaka).

MOODY, JAMES (1985) *Zambians Talking: Twenty-five English Conversations.* Lusaka: University of Zambia, Institute of African Studies.

MOORE, GERARD (1965) 'English words, African lives'. *Presence Africaine* 54, 90–101.

MORRISON, ANDREW (1989) 'World Englishes: implications for English language teaching in Zimbabwe'. Ngara, Emanuel/Andrew Morrison (eds), 190–9.

MOSHA, M. (1971) 'The national language question of Uganda'. *Journal of the Language Association of East Africa* 2 (2), 105–21.

MPHAHLELE, EZEKIEL (1963) 'Are we going to fold our arms and wait for that kingdom to come?' *Transition III* (2), 11–12. Repr. Riemenschneider, Dieter (1983) (ed.), 134–6.

MPHAHLELE, EZEKIEL (1964) 'The language of African literature'. *Harvard Educational Review* 34, 298–305.

MUDZI, ALICE KATHLEEN M. (1976) 'The effect of English on CiTonga, a Bantu language of Zambia'. MA thesis (Leeds).

MUFWENE, SALIKOKO S. (1986) 'The universalist and substrate hypotheses complement one another'. Muyksen, Peter/Neval Smith (eds), 129–62.

MUFWENE, SALIKOKO S. (1990) 'Transfer and the substrate hypothesis in creolistics'. *Studies in Second Language Acquisition* 12, 1–23.

MÜHLHÄUSLER, PETER (1986) *Pidgin and Creole Linguistics.* Oxford: Basil Blackwell.

MURRAY, M. (1963) 'English in the Sudan: trends and policies, relations with Arabic'. Spencer, John (ed.), 86–95.

MUSISI, C. HEATON, J. (1970) 'Research in English medium problems in Uganda primary schools'. Gorman, Thomas P. (ed.), 30–6.

MUSONDA, MOSES (1978) 'A study of language use among local students at the university of Zambia'. Ohannessian, Sirarpi/Mubanga E. Kashoki (eds), 228–43.

MUTHIANI, JOSEPH (1979) 'Sociopsychological base of language choice and use: the case of Swahili, vernaculars and English in Kenya'. McCormack, William C./Stephen A. Wurm (eds), 377–88.

MUYSKEN, PIETER/NOVAL SMITH (eds) (1986) *Substrata versus Universals in Creole Genesis*. Amsterdam: John Benjamins.

MYTTON, GRAHAM (1978) 'Language and the media in Zambia'. Ohannessian, Sirarpi/Mubanga E.Kashoki (eds), 207–27.

NAMA, CHARLES A. (1990) 'A critical analysis of the translation of African literature'. *Language & Communication* 10, 75–86.

NARTY, JONAS N.A. (1982) 'Code-switching, interference or faddism? Language use among educated Ghanians'. *Anthropological Linguistics* 24, 183–92.

NDAHI, K. (1977) 'The place of grammar in the teaching of English'. *The Nigerian Language Teacher*, 12–24.

NEALE, BARBARA (1971) 'Asians in Nairobi: a preliminary survey'. Whiteley, Wilfried H. (ed.), 334–46.

NEALE, BARBARA (1974) 'Language use among the Asian communities'. Whiteley, Wilfried H. (ed.), 263–317.

NELSON, C.L. (1984) 'Intelligibility: the case of non-native varieties of English'. PhD thesis (Illinois at Urbana-Champaign).

NELSON, CECIL L. (1988) 'The pragmatic dimension of creativity in the other tongue', *World Englishes* 7, 173–81.

NGARA, E.A. (1974) 'A redefinition of the role of the English language in African universities'. *Bulletin of the Association of African Universities* 1 (2), 35–42.

NGARA, E.A. (1975) 'Comments on the teaching of English in Botswana, Lesotho and Swaziland'. *Education in Botswana, Lesotho and Swaziland* 9, 4–14.

NGARA, E.A. (1982) *Bilingualism, Language Contact and Language Planning*. Gwelo: Mambo Press.

NGARA, E.A. (1983) 'Non-contrastive errors in African English: Types and significance'. *IRAL (International Review of Applied Linguistics)* 21, 35–45.

NGARA, EMANUEL/ANDREW MORRISON (eds) (1989) *Literature, Languages and the Nation*. Harare: ATOLL in association with Baobab Books.

NGUGI WA THIONG'O (1986) *Decolonizing the Mind. The Politics of Language in English Literature*. London: James Currey.

NIEDZELSKI, HENRY (1983) 'Teaching English in Francophone Africa'. *World Language English* 2, 219–24.

NIVEN, ALASTAIR (ed.) (1976) *The Commonwealth Writer Overseas. Themes of Exile and Expatriation*. Bruxelles: Didier.

NORRISH, JOHN A. (1978) 'A language and study skills course in the University of Ghana'. *English Language Teaching Journal* 32 (2), 127–33.

NSIBAMBI, APOLO (1971) 'Language policy in Uganda'. *African Affairs* (London) 70, 62–71.

NSONTA, PAUL M. (1973) 'Some observations on language use in churches in Zambia'. *Bulletin of the Zambia Language Group* 2 (1), 12–29.

NWAEGBE, W.D.O. (1978) 'The future of English in Nigeria'. *Nigerian Journal of the Humanities* 2, 34–41.

NWOGA, DONATUS (1965) 'Onitsha market literature'. *Transition* 4, 26–33.

NWOYE, ONUIGBO GREGORY (1978) 'Language planning in Nigeria' PhD thesis (Georgetown).

O'BARR, W.M. (1976) 'Language use and language policy in Tanzania: an overview'. O'Barr, W.M./J.F. O'Barr (eds), 31–48.

O'BARR, WILLIAM/JEAN F. O'BARR (1976) Language and Politics. The Hague: Mouton.

O'DOWD, M.C. (1974) 'The English-speaking South African and the problem of identity'. Optima 24, 113–28.

O'HAGAN, CHARLES (1962) 'English-medium teaching in Kenya'. Overseas Education 34 (3), 99–106.

OBIECHINA, EMMANUEL N. (1973) 'The problem of language in African writing: the example of the novel'. The Conch 5 (12), 11–28.

OBIECHINA, EMMANUEL N. (1974) 'Variety differentiation in English usage'. Journal of the Nigeria English Studies Association 6, 77–94.

OBILADE, ANTHONY O. (1978) 'Pidgin English as a medium of instruction: the Nigerian experience'. Africana Marburgensia 13, 59–69.

OBILADE, ANTHONY O. (1984) 'On the nativization of the English language in Nigeria'. Anthropological Linguistics 26, 170–85.

OBOTE, MILTON (1967) 'Language and national identification. Address'. East Africa Journal 4, 1. Repr. Mazrui, Ali (ed.) (1975), 210–15.

ODUMUH, ADAMA E. (1981) 'Aspects of the semantics and syntax of "Educated Nigerian English"'. PhD thesis (Ahmadu Bello University, Zaria, Nigeria).

ODUMUH, ADAMA E. (1984) 'Educated Nigerian English as a model of standard Nigerian English'. World Language English 3, 231–5.

ODUMUH, ADAMA E. (1987) Nigerian English (NigE). Selected Essays. Zaria: Ahmadu Bello University Press Ltd.

OGALI, OGALI A. (1980) Veronica My Daughter and Other Onitsha Market Plays and Stories. Washington: Three Continents Press.

OHANNESSIAN, SIRARPI (1978) 'Zambian languages in secondary schools: attitudes of teachers in training'. Ohannessian, S./M.E. Kashoki (eds), 376–97.

OHANNESSIAN, SIRARPI/KASHOKI, MUBANGA E. (1978) Language in Zambia. London: Oxford University Press for the International African Institute.

OHANNESSIAN, SIRARPI/CHARLES A. FERGUSON/EDGAR C. POLOMÉ (1975) Language Surveys in Developing Nations. Papers and reports on sociolinguistic surveys. Arlington, Virgina: Center for Applied Linguistics.

OJAIDE, TANURE (1978) 'My poetry: English language and the African tradition'. World Englishes 6, 165–9.

OJERINDE, ADEDIBU (1980) 'Close tests as a measure of English language proficiency among Nigerian primary-school pupils'. English Language Teaching Journal 35, 62–6.

OJO, VALENTINE (1977) 'English–Yoruba language contact in Nigeria'. PhD thesis (Tübingen).

OKANLAWON, BIDEMI O. (1984) 'A study of the acquisition of some aspects of English by Nigerian learners'. PhD thesis (Edinburgh).

OKANLAWON, BIDEMI O. (1987) 'A study of the acquisition of the article system of English by Nigerian learners'. *Journal of English as a Second Language* 1, 47–60.

OKARA, GABRIEL (1963) African speech . . . English words. *Transition* III (10), 15–16. Repr. Riemenschneider, Dieter (ed.) (1983), 136–8.

OKONKWO, C.J.E. (1975) 'A function-oriented model for initial language planning in Sub-Saharan Africa'. *Ohio State University Working Papers in Linguistics* 19, 37–52.

OKUDZETO, SAM (1978) 'Language and the judicial system in Ghana'. *West African Journal of Modern Languages* 3, 66–70.

OLAGOKE, D. OLU (1975) 'An error analysis of the English of Lagos university students'. PhD thesis (Edinburgh).

OLIVER, ROLAND/J.D. FAGE (5th Edition 1975) *A Short History of Africa.* Harmondsworth: Penguin African Library.

OLUIKPE, BENSON O. (1979) 'Noun phrase in legal English. A grammatical sketch'. Ubahakwe, Ebo (ed.), 200–26.

OLUIKPE, BENSON O. (1984) 'Negation in English and Igbo'. *IRAL (International Review of Applied Linguistics in Language Teaching* 22, 219–28.

OMOLEWA, MICHAEL (1975) 'The English language in colonial Nigeria 1862–1960: a study of the major factors which promoted the English language'. *Journal of the Nigerian English Studies Association* 7, 103–17. Repr. (1978) 'The ascendancy of English in Nigerian schools, 1862–1960. A study of language educational policy in colonial Nigeria'. *West African Journal of Modern Languages* 3, 86–97.

OMOLEWA, MICHAEL (1979) 'The emergence of non-standard English in Nigeria 1842–1926'. Ubahakwe, Ebo (ed.), 14–26.

OMONDI, LUCIA (1979) 'Paralinguistics: A survey of non-verbal communication with particular reference to Zambia and Kenya'. *Journal of the Language Association of East Africa* 4 (1), 19–41.

OMONDI, LUCIA (1980) 'Language and culture: the relevance of linguistics to the Kenya situation'. *Journal of East African Research and Development* 10 153–64.

OSBISTON, RACHEL (ed.) (1987) *Communication Skills for the Public Sector.* Lusaka: National Institute of Public Administration.

OSISANYA, DORCAS (1974) 'The Teaching of Informal Varieties'. *Journal of the Nigerian Studies Association* 6, 100–9.

OWOMOYELA, OYEKAN (1979) *African Literatures: An Introduction.* Waltham, Mass.: African Studies Association (Crossroads Press).

PAI, A. DADA/T. ODERINDE (1979) 'An empirical study of the acceptability of four accents spoken in Nigeria'. Ubahakwe, Ebo (ed.), 242–56.

PARKIN, DAVID (1971) 'Language choice in two Kampala housing states'. Whiteley, Wilfried H. (ed.), 347–63.

PARKIN, DAVID J. (1974) 'Status factors in language adding: Bahati housing estate in Nairobi'. Whiteley, Wilfred H. (ed.), 147–65.

PARKIN, DAVID J. (1977) 'Emergent and stabilized multilingualism: polyethnic peer groups in urban Kenya'. Giles, H. (ed.) *Language, Ethnicity and Intergroup Relations.* London: Academic Press, 185–209.

PAUSEWANG, SIEGFRIED (1973) *Methods and Concepts of Social Research in a Rural Developing Society*. München: Weltforum Verlag.

PEMAGBI, JOE (1989) 'Still a deficient language? A description and glossary of the 'New English' of Sierra Leone'. *English Today* 17 (5), 20–4.

PERREN, G.E. (1956) 'Some problems of oral English in East Africa'. *English Language Teaching* 11, 3–10.

PERREN, G.E. (1958) 'Bilingualism, or replacement? English in East Africa'. *English Language Teaching* 13, 18–22.

PETTMANN, CHARLES (1913, repr. 1968) *Africanderisms. A Glossary of South African Colloquial Words and Phrases and of Place and Other Names*. London: Longmans, Green and Co.

PHILLIPSON, ROBERT/TOVE SKUTTNAB-KANGAS/HUGH AFRICA (1986) 'Namibian educational language planning: English for liberation or neocolonialism?' Spolski, Bernard (ed.) *Language and Education in Multilingual Settings*. Clevedon, UK: Multilingual Matters, 77–95.

PLATT, JOHN (1986) 'Quantitative analysis and the New Englishes', *World Englishes* 5, 85–7.

PLATT, JOHN/HEIDI WEBER/MIAN LIAN HO (1984) *The New Englishes*. London/Boston/Melbourne/Henley: Routledge & Kegan Paul.

PLATT, JOHN/HEIDI WEBER (1980) *English in Singapore and Malaysia. Status: Features: Functions*. Kuala Lumpur: Oxford University Press.

POLOMÉ, EDGAR C. (1979) 'Tanzanian language policy and Swahili'. *Word* 30, 160–71.

POLOMÉ, EDGAR C. (1980) 'Tanzania: a socio-linguistic perspective?'. Polomé, Edgar C./C.P. Hill (eds) (1980), 103–38.

POLOMÉ, EDGAR C. (1982) 'Rural versus urban multilingualism in Tanzania'. *International Journal of the Sociology of Language* 34, 167–81.

POLOMÉ, EDGAR C. (1982) 'Sociolinguistically orientated language surveys: reflections on the survey of language use and language teaching in Eastern Africa'. *Language in Society* 11, 265–83.

PONGWENI, ALEC J.C. (1990) 'The pronunciation of English vowels by Shona speakers: problems and causes'. Ramsaran, Susan (ed.) (1990), 231–42.

POVEY, JOHN (1969) 'The English language of the contemporary African novel'. *Critique* 11, 79–86.

POVEY, JOHN (1976) 'The role of English in Africa: A survey'. *English in Africa* 3, 13–22. Repr. *Workpapers on Teaching English as a Second Language* 10, 79–87.

PRATOR, CLIFFORD (1967) 'The survey of language use and language teaching in Eastern Africa'. *Linguistic Reporter* 9, 1–28.

PRATOR, CLIFFORD (1975) 'The survey of language use and language teaching in Eastern Africa in retrospect'. Ohannessian, Sirarpi/Charles A. Ferguson/Edgar E. Polomé (eds) (1975), 145–58.

PRATOR, CLIFFORD H. (1968) 'The British heresy in TESL'. Fishman, Jushua A./Charles A. Ferguson/Jyotirindra Das Gupta (eds), 459–76.

PRESTON, DENNIS R. (ed.) (1989) *Sociolinguistics and Second Language Acquisition*. Oxford: Basil Blackwell.

PRIDE, JOHN (ed.) (1982) *New Englishes*. Rowley, Mass.: Newbury House.

QUIRK, RANDOLPH (1990) 'Language varieties and standard language', English Today **21**, 3–10.

QUIRK, RANDOLPH/SIDNEY GREENBAUM/GEOFFREY LEECH/JAN SVARTVIK (1985) *A Comprehensive Grammar of the English Language*. London: Longman.

RADFORD, W.L. (1970) 'The teaching of English in Kenya secondary schools: problems and possibilities'. Gorman, Thomas P. (ed.), 84–9.

RAMSARAN, SUSAN (ed.) (1990) *Studies in the Pronunciation of English*. Cambridge: Cambridge University Press.

REA, PAULINE M. (ed.) (1980) 'Language for Education. Communication Skills Unit. 10th Anniversary of the University of Dar es Salaam'. University of Dar es Salaam.

REAGAN, TIMOTHY G. (1987) 'The politics of linguistic apartheid: language policies in black education in South Africa'. *The Journal of Negro Education* **56** (3), 299–312.

REH, MECHTHILD (1981) *Problems of Linguistic Communication in Africa*. Hamburg: Helmut Buske.

REH, MECHTHILD/BERND HEINE (1982) *Sprachpolitik in Afrika*. Hamburg: Buske.

RICE, FRANK A. (ed.) (1962) *A study in the role of second languages in Asia, Africa and Latin America*. Washington DC: Center for Applied Linguistics.

RICHMOND, EDMUND B. (1980) 'Literacy and language teaching in Gambia'. *The Modern Language Journal* **64**, 416–21.

RICHMOND, EDMUND B. (1989) 'African English expressions in the Gambia'. *World Englishes* **8**, 223–8.

RICKFORD, JOHN R. (1987) 'The haves and the have nots: sociolinguistic surveys and the assessment of speaker competence'. *Language in Society* **16**, 149–78.

RIEMENSCHNEIDER, DIETER (ed.) (1983) *Grundlagen zur Literatur in englischer Sprache: West- und Ostafrika*. München: Fink.

ROMAINE, SUZANNE (1988a) 'Contributions from pidgin and creole studies to a sociolinguistic theory of language change'. *International Journal of the Sociology of Language* **71**, 59–66.

ROMAINE, SUZANNE (1988b) *Pidgin and Creole Languages*. London: Longman.

ROWLANDS, E.C. (1963) 'Yoruba and English, a problem of coexistence'. *African Language Studies* **4**, 208–14.

RUBAGUMYA, CASMIR M. (1986) 'Language planning in the Tanzanian educational system: problems and prospects'. *Journal of Multilingual and Multicultural Development* **7**, 283–300.

RUBAGUMYA, CASMIR M. (ed.) (1990) *Language in Education in Africa: A Tanzanian Perspective*. Cleveland: Multilingual Matters Ltd.

RUFAI, ABBA. (1977) 'The question of a national language in Nigeria: problems and prospects'. Kotey, Paul F.A./Haig Der-Houssikian (eds), 68–83.

RUGEMALIRA, J.M. (1990) 'The Communication Skills Unit and the language problem at the University of Dar es Salaam'. Rubagumya, Casmir M. (ed.), 105–22.

RUGEMALIRA, J.M/C.M. RUBAGUMYA/M.K. KAPINGA/A.F. LWAITAMA/J. TETLOW (1990) 'Reflections on recent developments in language policy in Tanzania'. Rubagumya, Casmir M. (ed.), 25–35.

RUZICKA, K.F. (1953) 'Lehnwörter im Swahili. I. Arabische und englische Lehnwörter'. Archiv Orientalni 21, 582–603.

RYNKIEWICH, M.A./J.P. SPRADLEY (1971) Ethnics and Anthropology: Dilemmas in Fieldwork. New York: Wiley.

SAAH, KOFI (1986) 'Language use and attitudes in Ghana' Anthropological Linguistics 28, 367–77.

SAHGAL, ANJU/R.K. AGNIHOTRI (1985) 'Syntax – the common bond. Acceptability of syntactic deviances in Indian English'. English World-Wide 6, 117–29.

SALAMI, A. (1968) 'Defining a "Standard Nigerian English"'. Journal of the Nigeria English Studies Association 2 (2), 99–106.

SALAMI, A. (1969) 'English loan words in Yoruba'. PhD thesis (London).

SALAMI, A. (1972) 'Vowel and consonant harmony and vowel restriction in assimilated English loanwords in Yoruba'. African Language Studies 13, 162–81.

SALAMI, L. OLADIPO (1986) 'Prospects and problems of urban sociolinguistic survey in Africa: notes from Ife-Ife, Nigeria'. Anthropological Linguistics 28, 473–82.

SANDELL, LIZA (1982) English Language in Sudan: A History of its Teaching and Politics. London: Ithaca Press.

SCHLEMMER, LAWRENCE (1976) 'English-speaking South Africans today: identity and integration into the broader national community'. de Villiers, André (ed.), 91–135.

SCHMIED, JOSEF (1983) 'Englisch in Afrika und Vorderasien'. Englisch-Formen und Funktionen einer Weltsprache. Bamberg: Universitätsbibliothek, 87–116.

SCHMIED, JOSEF (1985a) Englisch in Tansania. Sozio- und interlinguistische Probleme. Heidelberg: Groos.

SCHMIED, JOSEF (1985b) 'Attitudes towards English in Tanzania'. English World-Wide 6, 237–69.

SCHMIED, JOSEF (1986) 'English in Tanzanian education'. Bayreuth African Studies Series 5, 63–114.

SCHMIED, JOSEF (1990a) 'Accepted language behaviour as a basis for language teaching: a comparison of English in Kenya and Tanzania'. Rubagumya, C.M. (ed.), 123–32.

SCHMIED, JOSEF (1990b) 'The English language and African identities'. The Cambridge Review III/2309, 57–60.

SCHMIED, JOSEF (1990c) 'Corpus linguistics and non-native varieties of English'. New Englishes 9, 255–68.

SCHMIED, JOSEF (1990d) 'Language use, attitudes, performance and sociolinguistic background: a comparison of English in Kenya, Tanzania and Zambia'. English World-Wide 10, 217–38.

SCHMIED, JOSEF (1991a) 'National and subnational features in Kenyan English'. Cheshire, Jenny (ed.), 420–32.

SCHMIED, JOSEF (1991b) 'The status of English in Kenya and Tanzania'. Bammesberger, Alfred/Teresa Kirchner (eds) *Language and Civilisation*. Frankfurt: Lang.

SCHMIED, JOSEF (ed.) (1989) *English in East and Central Africa* 1. Bayreuth African Studies Series 15.

SCHMIED, JOSEF (ed.) (1990) *Linguistics in the Service of Africa*. Bayreuth African Studies Series 18.

SCHMIED, JOSEF (ed.) (1991) *English in East and Central Africa* 2. Bayreuth African Studies Series 22.

SCHNEIDER, GILBERT D. (1967) 'West African Pidgin English – an overview: phonology, morphology'. *Journal of English Linguistics* 1, 49–56.

SCHNEIDER, GILBERT D. (1970) 'West African Pidgin English'. Athens, Ohio.

SCHUMANN, JOHN H. (1978) *The Pidginization Process: A Model for Second Language Acquisition*. Rowley: Newbury House.

SCHURING, G.K. (1979) *A multilingual society: English and Africans among Blacks in the RSA*. Pretoria: South African Human Sciences Research Council.

SCOTT, MARGARET SUE/G. RICHARD TUCKER (1977) 'Error analysis and English-language strategies of Arab students'. *Language Learning* 24, 69–97.

SCOTTON, CAROL MYERS (1972) *Choosing a lingua franca in an African capital*. Edmonton/Champaign: Linguistic Research Inc.

SCOTTON, CAROL MYERS (1976a) 'Strategies of neutrality: language choice in uncertain situations'. *Language* 52, 919–41.

SCOTTON, CAROL MYERS (1976b) 'The role of norms and other factors in language choice in work situations in three African cities (Lagos, Kampala, Nairobi)'. Verdoodt, Albert/Rolf Kjolseth (eds), *Language in Sociology*. Louvain: ed. Peeters, 201–31.

SCOTTON, CAROL MYERS (1978) 'Language in East Africa: linguistic patterns and political ideologies'. Fishman, Joshua A. (ed.), 719–59.

SCOTTON, CAROL MYERS (1982) 'Language use in Kenya: an urban-rural comparison of the Luyia'. *International Journal of the Sociology of Language* 34, 121–36.

SCOTTON, CAROL MYERS (1983) 'The negotiation of identities in conversation: a theory of markedness and code choice'. *International Journal of the Sociology of Language* 44, 115–36.

SCOTTON, CAROL MYERS (1986) 'Diglossia and code switching'. Fishman, Joshua A. (ed.), 402–15.

SCOTTON, CAROL MYERS (1989), 'Codeswitching with English: Types of switching, types of communities'. *World Englishes* 8, 333–46.

SCOTTON, CAROL MYERS/W. URE (1977) 'Bilingual strategies: the social functions of code-switching'. *International Journal of the Sociology of Language* 13, 5–20.

SCOTTON, CAROL MYERS/W. URE (1982) 'The linguistic situation and language policy in Eastern Africa'. *Annual Review of Applied Linguistics* 3, 8–20.

SEBEOK, THOMAS A. (ed.) (1971) *Current Trends in Linguistics, Vol. 7: Linguistics in Sub-Saharan Africa*. The Hague and Paris: Mouton.

SENGHOR, LEOPOLD S. (1975) 'The essence of language: English and French'. *Cultures* 2 (2), 75–98.

SERPELL, ROBERT (1978a) 'Learning to say it better: a challenge for 5Zambian education'. *Bulletin of the Zambia Language Group*. Repr. Pride, John B. (ed.) (1982), 100–18.

SERPELL, ROBERT (1978b) 'Some developments in Zambia since 1971'. Ohannessian, Sirarpi/Mubanga E. Kashoki (eds), 424–47.

SEY, K.A. (1973) *Ghanaian English: An Exploratory Survey*. London: Macmillan.

SHNUKAL, ANNA/LYNELL MARCHESE (1983) 'Creolization of Nigerian Pidgin English: a progress report'. *English World-Wide* 4, 17–26.

SIACHITEMA, ALICE K. (1986) 'Attitudes towards the use of English in three neighbourhoods of Lusaka'. PhD thesis (Edinburgh).

SIACHITEMA, ALICE K. (1991) 'The social significance of language use and language choice in a Zambian urban setting: an empirical study of three neighbourhoods in Lusaka'. Cheshire, Jenny (ed.), 474–90.

SIBANDA, BEKI (1981) 'The question of a national language in Zimbabwe'. *Fourah Bay Studies in Language and Literature* (English Dept. Fourah Bay College, University of Sierra Leone) 2, 69–89.

SILVA, PENNY (1978) 'The 1820 settlement: some aspects of its influence on the vocabulary of South African English'. *English in Africa* 5, 61–70.

SIMUKOKO, YOUNGSON T. (1979) 'Second language learning and description: a theoretical frame of reference for studying Zambian English'. *The Bulletin of the Zambia Language Group* 4, 1–17.

SIMUKOKO, YOUNGSON T. (1981) 'Some aspects of the English of Bantu speakers in urban primary schools in Zambia'. PhD thesis (Edinburgh).

SINGLER, JOHN V. (1976–77) 'Language in Liberia in the nineteenth century: the settlers' perspective'. *Liberian Studies Journal* 7 (2), 73–85.

SINGLER, JOHN V. (1981) 'An introduction to Liberian English'. Peace Corps East Lansing: Michigan State University.

SINGLER, JOHN V. (1984) 'Variation in tense-aspect-modality in Liberian English'. PhD thesis (University of California, Los Angeles).

SINGLER, JOHN V. (1989) 'Plural marking in Liberian Settler English 1820–1980', *American Speech* 64, 40–64.

SINGLER, JOHN VICTOR (1991) 'Social and linguistic constraints in Liberian English'. Cheshire, Jenny (ed.), 545–62.

SMITH, BERNARD (1987) 'Arabic speakers'. Swan, Michael/Bernard Smith (eds), 142–57.

SMITH, LARRY S./CECIL L. NELSON (1985) 'International intelligibility of English: directions and resources.' *World Englishes* 4, 333–42.

SMITH, DAVID M./ROGER W. SHUY (ed.) (1972) *Sociolinguistics in Cross-Cultural Analysis*. Washington, DC: Georgetown University Press.

SMOCK, DAVID R. (1975) 'Language policy in Ghana'. Smock, David/Kwamena Bentsi-Enchill (ed.), 169–88.

SMOCK, DAVID/KWAMENA BENTSI-ENCHILL (eds) (1975) *The Search for National Integration in Africa*. New York: The Free Press.

SOW, ALFA IBRAHIM (1977) *Langues et Politique de Langues en Afrique Noire. L'Experience de l'Unesco*. Nubia: UNESCO.

SOYINKA, WOLE (1975). 'Aesthetic illusion: prescriptions for the suicide of poetry'. *Third Press Review* 1, 65–8.

SOYINKA, WOLE (1977). 'The scholar in African society'. *FESTAC Colloquium Proceedings*. Lagos. Document No. Col. PL/05 English Original, 44–53.

SPENCER, JOHN (1971a) 'West Africa and the English language'. Spencer, John (ed.), 1–34.

SPENCER, JOHN (1971b) 'Colonial language policies and their legacies'. Berry Jack/Joseph H. Greenberg (eds), *Current Trends in Linguistics 7: Linguistics in Sub-Saharan Africa*. The Hague: Mouton, 537–47. Repr. 'Colonial language policies and their legacies in Sub-Saharan Africa'. Fishman, Joshua A. (ed.) (1974) *Advances in Language Planning*. The Hague: Mouton, 163–75.

SPENCER, JOHN (1985) 'Language and development in Africa: The unequal equation'. Wolfson, Nessa/Joan Manes (eds), 387–97.

SPENCER, JOHN (1988) 'Reflections on language and development in tropical Africa'. Klegraf, Josef/Dietrich Nehls (eds) *Essays on the English Language and Applied Linguistics* (Studies in descriptive linguistics Vol. 18) Heidelberg: Julius Groos, 479–88.

SPENCER, JOHN (1991) 'Africa's contribution to the lexicon of English'. Bammesberger, Alfred/Teresa Kirchner (eds) *Language and Civilisation*. Frankfurt: Lang.

SPENCER, JOHN (ed.) (1963) *Language in Africa*. Cambridge/London: Cambridge University Press.

SPENCER, JOHN (ed.) (1971) *The English language in West Africa*. London: Longman.

SRIDHAR, KAMAL K. (1985) 'Sociolinguistic theory and non-native varieties of English', *Lingua* 68, 39–58.

SRIDHAR, KAMAL K./S.N. SRIDHAR (1986) 'Bridging the paradigm gap: second language acquisition theory and indigenized varieties of English'. *World Englishes* 5 (1), 3–14.

STOOPS, YVETTE (1979) 'The Afrikaner and his language (Remarks on R. Angogo "Language and Politics in South Africa")'. *Studies in African Linguistics* 10, 313–16.

STREVENS, PETER (1971) 'The medium of instruction (mother-tongue/second language) and the formation of scientific concepts'. *IRAL (International Review of Applied Linguistics in Language Teaching)* 9, 267–74.

STREVENS, PETER (1982a) 'The localized forms of English'. Kachru, Braj B. (ed.), 23–30.

STREVENS, PETER (1982b) 'World English and the world's Englishes – or, whose language is it anyway?' *Journal of the Royal Society of Arts* 130, 418–31.

STUBBS, MICHAEL (1986) *Educational Linguistics*. Oxford: Basil Blackwell.

SWAN, MICHAEL/BERNARD SMITH (eds) (1987) *Learner English. A Teacher's Guide to Interference And Other Problems.* Cambridge: Cambridge University Press.

TABOURET-KELLER, ANDRÉ (1971) 'Language use in relation to the growth of towns in West Africa: a survey'. *International Migration Review* 5, 180–203.

TADADJEU, MAURICE (1975) 'Language planning on Cameroon: toward a triblingual education system'. *Ohio Working Papers in Linguistics* 19, 53–75.

TADADJEU, MAURICE (1977) 'Cost-benefit analysis and language education planning in Sub-Saharan Africa'. Kotey, Paul F.A./Haig Der-Houssikian (eds), 3–34.

TADADJEU, MAURICE (1980) *A Model for Functional Trilingual Education Planning in Africa.* Paris: UNESCO.

TAIWO, C.O. (1976) 'Nigeria: language problems and solutions'. *Prospecte* 6, 406–15.

TAIWO, C.O. (1979) 'Varieties of English in Nkem Nwankwo's novels'. Ubahakwe, Ebo (ed.), 54–76.

TAYLOR, DAVID S. (1988) 'The meaning and use of the term "competence" in linguistics and applied linguistics'. *Applied Linguistics* 9, 148–68.

THOMASON, SARAH G./TERRENCE KAUFMAN (1988) *Language Contact, Creolization, and Genetic Linguistics.* Berkeley: University of California Press.

THOMPSON, P. DRUMMOND (1963) 'English in the Commonwealth: Nigeria'. *English Language Teaching* 17, 152–8.

THORBERG, YNGVE (1970) *English in a multilingual society. A Study of interference phenomena in East African English, with special reference to the language learning situation.* Stockholm Theses in English 3.

THUMBOO, EDWIN (1986) 'Language as power: Gabriel Okara's *The Voice* as a paradigm'. *World Englishes* 5, 249–64.

THUMBOO, EDWIN (1987) 'The literary dimension of the spread of English: creativity in a second language'. *Georgetown University Round Table on Language and Linguistics* (Washington), 361–401.

TIFFEN, BRIAN W. (1968) 'Language and education in Commonwealth Africa'. Dakin J./Brian Tiffen/H.G. Widdowson (eds), 63–113.

TIFFEN, BRIAN W. (1974a) 'The Intelligibility of Nigerian English'. PhD thesis (London).

TIFFEN, BRIAN W. (1974b) 'The intelligibility of African English'. *ELT Documents* 2, 10–12.

TIFFEN, BRIAN W. (1975) 'English versus African languages as the medium of education in African primary schools'. Bram, G.N./M. Hiskett (eds) *Conflict and Harmony in Education in Tropical Africa.* London: Allen & Unwin, 319–35.

TINGLEY, CHRISTOPHER (1981) 'Deviance in the English of Ghanaian newspapers'. *English World-Wide* 2, 39–62.

TODD, LORETO (1974) *Pidgins and Creoles.* London/Boston: Routledge & Kegan Paul.

TODD, LORETO (1979) 'Cameroonian: a consideration of "What's in a name?"' Hancock, Ian F. et al. (eds), 281–94.

TODD, LORETO (1982a) Cameroon. (Varieties of English around the world T1.) Heidelberg: Groos.

TODD, LORETO (1982b) 'English in Cameroon: education in a multilingual society'. Pride, John B. (ed.), 119–37.

TODD, LORETO (1982c) 'The English language in West Africa'. Bailey, Richard/Manfred Görlach (eds), 281–305.

TODD, LORETO (1984) 'Language options for education in a multilingual society: Cameroon'. Kennedy, Ch. (ed.) Language Planning and Language Education. London: Allen & Unwin, 160–71.

TODD, LORETO (1984) Modern Englishes: Pidgins and Creoles. London: Deutsch.

TODD, LORETO/IAN HANCOCK (1986) International English Usage. A Comprehensive Survey of Written and Spoken English World-Wide. Beckenham: Croom Helm.

TOMORI, S.H.O. (1967) 'A study in the syntactic structures of the written English of British and Nigerian grammar school pupils'. PhD thesis (London).

TOMORI, S.H.O. (1977) 'A diachronic and synchronic study of the motivation for learning English in Nigeria'. English Language Teaching 31, 149–58.

TONKIN, ELIZABETH (1979) 'Uses of pidgin in the early literate English of Nigeria'. Hancock, Ian et al. (eds), 303–8.

TREFFGARNE, CAREW (1975) The Role of English and French as Languages of Communication between Anglophone and Francophone West African States. London: Africa Educational Trust.

TREGIDGO, P.S. (1959) Practical English Usage for Overseas Students. London: Longmans.

TREGIDGO, PHILIP (1987) 'Speakers of West African languages'. Swan, Michael/Bernard Smith (eds), 185–93.

TRIPATHI, P.D. (1990) 'Zambianization'. English Today. 34–8.

TRUDGILL PETER J./HANNAH (1982) International English. London: Edward Arnold.

TUCKER, A.N. (1947/48) 'Foreign sounds in Swahili'. Bulletin of the School of Oriental and African Studies (London), 11/12, 214–32.

UBAHAKWE, EBO (1974) 'Bookish English among Nigerian students'. Journal of Nigerian English Studies Association 6 (1), 38–51.

UBAHAKWE, EBO (1979) 'The dilemma in teaching English in Nigeria as a language of international communication'. English Language Teaching Journal 34, 156–63.

UBAHAKWE, EBO (1988) 'Towards a harmonized ETL programme in Nigeria'. Journal of English as a Second Language 2, 64–79.

UBAHAKWE, EBO (ed.) (1979) Varieties and Functions of English in Nigeria. Ibadan: African Universities Press.

UFOMATA, T. (1986) 'The phonological influence of English upon Yoruba'. PhD thesis (London).

UFOMATA, T. (1990) 'Acceptable models for TEFL (with special reference to Nigeria)' Ramsaran, Susan (ed.) (1990), 212–16.

UNESCO (1953) 'African Languages and English in Education. A Report of a Meeting of Experts'. Paris: UNESCO.

UNESCO (1964) *Education in Northern Rhodesia: A Report and Recommendations prepared by the UNESCO Planning Mission 1963*. Lusaka: Government Printer.

UNESCO (1972) 'The role of linguistics and sociolinguistics in language education and policy'. Paris: UNESCO.

UNITED NATIONS (1981) 'Toward a Language Policy for Namibia. English as the Official Language: Perspectives and Strategies'. Lusaka: UN Institute for Namibia.

UNIVERSITY OF CAMBRIDGE LOCAL EXAMINATION SYNDICATE (1986) *General Certificate of Education 1987*. Regulations and syllabuses for private candidates in Zimbabwe. Harare: Academic Books Zimbabwe.

URE, JEAN (1979) 'Language choice and socialization in a multilingual community: language use among primary school teachers in Ghana'. McCormack, William C./Stephen A. Wurm (ed.), 263–83.

VAN DEN BERGHE, PIERRE L. (1968) 'Language and "nationalism" in South Africa'. Fishman, Joshua A./Charles A. Ferguson/Jyotirindra Das Gupta (eds), 215–24.

VAN WYK, E.B. (1978) 'Language contact and bilingualism'. Lanham, L.W./K.P. Prinsloo (eds), 29–52.

VENTER, J.A. (1975) 'Twelve years of English teaching in Afrikaans schools'. *English Usage in Soth Africa* 6 (2), 1–12.

VIERECK, WOLFGANG (1987) 'English as an international language'. *Indogermanische Forschungen* 92, 172–95.

VIERECK, WOLFGANG/WOLF-DIETRICH BALD (eds) (1986) *English in Contact with Other Languages*. Budapest: A. Kiadó.

VILJOEN, W.J. (1923) 'How we solved the language problem in South Africa'. *Journal of the Africa Society* 23 (89), 1–5.

VILLIERS, ANDRÉ DE (ed.) (1976) *English-speaking South Africa Today*. Cape Town: Oxford University Press.

VORSTER, J. PROCTOR, L. (1975) 'Black attitudes to white languages in South Africa'. *Journal of Psychology* 92, 103–8.

VORSTER, J./L. PROCTOR (1976) 'Black attitudes to 'white' languages in South Africa: a pilot study'. *Journal of Psychology* 92, 193–8.

WALI, OBIAJUNWA (1963) 'The dead end of African literature?' *Transition* III (10) 13–15. Repr. Riemenschneider, Dieter (ed.) (1983), 130–3.

WALSH, N.G. (1967) 'Distinguishing types and varieties of English in Nigeria'. *Journal of the Nigerian English Studies Association* 2, 47–55.

WARDHAUGH, RONALD (1987) *Languages in Competition: Dominance, Diversity, and Decline*. Oxford: Basil Blackwell.

WARNER, ALAN (1963) 'A new English in Africa?' *Review of English Literature* (London) 14, 45–54.

WATTS, H.L. (1976) 'A social and demographic portrait of English-speaking white South Africans'. Villiers, André de (ed.), 41–90.

WEBB, VICTOR N. (1983) 'On the South African English vowel system'. *Stellenbosch Papers in Linguistics* 10, 134–64.

WEBB, VICTOR N.C. (1979) 'Language attitudes in a segregated society. The Afrikaans-speaking coloured community in Port Elizabeth, South Africa'. *Sociologia Internationalis* 17, 103–40.

WEINSTEIN, BRIAN (1983) *The Civic Tongue: Political Consequences of Language Choices*. New York: Longman.

WELCH, F. (1974) 'The danger of de-standardizing English'. *Lugha* (Dar es Salaam) 4, 12–16.

WELLS, J.C. (1982) *Accents of English*. 3 vols, Cambridge: Cambridge University Press.

WELLS, J.C. (1987) 'Phonological relationships in Caribbean and West African English'. *English World-Wide* 8, 61–8.

WELMERS, WM. E. (1971) 'Christian missions and language policies'. Sebeok, Thomas A. (ed.), 559–69.

WHITELEY, WILFRIED H. (1963) 'Loan-words in Kamba. A preliminary survey'. *African Language Study* 4, 146–65.

WHITELEY, WILFRIED H. (1968) 'Ideal and reality in national language policy: A case study from Tanzania'. Fishman, Joshua A./Charles A. Ferguson/Jyotirindra Das Gupta (eds), 327–44.

WHITELEY, WILFRIED H. (1969a) *Swahili. The Rise of a National Language*. London: Methuen.

WHITELEY, WILFRIED H. (1969b) 'Loanwords in linguistic description: a case study from Tanzania, East Africa'. Rauch, Irmengard/Charles T. Scott (ed.) *Approaches in Linguistic Methodology*. Madison, Milwaukee, London: The University of Wisconsin Press 125–43.

WHITELEY, WILFRIED H. (1971) 'Language policies of independent African states'. Sebeok, Thomas S. (ed.), 548–58.

WHITELEY, WILFRIED H. (1973) 'Sociolinguistic surveys at the national level'. *Monograph Series on Language and Linguistics* (Georgetown University) 25, 162–80.

WHITELEY, WILFRIED H. (ed.) (1971) *Language Use and Social Change. Problems of Multilingualism with Special Reference to Eastern Africa*. London: Oxford University Press.

WHITELEY, WILFRIED H. (ed.) (1974) *Language in Kenya*. Nairobi: Oxford University Press.

WILLIAMS, DAVID (1982) 'Attitudes towards varieties of Nigerian spoken English'. *World Language English* 3, 6–10.

WILLIAMS, JESSICA (1987) 'Non-native institutionalized varieties of English'. *English World-Wide* 8, 161–99.

WILLIAMS, R.T. (1989) 'The (mis)identification of regional and national accents of English: pragmatic, cognitive and social aspects'. García, Ofelia/Ricardo Otheguy (eds), 55–82.

WILLMOTT, M.B. (1979) 'Variety signifiers in Nigerian English'. *English Language Teaching Journal* 33, 227–33.

WINGARD, PETER (1963) 'Problems of the media of instruction in some Uganda school classes: a preliminary survey'. Spencer, John (ed.), 96–115.

WOLFSON, NESSA/JOAN MANES (eds) (1985) *Language of Inequality*, Berlin: Mouton.

WOLL, HANS (1967) 'Language, ethnic identity and social change in Southern Nigeria'. *Anthropological Linguistics* 9, 18–25.

WONG, IRENE F.H. (1982) 'Native-speaker English for the Third World today?'. Pride, John (ed.), 259–86.

WRIGHT, EDGAR (1976) 'The bilingual, bicultural African writer'. Niven, Alastair (ed.), 107–19.

WRIGHT, SUSAN (1987) ' "Now now" not "just now": the interpretation of temporal deictic expressions in South African English.' *African Studies* 46, 163–77.

YAHYA-OTHMAN, SAIDA (1989) 'When international languages clash: the possible detrimental effects of the conflict between English and Kiswahili in Tanzania'. Ngara, Emanuel/Andrew Morrison (eds), 165–74.

YANKSON, KOFI (1974) 'The use of pidgin in "No longer at Ease" and "A Man of the People" '. *Asemka* 1 (2), 68–80.

YANKSON, KOFI E. (1989a) *Error Analysis: A Study of Undergraduate Interlanguage.* Enugu: Fourth Dimension Publishing Co. Ltd.

YANKSON, KOFI E. (1989b) *Better English through Concord for West African Students,* Uruowulu-Obosi (Nigeria): Pacific Publishers.

YANKSON, KOFI E. (1990) *Chinua Achebe's Novels. A Sociolinguistic Perspective.* Uruowulu-Obosi (Nigeria): Pacific Publishers.

YATES, BARBARA A. (1980) 'The origins of language policy in Zaire'. *The Journal of Modern African Studies* 18, 257–97.

YOUNG, DOUGLAS (1978) 'English in education'. Lanham, L.W./K. Prinsloo (eds), 187–214.

YOUNG, P. (1969/70) 'The language of West African writing in English, with special reference to Nigerian prose fiction'. PhD thesis (Durham).

YOUNG, PETER (1971) 'The language of West African literature in English'. Spencer, John (ed.), 165–84.

ZIMMERMANN, W. (1984) 'Language planning, language policy and education in Namibia'. *International Education Journal* 1, 181–96.

ZUENGLER, JANE E. (1982) 'Kenyan English'. Kachru, Braj. B. (ed.), 112–24.

ZUENGLER, JANE E. (1985) 'English, Swahili, or other languages? The relationship of educational development goals to language of instruction in Kenya and Tanzania'. Wolfson, Nessa/Joan Manes (eds), 241–54.

Index

257